The Virgil Michel Series

Virgil Michel, O.S.B., a monk of Saint John's Abbey in Collegeville, Minnesota, was a founder of the Liturgical Movement in the United States in the 1920s and fostered its development until his death in 1938. Michel's writing, editing, teaching, and preaching centered on the relationship between liturgy and the life of the faithful—the Body of Christ.

The Pueblo Books imprint of The Liturgical Press honors Virgil Michel's life and work with a monograph series named for him. The Virgil Michel Series will offer studies that examine the connections between liturgy and life in particular communities, as well as works exploring the relationship of liturgy to theology, ethics, and social sciences. The Virgil Michel Series will be ecumenical in breadth and international in scope, recognizing that liturgy embodies yet transcends cultures and denominations.

Series Editor: Don E. Saliers

Don E. Saliers, who teaches regularly at St. John's University in the summer program, is William R. Cannon Distinguished Professor of Theology and Worship at Emory University, Atlanta, Georgia.

Christian Scharen

Public Worship
and
Public Work

Character and Commitment
in Local Congregational Life

Virgil Michel Series
Don E. Saliers, Editor

A PUEBLO BOOK

Liturgical Press Collegeville, Minnesota

www.litpress.org

A Pueblo Book published by the Liturgical Press

Design by Frank Kacmarcik, Obl.S.B.

Library of Congress Cataloging-in-Publication Data

Scharen, Christian Batalden.
    Public worship and public work : character and commitment in local
        congregational life / Christian Scharen.
            p. cm.—(Virgil Michel series)
        "A Pueblo book."
        Includes bibliographical references and index.
        ISBN 0-8146-6193-9 (pbk.)
        1. Public worship. 2. Christian ethics. 3. Social ethics. 4.
    Christianity and culture—United States. I. Title. II. Series.

BV15.S332 2004
250'.973—dc22

2003026382

TO DANIEL, MARTIN, AND SUSAN

Contents

Illustrations

Acknowledgments

From the beginnings of this project I received strong support and encouragement from my scholarly mentors Don E. Saliers and Steven M. Tipton. Steve wrote in the acknowledgments of his own dissertation in book form *(Getting Saved from the Sixties)* that he wished to thank his mentors and teachers, yet could "only begin to return their kindness by extending it to others." In my case, he has paid on this due, providing generous engagement with my ideas that still extends beyond what I have been able to wrestle down on paper here. Don has been at turns teacher, mentor, and model as I have tried to find ways to keep my academic research and writing accountable to the life of the church. His own pioneering work in this area has influenced me more than I can express.

Others have been helpful to me as teachers and friends, as well as critics of this work at one stage or another: Nancy Eiesland, Elizabeth Bounds, Nancy Ammerman, Michael Aune, Robert Bellah, Jon Gunnemann, James Gustafson, Stanley Hauerwas, Timothy Jackson, Paul Lichterman, Charles Matthews, William McKinney, Donna Simone, Ted Smith, and Martha Stortz. Diane Wolf and Cynthia Kolb read the penultimate draft, marking up the manuscript with the valuable comments of a retired high school English teacher and a pastor, respectively. Such generosity saved me from many more mistakes than those you may still find, dear reader, and the author takes credit for all those that remain.

I am grateful to Therese Lysaught and the Society of Christian Ethics for the opportunity to put together a panel on the subject of worship and ethics while I was not yet officially a member. Early versions of chapters 1, 3, and 6 provided material for "Lois, Liturgy, and Ethics," *Annual of the Society of Christian Ethics* 20 (2000) 275–305.

I am grateful to Emory's Graduate School of Arts and Sciences for funding in 1999–2000 through the Andrew Mellon Dissertation

Fellowship in Southern Studies. Thanks to the Louisville Institute and its director, James Lewis, for kind support and for the funding provided by a 2000–2001 Louisville Dissertation Fellowship in American Religion (grant #2000019).

Graham Reside and Robert Jones were more than generous— they were mercilessly critical! What are friends for? In our every Friday meetings we discussed our respective projects. Their support was constant, and as a result of the process they know my work better than almost anyone else, including me.

Sonja, my dear partner in life, has strongly supported my process of research and writing. During my work on this project, we have welcomed our son Isaiah and our daughter Grace into our family. Their presence in our lives has made this time immeasurably richer and has likely made the book stronger for the joy they brought to my days, counterbalancing my work with time to coo or play firefighter or make a trip to the zoo. It is in large part Isaiah's doing that this book has pictures in it. They are his favorite part. I'm also grateful for family support beyond the nucleus of our home. Albert and Vicki Scharen offered moral support and encouragement. Paul, LaVonne, and Maren Batalden offered refuge for Sonja, Isaiah, and Grace for weeks at a time while I worked on this project and provided other forms of encouragement to boot.

My case congregations and their fine leaders, the Reverends John Adamski, James Davis, and Ted Wardlaw, all were kind in welcoming me and opening their churches and lives to my sometimes fumbling questions. As of the summer of 2003, only James Davis remains; Ted Wardlaw has moved to Austin Presbyterian Seminary, where he serves as president, while John Adamski has moved to Our Lady of Lourdes, where he serves as pastor. But the congregations endure, and to the Catholic Shrine, Big Bethel A.M.E., and Central Presbyterian, thank you and I trust that some of the commitments you hold so dear show through in what is written about you here.

Lastly, I dedicate the book to three remarkable pastors who shepherded me while I was in college and even in the years since: Susan Briehl, Martin Wells, and Dan Erlander. Susan, Martin, Dan, this volume is dedicated to you with heartfelt gratitude for first showing me that liturgy and ethics must always be held in the tension that is the Christian life. That is a lesson worth reflecting on; better yet, it is a lesson worth living.

Part One

Introduction

Public Worship and Public Work

As I drove out toward Stone Mountain, I reflected on the uniqueness of Greater Atlanta. This city, home to Martin Luther King Jr., had emerged from the civil-rights era as a powerhouse city for African Americans. Just a few decades ago the suburban community of Stone Mountain was best known for its Confederate theme park, complete with huge granite carvings of Civil War generals, and its role in the rebirth of the Ku Klux Klan. Today Stone Mountain is among the top five fastest growing African American suburban communities in the nation. Complete with cul-de-sac homes and its own golf course, this community has become a case study in the changing fortunes of Atlanta's black middle class.

That afternoon I was headed to interview the senior minister of a booming, suburban African Methodist Episcopal church of over two thousand members. They had recently relocated from the center of Decatur, the DeKalb County seat, to this major thoroughfare in Stone Mountain. I was curious about the effect of the move on the culture of the congregation, and especially its historic mission of spiritual and social uplift for the less fortunate. After settling in the pastor's office, I asked what the new members, predominately aged 25 to 45, were looking for. Pausing to push back from his desk in his large leather chair, he looked up at the ceiling and said, "Service." In an attempt to clarify, I said, "They want to serve?" And he quickly laughed out loud and looked at me, responding in rapid fire, "No, they want to *be* served." I begin with this brief anecdote because it so sharply portrays the basic worry underlying this book: regardless of race and ethnicity, the marriage of religion and middle-class private life in recent decades has led to a decline in the public voice and concern of churches for the public life of their communities. Stating my reasons for such a worry serves well as a means of introduction.

First, my understanding of the church's responsibility in public life is indelibly shaped by my roots in the Lutheran tradition. Understanding my own church's history predisposes me to worry about a church that does not critically participate in civic life but rather puts forth arguments for "the church" apart from its responsibility for public life. Such an argument, most notoriously articulated by German Lutheran theologians Paul Althaus and Werner Elert in their 1934 "Ansbach Proposal," led the German church to support Hitler.

Karl Barth's "Barmen Declaration," written a few months earlier that same year, proclaimed the radical freedom and responsibility of Christians to Jesus Christ as Lord of all human life, including the sphere of politics. Althaus and Elert's response to Barth separated the church into a spiritual sphere, stripping it of any responsibility toward the political save the responsibility to "assist the Führer in his work through our respective vocations and professions."[1] The wound of this experience has fueled a small industry of theological work for the post–World War II generation of Lutheran social ethicists in order to work out a solid Lutheran basis for a properly theological responsibility of the church in and for public life.[2]

Second, my concerns arise as, over the course of recent decades, interrelated social and generational changes threaten to undermine the public commitments that American congregations enable and enact. During the last quarter century, American churches faced two powerful social realities:

- the increasingly dominant influence of individualism
- a vast religious restructuring

While the influence of individualism is rooted in changes in the family and the economy, its influence played into the complex process of religious restructuring that strongly destabilized the

[1] Paul Althaus and Werner Elert, "The Ansbach Proposal as a Response to the Barmen Theological Declaration," 189–192, in Karl H. Hertz, ed., *Two Kingdoms and One World: A Sourcebook in Christian Ethics* (Minneapolis: Augsburg, 1976).

[2] The indispensable book is William Lazareth, *Christians in Society: Bible, Luther, and Social Ethics* (Minneapolis: Fortress, 2001).

public role of the church in the United States.[3] These main changes are manifested in a society composed not only of an increasingly mobile, affluent, and educated professional middle class but also of an increasingly insecure middle-middle class and a significant, increasingly worse-off, very poor class.[4] Let me give brief examples of these two broad social changes here.

Individualism and Its Effects

First, many sociologists have attempted to map the impact of recent generational changes, most significantly the complicated set of changes reflected in the lives of the so-called baby boom generation, who were born between 1946 and 1964 and came of age during the 1960s and 1970s. This generation was marked by much higher enrollment in higher education, rising from 2.6 million in 1950 to 8.6 million in 1970. Throughout this period, survey research correlates the variable of higher education with a cultural revolution expressed especially in a new egalitarianism that played out in relation to a host of social issues ranging from war to drugs to racism.[5] Out of such a "new morality" one can find the growth of expressive individualism, a way in which these egalitarian values are expressed, based upon intuitive and experiential bases and as a part of the integrity of one's self-expression.

Intertwined with these cultural changes are the institutional changes wrought by the rise of a post-industrial economy. Economic changes shifted the model of traditional, lifelong patterns of work and family life in a particular town to a model of high geographic and occupational mobility, especially for those who have more education and who hold professional jobs. Such economic changes have broken individuals free from "ascriptive" ties to

---

[3] Robert N. Bellah and others, *Habits of the Heart: Individualism and Commitment in American Life* (Berkeley: University of California Press, 1985); Robert Wuthnow, *The Restructuring of American Religion: Society and Faith Since World War II* (Princeton: Princeton University Press, 1988).

[4] William Julius Wilson, *The Bridge over the Racial Divide: Rising Inequality and Coalition Politics* (Berkeley and New York: University of California and Russell Sage Foundation, 1999); see also Edward N. Wolff, "The Rich Get Richer and Why the Poor Don't," *The American Prospect* 12 (February 12, 2001) 15–16.

[5] Wuthnow, *Restructuring of American Religion,* 155ff.

family, friends, and organizational membership, leaving in its place a dominant mode of "achieved," voluntary, and chosen ties.

For example, family has changed dramatically in consort with such broad economic and cultural changes. Today half of marriages end in divorce; families have less time together, given that more families have two or more wage earners; they rarely live near extended relatives and often do not even sit together for one meal a day. Such tectonic shifts give rise to the view, reported by Americans in social survey after social survey, that people are more selfish today, that community and family are in crisis, and that our society is facing a moral crisis.[6]

Religious Restructuring and the Loss of Public Vision
At the same time, these cultural and social institutional shifts have accompanied what Phillip Hammond calls the "third disestablishment" of the Christian church in the United States. According to Hammond's time line, the first disestablishment was the Bill of Rights, insofar as it prohibits any state-supported religion. The second disestablishment ended the cultural dominance of Protestantism through the massive Catholic immigration and the rise of a scientific worldview, both expanding throughout the nineteenth century and peaking in the early decades of the twentieth. A third disestablishment was rooted in the upheaval of the 1960s, Hammond argues. Here traditional religious organizations generally were rejected, and a new individual and mystical quest for spirituality became popular. In this movement traditional religious traditions were likely to be important, if important at all, in individual and not in collective ways.[7]

During this era of the third disestablishment, Wuthnow traces additional roots of restructuring that impacted the public voice of churches. According to Wuthnow's research, rising educational achievement in the baby boomer generation both made various denominations look more like one another and led to more salient di-

---

[6] Robert Wuthnow, *Restructuring of American Religion,* and *Loose Connections: Joining Together in America's Fragmented Communities* (Cambridge, Mass.: Harvard University Press, 1998).

[7] Phillip E. Hammond, *Religion and Personal Autonomy: The Third Disestablishment in America* (Columbia: University of South Carolina Press, 1992) 9ff.

vides within them between the more and less educated, and also those more and less liberal on a host of social issues. The public voice of such denominations, Wuthnow argues, was eclipsed during the 1980s by "special purpose groups" that tend to be focused on a single issue and mainly require payment of membership dues and possibly letter writing in support of Washington lobbyists (for example, the National Rifle Association, Bread for the World, Greenpeace).[8]

Some scholars interpret a key source of growing individualism and religious restructuring to be the loosening of the social interconnectedness of our moral communities and virtues. For example, Robert Bellah and his research team found an important and widespread shift in the mode of commitments people make, from conscientiously choosing to live and act in ways that are "good in themselves" to choosing freely to do or experience something "because I like it." In *Habits of the Heart,* Bellah and his co-authors designate the latter style as an aspect of expressive individualism. Expressive individualism, they argue, privileges "a unique core of feeling and intuition inside every person that should unfold or be expressed if individuality is to be realized."[9] With the spread of such culturally constituted ways of understanding our experience and justifying our decisions, we will weaken the moral coherence of our character and the institutions that form them.[10] Yet such commitments and the institutions that sustain, and are sustained by, them require some places in which such moral communities and the virtues of public commitment can be nurtured.

Churches and Public Life
Historically, American churches have been a central site of communal concern and public engagement. Yet recent research shows that such cultural shifts as noted above present new challenges to congregations that may be tempted to provide intimate havens of personal solace and spiritual connection while neglecting their sense of public-spiritedness, in whatever form it might take within this

---

[8] Wuthnow, *Restructuring of American Religion,* 71–131.

[9] Bellah and others, *Habits of the Heart,* 33–35 and 334.

[10] Robert N. Bellah and others, *The Good Society* (New York: Alfred A. Knopf, 1991); Hammond, *Religion and Personal Autonomy;* Wuthnow, *Loose Connections.*

or that denomination or tradition. Bellah and his co-authors captured an extreme case of such religious privatization most memorably in their evocation of Sheila Larson and her religion of "Sheilaism," consisting of "her own little voice" shorn of any objective or institutional grounding whatsoever.[11] Their worry lies in the extent to which Sheila represents the effects of broad cultural changes leading to what they, in an introduction to the tenth anniversary edition of *Habits of the Heart*, termed a "crisis of civic membership."[12]

Robert Putnam's striking book *Bowling Alone: The Collapse and Revival of American Community* is the most recent in this line of argument that American society, including the church, faces a pressing challenge in responding to shifts over the last thirty to fifty years in levels and kinds of civic commitment, participation, and connection.[13] In this work Putnam argues that such shifting styles of commitment rooted in social and generational change have accompanied dramatic declines since the 1950s in bowling leagues and all sorts of other community groups. He argues that this decline affects our national stock of "social capital," a term meant to measure social interconnectedness that both benefits individuals and has a general effect on social life.[14] While in itself a neutral concept, positive things such as mutual support, cooperation, trust, and institutional effectiveness rely on social capital—it works as a

[11] Bellah and others, *Habits of the Heart*, 221; see also Bruce A. Greer and Wade Clark Roof, "Desperately Seeking Sheila: Locating Religious Privatism in American Society," *Journal for the Scientific Study of Religion* 31 (1992) 346–352.

[12] Robert N. Bellah and others, "Individualism and the Crisis of Civic Membership," *Chiristian Century* (May 8, 1996) 514–515.

[13] The debate on Putnam's "bowling alone" thesis has been controversial from the first article he published by that title; see Robert Putnam, "Bowling Alone: America's Declining Social Capital," *Journal of Democracy* (January 1995) 65–78. For entry into a debate, see Theda Skocpol and Morris P. Fiorina, eds., *Civic Engagement in American Democracy* (Washington, D.C.: Brookings Institution Press, 1999).

[14] Robert D. Putnam, *Bowling Alone: The Collapse and Revival of American Community* (New York: Simon and Schuster, 2000) 18–24. Putnam derives his use primarily from James Coleman and Pierre Bourdieu. For an overview of the concept, see Michael Woolcock, "Social Capital and Economic Development: Towards a Theoretical Synthesis and Policy Framework," *Theory and Society* 27 (1998)151–208.

lubrication for social life. Putnam distinguishes between bonding capital—the strong ties of one's family and friends—and bridging capital—the weaker ties to acquaintances beyond one's everyday connections. Social capital is built up through the multitude of ways that we get together with others, from Boy Scouts to family dinners to churchgoing.

Churches, according to Putnam, are an especially key institution, for regular worship is one of the strongest predictors of general social connectedness and concern.[15] Churches both inspire altruism in their members and engage in significant social service, as well as fostering social movements and new programs. As he examines a wide spectrum of evidence, Putnam concludes that while Evangelical and Hispanic Catholic church membership is growing, the broad mainline churches, including the traditional African American communions, are shrinking, and those who are members spend about half as much time on church activities as they did in 1950.[16] These trends are particularly significant because, although Evangelical and new immigrant churches effectively produce bonding capital, they are not nearly as likely as mainline churches to foster civic engagement in the broader community (bridging capital). Given these findings, Putnam concludes that churches on the whole "reinforce rather than counterbalance the ominous plunge in social connectedness in the secular community."[17]

FROM CHURCH TO CHURCHES

My fundamental concern, then, lies in thinking through the public role of the church, theologically and sociologically.[18] In order to engage debates noted just above regarding the relative fraying of the United States' civic fabric and the possible contribution of public-minded churches to its repair, I turned to literature on the

[15] "Religiosity rivals education as a powerful correlate of most forms of civic engagement." Putnam, *Bowling Alone*, 67.

[16] Ibid, 70ff.

[17] Ibid, 78–79.

[18] One needs to ask these together, explicitly, or they will nonetheless be present in a covert way. See Robert Bellah, *Beyond Belief: Essays on Religion in a Post-Traditional World* (New York: Harper and Row, 1970) 206; Further, see Alasdair MacIntyre, *After Virtue: A Study in Moral Theory*, 2nd ed. (Notre Dame: University of Notre Dame Press, 1984) 23.

relation of worship and social ethics, a literature not usually noted in discussions of the church in public life. Yet, despite its relative neglect, this literature shows a growing consensus of liturgists and ethicists that Christian worship shapes people and communities committed to the broader public good, to acts of justice and peace in the world. One influential ethicist, Stanley Hauerwas, has argued forcefully that the church's worship *is* a social ethic, a public commitment par excellence. While approaching their subject in different ways, recent writers on the relation of Christian social ethics and worship have largely followed Hauerwas in arguing some form of an Aristotelian or "character ethics" approach, suggesting that worship of God forms people for Christian living in the world.

My study, then, takes up this basic question: Does Christian worship form a people committed to the good of a broader public life? Yet immediately I began to ask myself: Whose worship? Formed how? Engaged in which public? These critical questions persisted because, athough I was attracted to the ideal portrait of worship forming public-minded Christians, I also knew that actual churches in the United States vary greatly according to their interest and ability in having such a civic impact. For example, in their massive study of civic participation, Sydney Verba and his colleagues found that churches can be remarkable sources of public spiritedness and action, but this effect was most prominent for relatively uneducated members of churches that encourage lay leadership and public speaking (for example, African American churches).[19] As I initially envisioned it, then, this study was to test claims about the relation of worship and social-ethical commitment grounded in careful case studies of congregational life, worship, and work. Only in such case study could I begin to see if and how particular churches foster and sustain civic commitment. Such case studies formed the heart of my field work and my report of it here.

The title *Public Worship and Public Work* is a play on the Greek word for "liturgy" *(leitourgía)*, which originally described service performed by people on behalf of the city. It was literally "public work" *(leitos:* public, common people; and *ergos,* performing a task,

[19] Sidney Verba, Kay Lehman Schlozman, and Henry E. Brady, *Voice and Equality: Civic Voluntarism in American Politics* (Cambridge, Mass.: Harvard University Press, 1995) 320ff.

working). The term was adopted to describe service to God in the temple and later in Christian worship. It referred to the priest, surely, but also the actions of the members gathered in the worship service and their everyday acts of love and mercy shown toward others.[20] Thus I intend the double meaning in liturgy: public work in the sense of communal praise of God, but also in the sense of the witness and social impact of such a communal act done "publicly."

Let me be clear, however, that my primary question is not the "proper role of religious presence in public life" (a question deriving from the liberal assumption of religion as private and depending on an outdated view of secularization).[21] Rather, I understand Christianity to have an internal and properly theological responsibility in public life. Since Christian faith compels care for the well-being of society, and American public life and democratic polity depend on religious participation in public life, my concern centers on understanding what sorts of churches form and sustain common civic commitment, a commitment that can contribute to the renewal of our frayed social fabric. Something like the three congregations discussed below and their patterns of public worship and public work are needed in order for the church to fulfill its proper role as church in society by which, in Augustine's classic formulation, it makes "use of the earthly peace and defends and seeks the compromise between human wills."[22]

However, it is worth noting at the outset that this way of addressing the question of the church in American society has been vigorously attacked by one of the key figures in contemporary theology and in the debates over liturgy and ethics, Stanley Hauerwas. While I agree with such writers as Hauerwas, George Lindbeck, and John Milbank that the church's integrity depends in part on its

[20] "Leitourgía" in William F. Arndt and F. Wilbur Gingrich, eds., A Greek-English Lexicon of the New Testament and Other Early Christian Literature (Chicago: University of Chicago Press, 1952) 472.

[21] For such an argument, see Ronald F. Thiemann, Constructing a Public Theology: The Church in a Pluralistic Culture (Louisville: Westminster/John Knox, 1991), and Religion in Public Life: A Dilemma for Democracy (Washington, D.C.: Georgetown University Press, 1996).

[22] The City of God, bk. 19, ch.17. David Knowles, trans. (New York: Penguin Books, 1972) 878; and the best secondary text on this, R. A. Markus, Saeculum (New York: Cambridge University Press, 1988).

having a coherent culture distinct from that of its host society, I resist the more extreme implications of their social ethics, criticizing liberal theology and the assumption that the church should have a responsibility for the well-being of the United States or any actual society other than the church itself as Christ's Body.[23] My study, based as it is in fine-grained congregational study, adds nuance to such a polemical critique of liberal Christianity and its agenda for social ethics.

But why congregations, a reader might ask. Let me offer a brief rationale here. Robert Wuthnow's influential survey of religion and politics in America since World War II, *The Restructuring of American Religion,* in part documents the declining significance of denominationalism's public influence and the proliferation of what Wuthnow terms "special purpose groups."[24] Wuthnow argues that such groups may be "the ones that increasingly define the public role of American religion."[25] Yet, as he notes, such a fact is worth concern since these types of organizations are oriented toward recruiting individuals around a single cause, tend to have paper membership rather than local groups where members meet together to discuss, and thus play into the polarization of public debate and incivility noted by such recent books as James Davidson Hunter's *Culture Wars: The Struggle to Define America.*[26]

In the wake of Wuthnow's research on "special purpose groups," research on religion and public life has followed his lead, focusing on local ecumenical groups or national lobbies rather than congregations, where membership is more durable and tempered by face-to-face interaction over time.[27] Yet one lesson from the declining significance of denominationalism is, according to other au-

[23] The clearest statement may be Stanley Hauerwas and William H. Willimon, *Resident Aliens: Life in the Christian Colony* (Nashville: Abingdon, 1989).

[24] Wuthnow, *Restructuring of American Religion,* esp. chs. 5 and 6.

[25] Ibid., 121.

[26] New York: Basic Books, 1991.

[27] N. J. Demerath III and Rhys H. Williams, *A Bridging of Faiths: Religion and Politics in a New England City* (Princeton: Princeton University Press); John A. Coleman, "Deprivatizing Religion and Revitalizing Citizenship," in Paul Weithman, ed., *Religion and Liberalism* (Notre Dame: University of Notre Dame Press, 1997) 264–290; Richard L. Wood, *Faith in Action: God Meets Politics in the Inner City* (Baltimore: Johns Hopkins University Press, 2001).

thors, the increasing prominence of the congregation in American religious life.[28] Wuthnow himself has recently suggested that even many young people who otherwise exemplify the new style of commitment bemoaned by social critics nonetheless depend on local institutional grounding for their religious life and practices.[29] So while current research on religion and public life has somewhat neglected congregations, the overwhelming evidence is that over the course of American history the congregation is a major organizational expression of various groups' religious commitments, and in its activities, especially corporate worship, those commitments are sustained.[30] Engaging in congregational study allows a focus on just this aspect, corporate worship, and the contested literature about its effects on congregations' social-ethical commitments.

"IT'S THE COMMUNITY THAT MAKES THE CHURCH"

I began my fieldwork with questions derived explicitly from the character ethics paradigm, simply thinking that it had been too ideal in its vision of "the church," and thus empirical study could show how worship worked in more and less effective ways to form Christian communities and their civic commitments. I chose three churches with vital worship and public-spiritedness in downtown Atlanta—the Catholic Shrine of the Immaculate Conception, Big Bethel African Methodist Episcopal, and Central Presbyterian. I thought that these three would help me to see how strong formation happened, and I thought the worship in these three would hold the key.

As I studied the first congregation, the Shrine, I realized that the key issue in understanding congregational commitment to public life does not lie primarily in its worship. The turning point came as I unknowingly pursued my list of research questions about the

[28] Nancy Ammerman, *Congregation and Community* (New Brunswick, N.J.: Rutgers University Press, 1997); R. Stephen Warner, "The Place of the Congregation in the Contemporary American Religious Configuration," in James P. Wind and James W. Lewis, eds., vol. 2, *New Perspectives in the Study of Congregations,* 54–99 (Chicago: University of Chicago Press, 1994).

[29] Robert Wuthnow, "A Reasonable Role for Religion? Moral Practices, Civic Participation, and Market Behavior," in Robert W. Hefner, ed., *Democratic Civility: The History and Cross-Cultural Possibility of a Modern Political Ideal,* 113–129 (New Brunswick, N.J.: Transaction Publishing, 1998).

[30] Ammerman, *Congregation and Community,* 55.

formative power of liturgy on Christian character and ethical action one afternoon, talking with Betti, a Shrine Outreach committee member and executive director of Atlanta's Catholic Charities. Early in the conversation, we had this exchange:

CS: What about the Mass, about the liturgy and Sunday morning in your life as a Catholic? . . . Is that a draw to you, is it important in your work at Catholic Charities?

BK: Absolutely. It's not so much liturgy, okay? I love good liturgy, I love the Mass. . . . I converted to Catholicism almost thirty years ago, and what I was seeking when I was twenty years old and what I'm seeking now, when I'm almost fifty years old, are two entirely different things. Mass is good. Participating in the Eucharist is, you know, the seminal thing for a Catholic, it's what you do. But for me, what's important is community. And I guess what I've learned after thirty years is community is the core. It's the sharing of your life that matters *(laughing)*. But it's what comes out of the Mass.

CS: Do you notice that in your experience the character of the Mass relates to the character of the community?

BK: Always.

In retrospect, her comments seem quite clear to me: Pay attention to the character of the Shrine.

Obviously, at the time, I was still struggling to hear what she wanted me to understand. Near the end of our conversation, I suggested to her that the Shrine worship felt very reverent to me but not a formal reverence—people seemed to be reverent in all sorts of different ways, and this openness in part accounted for their acceptance of significant diversity within the parish. She answered, in part, that "if you need rigid structure and you need folks behaving in a very specific sort of 'churchy' way, then it's not the church for you." To which I responded, "But on the other hand, Father Adamski seems to be a pretty traditional liturgist," by which I meant "he's pretty 'churchy.'" And she quickly interrupted me, noting that we were talking about the identity of the community:

"This doesn't have to do with liturgy, this doesn't have to do with liturgy, this has to do with community, okay? Father John is a liturgical purist *(laughter)*. Our liturgy is about as pure as any liturgy you are going to get. In terms of the rubrics, it is absolutely according to the letter of the law. So, liturgy, liturgy is important, but again it's the community that makes the church, not the liturgy."

As we talked, she made it clear that the way I asked the question kept me from seeing the heart of the matter. She was trying valiantly to show me that the heart of the matter was not a direct link from liturgical action to ethical action; rather, the heart of the matter had something to do with the power of a congregation's communal identity.

In the aftermath of this realization, I felt as if I'd just been hit over the head by the obvious. What I needed to do was to take better account of the concrete and complicated identity of actual congregations, including influences from their religious traditions, but also key contextual and cultural influences exerting force on the formation of congregational identity. It is these multiple forces active in shaping a congregation's identity that then structure the range of possible styles of worship and social-ethical witness in a congregation.

Such an insight led me to the central argument of the book, which I then pursued with greater clarity through the rest of my fieldwork and writing. Discussions of liturgy and ethics have converged over the last decade into some version of a "linear model" of relating worship and ethics: participation in public worship forms one as a Christian, who then lives this out in public works of justice and mercy. This view fails to offer an adequate model for at least two key reasons. First, it neglects real churches by highlighting an ideal and normative church in its analysis. Second, it depends on a simple model of Christian formation.

In response, my main thesis is that *such a linear model has neglected the profound structuring effect of a congregation's communal identity in relation to the church's public worship and work.* This thesis has a number of key implications for the development of my argument in the book. In order to understand more clearly how congregations work to shape and sustain commitments to public life, I

- describe the multiple sources of congregational communal identity, drawing on cross-comparisons from case material to elaborate and illustrate;

15

- discuss how such a variegated identity structures a local "sense of public" and the ways and means available for acting on such a sensibility;
- propose a new "interactive model" for the relation of communal identity, worship, and public work as a way to speak in a more sophisticated way about how public worship and public work interrelate.

While limited in my ability to do so here, the concluding chapter will unpack the implications of these points, drawing on evidence developed in the case studies. On that basis, I can show that Christian formation through worship is hardly simple in itself and, in contrast to leading theological views, is remarkably interconnected with, rather than being in strong contrast to, "the world."

THE STRUCTURE OF THE BOOK

Chapter 1 discusses the development of various positions on the relation of liturgy and ethics, one site (neglected, at least in the church and public life literature) for examining the connection between church and public commitment. Increasingly, discussions on the topic have been dominated by character ethics and its most influential advocate, Stanley Hauerwas. This literature, upon close scrutiny, has two main shortcomings. It has focused too much on an ideal, normatively envisioned church and on a simple linear model of worship forming Christian public commitment. Yet, I argue, such a claim about formation through the practices of worship is provocative and suggestive for research, something that Hauerwas has in fact begun to argue himself. I therefore propose that my empirical study of real churches will yield a more complicated and more fruitful understanding of how church, worship, and public commitments connect.

In chapter 2 I explore various sociological studies that offer help in my effort to press ideal and simplistic theological construals of the connection between church, worship, and public commitment toward empirical realities. In the first half of the chapter, I critically engage research from congregational studies on the impact of organizational models that embody a structuring identity impacting what a congregation does and how it goes about it. Such research helps ground talk of the "church" by showing how particular

16

churches work in patterned and yet distinctly different ways to express a Christian "sense of public" in their social commitments.

Second, I interrogate research on ritual and moral formation to learn how moral community and social/public concern are produced through ritual action and how ritual fails to succeed in such formation. Beginning with the seminal work of Emilé Durkheim, I move beyond him to develop an approach focused on the ideas of formation through practice, *habitus,* and body techniques that offers a more powerful theoretical paradigm for thinking through the issues of formation raised in the liturgy and ethics material.

In introducing part 2 of the book, I discuss the three cases dealt with in chapters 3, 4, and 5—the Catholic Shrine of the Immaculate Conception, Big Bethel African Methodist Episcopal, and Central Presbyterian—in the context of a brief version of the changing fortunes of Atlanta's center city, where they have been since their founding in the 1840s. The congregations, and Atlanta itself, serve not as representative cases but rather as exemplars of issues of theoretical interest. Yet, as a theological and cultural study, it will be suggestive to other similarly located and influenced settings, particularly in urban settings in the United States. The study will be able to make some theoretical generalizations that move forward what is known and what needs to be known about the role of churches in public life.

Part 3 concludes the book by detailing the main argument regarding the key influences of communal identity and spelling out systematically the various implications of this claim, bolstered by material drawn from the case studies, for the larger theoretical and theological arguments of part 1.

Chapter One

Liturgy and Social Ethics: Characterizing a Debate

> Liturgy is social action. Through liturgy we are shaped to live rightly the story of God, to become part of that story, and are thus able to recognize and respond to the saints in our midst. Once we recognize that the church is a social ethic then we can appreciate how every activity of the church is a means and an opportunity for faithful service to and for the world.
>
> —Stanley Hauerwas, *Christian Existence Today*

Increasingly, Christian liturgists and social ethicists are raising questions about the relation between Christian social responsibility and the pattern and practice of common worship. At least in the United States,[1] Christian ethicists have tended to address this sort of question theoretically, tending to either (1) emphasize the importance of connecting liturgy and social ethics, especially seen as a concern for social justice, or (2) develop more or less sophisticated theories establishing the connection between worship and

---

[1] For a recent volume reporting on the state of the question in Germany and England, see Oswald Bayer and Alan Suggate, eds., *Worship and Ethics: Lutherans and Anglicans in Dialogue* (Berlin and New York: Walter de Gruyter, 1996).While I look primarily at literature from the United States, I discuss some authors from Great Britain (notably Robin Gill, and to a lesser extent, John Milbank) in part because the tremendous influence of Stanley Hauerwas on discussions there has woven together their conversations and those in this country.

social ethics.[2] The first, I will argue, has been dominant among Roman Catholics, and the second, among Protestants. While such a twofold typology is certainly too simple,[3] it is useful insofar as it helps to put certain things in focus.

In particular, such a typology allows the exposition of this chapter to set out the major normative claims regarding liturgy and ethics, all the while showing how these normative claims are rooted in descriptive accounts of human community, especially congregational worship. Yet these studies almost totally neglect the work of moving to study such normative claims in specific socio-cultural and institutionally embedded cases. Although such study has been neglected, it is clear that those who ask questions about liturgy's relation to ethical life have increasingly recognized the need for such study, and in the cases of Stanley Hauerwas and Robin Gill, have begun it. I will return to such questions in the conclusion of this chapter. I turn now to the first half of my typology: the Roman Catholic proposal that liturgy and social justice are fundamentally related.

A CATHOLIC SEARCH FOR LITURGY THAT DOES JUSTICE

Given the history of Catholic moral theology, one might find it odd that I would not begin here, on the Catholic side, with a discussion of virtue ethics. In a certain sense, it would be right, for it was the

[2] For example, Virgil Michel, who is widely credited for the Catholic emphasis on liturgy and social justice, went beyond simply stating the importance of holding the two together; his position entailed a sort of character ethic approach to the relation between worship and ethics not unlike what Stanley Hauerwas has proposed. See Michael J. Baxter, C.S.C., "Reintroducing Virgil Michel: Towards a Counter-Tradition of Catholic Social Ethics in the United States," *Communio* 24:499–528.

[3] This typology is more apt for looking back over the last half century. It is much less so as a map to the current debates, marked as they are by clear reversals of my division. For example, William Spohn, a Roman Catholic, wrote *Go and Do Likewise: Jesus and Ethics* (New York: Crossroad, 1998), proposing a carefully nuanced virtue ethic approach to these questions; and James M. Childs, a Lutheran, authored *Preaching Justice: The Ethical Vocation of Word and Sacrament Ministry* (Harrisburg, Pa.: Trinity Press International, 2000), arguing strongly for the relationship between liturgy and justice. Spohn and Childs still serve to make my larger point, even so neither seeks to subject his normative claim to the fire of empirical grounding.

great Catholic theologian Thomas Aquinas who rehabilitated Aristotle's virtue ethics for use in Christian thought.[4] However, from the Council of Trent in the sixteenth century up to the era of the Second Vatican Council, Catholic moral theology tended to be the domain of the "manuals" guiding confessors and training seminarians in the sacrament of penance. They were, in effect, very detailed books of laws regarding sin and penance; notions of grace and the virtues, so prominent in Aquinas's moral theology, virtually disappear.[5]

Rather than the manualist tradition, one must turn to the traditions of social encyclicals to see the roots of a position on liturgy and social justice. In the context of industrial and political revolutions, social change on a vast scale, and ecclesial retrenchment across Europe, it is nothing short of remarkable that Pope Leo XIII's 1891 encyclical *Rerum Novarum* so strongly focused the attention of the church on the plight of the poor and the necessity of the church's stand for justice on their behalf.[6] While Leo himself did not connect his concern for the plight of the workers in a new economic world to the church's liturgy, his influence in beginning such a conversation was essential.

It was an American Benedictine priest, Dom Virgil Michel, a monk of St. John's Abbey, Collegeville, Minnesota, who a generation after Leo connected the nascent tradition of social teachings initiated by Leo to the power of liturgy.[7] In his most famous formulation of the issue, Virgil wrote that "Pius X tells us that the liturgy is the indispensable source of the true Christian spirit; Pius XI tells us that the true Christian spirit is indispensable for social regeneration.

---

[4] Thomas Aquinas, *Treatise on the Virtues,* trans. John A. Oesterle (Notre Dame: University of Notre Dame Press, 1984).

[5] Charles E. Curran, *The Origins of Moral Theology in the United States: Three Different Approaches* (Washington, D.C.: Georgetown University Press, 1997) 12–18; *The Catholic Moral Tradition Today: A Synthesis* (Washington, D.C.: Georgetown University Press, 1999) 110f.

[6] Leo XIII, *Rerum Novarum: The Condition of Labor,* in *Catholic Social Thought: The Documentary Heritage,* ed. David J. O'Brien and Thomas A. Shannon (Maryknoll, N.Y.: Orbis Books, 1992) 14–39.

[7] This section owes much to Mark Searle, "The Liturgy and Catholic Social Doctrine," in *The Future of the Catholic Church in America* (Collegeville, Minn.: Liturgical Press, 1991) 43–75.

Hence, the conclusion: The liturgy is the indispensable basis of social regeneration."[8] As Michel well knew, however, neither Pius X or Pius XI made this same connection.

Pius X launched the modern liturgical movement and at the same time was a leading advocate of retrenchment against the modern world. His aim of returning the whole of society under the authority of the Catholic church could, he felt, be achieved through a full-scale immersion in the liturgical life of the church, "the indispensable source of the true Christian spirit."[9] However, leaders in the liturgical movement, notably Michel's friend and mentor, the Belgian Benedictine Lambert Beauduin, happily took up Pius X's rhetoric and put it to their own uses, urging attention to participation in liturgy, as opposed to various individual devotions, as the font of the church's life.

Pius XI, widely credited with introducing the term "social justice" into the Catholic lexicon, offered no less than an alternative model of society as an organic and interrelated whole, a vision rooted in St. Paul's writing on the "Mystical Body of Christ." In *Quadragesimo Anno*, Pius XI proposed this reorganization of society; but because it drew its model from the church's life in Christ, where the members are all integral to the whole, such a societal reorganization required "a profound renewal of the Christian spirit."[10] However, Pius didn't see with the force Michel did how such a renewal must be grounded in the liturgy of the church. It was Michel's genius to make this claim.

Michel centered his connection of liturgy and social justice on his deployment of the concept of "the Mystical Body," a concept he learned during his years of study in Europe. He thought it particularly well suited to the situation of the American Catholic church, one that he felt was too dominated by "the atmosphere of individ-

[8] Virgil Michel, "Liturgy, the Basis of Social Regeneration," *Orate Fratres* 9 (1935) 346.

[9] Pius X, *E Supremi Apostolatus* (October 4, 1903), no. 9, in *All Things in Christ: Encyclicals and Selected Documents of Saint Pius X*, ed. Vincent A. Yzermans (Westminster, Md.: Newman Press, 1954) 8.

[10] Pius XI, *Quadragesimo Anno: After Forty Years*, in *Catholic Social Thought: The Documentary Heritage*, ed. David J. O'Brien and Thomas A. Shannon (Maryknoll, N.Y.: Orbis Books, 1992) 42–79.

ualism rampant in the world today." Through participation in communion, he argued,

"we are united anew with all the members of the Mystical Body of Christ; we are imbued with the all embracing love of Christ for God, and of God for man. We are more completely integrated socially in the holy family of God our Father through Christ our Head and divine Brother, and we are freshly equipped to withstand the pagan way of selfish individualism in our daily thoughts, words, and deeds."[11]

From an emphasis on the ideal organization of the church as a social body of a supernatural sort, he made the move to suggest that this should also be the best model for society to follow.

However, Michel was not simply suggesting a return to a Christendom model of the social order subject to the church and modeled on it in a formal way. Rather, it was through bodily participation in the Mystical Body that people would learn its basic mode of social relationships, in which each individual feels a connection to and responsibility for the good of the whole. "The mystical body teaches the fullest responsibility on the part of each member for the good of the whole work of Christ as entrusted by him to his body which is the Church."[12]

One learns this, not as a cognitive proposition or dogma, but affectively, if you will, through bodily participation in liturgy.[13] Michel urged active participation for just such a reason—in the active participation of the laity, he thought, such a social sensibility could be imbued.

[11] Virgil Michel, "The Social Nature of Communion," in *The Social Problem, Book Four: The Mystical Body and Social Justice* (Collegeville, Minn.: St. John's Abbey Press, 1938) 11–16.
[12] Virgil Michel, *The Christian in the World* (Collegeville, Minn.: Liturgical Press, 1939) 77.
[13] Such attention to bodily participation, undoubtably rooted in his study of Aquinas's theory of habituation, again exemplifies the ways in which Michel was ahead of his time. In addition to the literature on character ethics below, see Louis-Marie Chauvet and François Kabasele Lumbala, eds., *Liturgy and the Body,* Concilium 1995/3 (Maryknoll, N.Y.: Orbis Books, 1995); Bruce T. Morrill, ed., *Bodies of Worship: Explorations in Theory and Practice* (Collegeville, Minn.: Liturgical Press, 1999).

"Active participation in the liturgy is the means to familiarize the faithful with the mystical body doctrine. He who lives the liturgy will in due time feel the mystical body idea developing in his mind and growing upon him, will come to realize that he is drinking at the very fountain of the true Christian spirit which is destined to reconstruct the Social Order."[14]

Liturgy was so essential, in other words, exactly because it does not merely teach the doctrine of the mystical body; rather, the liturgy "has us live this spirit in all its enactments. In the liturgy the teaching is inseparable from putting into practice."[15] And such practice, Michel saw, made liturgy "the ordinary school of the development of the true Christian."[16] Liturgy did not directly do anything to change or even suggest change in the social order; rather, by its rehearsal of a divine model of social life, it shaped the sensibilities of Christians who would, he believed, serve as the basis for a broad social regeneration.

Michel died in 1938, when he was only forty-eight and a quarter century before John XXIII opened the Second Vatican Council. For complicated reasons, not the least of which is Michel's absence from the proceedings, neither of the most important documents for furthering the church's work on social justice and on liturgical renewal made explicit the connections Michel saw as so essential.[17] According to one commentator, R. Kevin Seasoltz,

---

[14] Virgil Michel, "With Our Readers," *Orate Fratres* 5 (1930) 431.

[15] Virgil Michel, "The Liturgy as the Basis of Social Regeneration," *Orate Fratres* 9 (1934) 541. It is worth noting that during his years in Europe, in addition to study in Rome on the liturgy and travel to various great Benedictine centers of liturgical renewal, he spent a year in Louvain studying the philosophy of Thomas Aquinas and could not have avoided gaining some appreciation for the virtue approach to human action found there. See Paul Marx, O.S.B., *Virgil Michel and the Liturgical Movement* (Collegeville, Minn.: Liturgical Press, 1957) 33–34.

[16] Virgil Michel, "Christian Culture," *Orate Fratres* 13 (1938) 303.

[17] Mark Searle notes that Pius XII used the idea of the Mystical Body in his efforts at retrenchment within a more traditional notion of the church, especially in its institutional identity and power. This, Searle argues, was out of touch with the mood of *aggiornamento* set by John XXIII and thus was dropped in favor of an image of the church as a pilgrim people of God. See Searle, "The Liturgy and Catholic Social Doctrine," 56.

"The Constitution on the Sacred Liturgy affirmed the importance of liturgy for the life of the church but it failed to delineate the link between liturgy and social life or the role of the church in the world. Likewise, the Constitution on the Church in the Modern World failed to mention the role of liturgy in forwarding the redemptive work of God in the world."[18]

It seemed that Michel's legacy was floundering and in danger of slipping beyond the church's active memory.

However, a growing number of students of liturgy, at first his friends and later those who came under the sway of his voluminous writings, faithfully reasserted his positions.[19] In large part because Vatican II did not affirm the connections between liturgy and justice that Virgil Michel held dear, much writing inspired by Michel took the form of an assertion: "But! Liturgy and social justice *should* be connected!"[20] Strong critiques of liturgy from Third World liberation theologians only added to this tendency; those promoting liturgical renewal were anxious not to be viewed as promoting the church and its liturgy shorn of its social context and implications, especially for the poor.[21] On the occasion of the fiftieth year of Michel's death, Mark Searle argued that although we cannot simply recover Michel's means of linking liturgy to social justice today, his work "challenges us to recover for our own time that profound link that he articulated for us."

Searle died in 1992, but he and others in recent years began thinking through the terms of such a link between liturgy and social justice. Catholic ethicist Kenneth Himes, after summarizing

---

[18] R. Kevin Seasoltz, "Justice and the Eucharist," *Worship* 58 (1984) 508.

[19] One should be mentioned above all. Father Paul Marx, O.S.B., a friend and fellow Benedictine at St. John's Abbey, wrote what remains today the most comprehensive study of Michel's life and work (see note 15 above) and carried on his labors for liturgical renewal and social regeneration.

[20] Mark Searle, ed., *Liturgy and Social Justice* (Collegeville, Minn.: Liturgical Press, 1980); Kathleen Hughes, R.S.C.J., and Mark R. Francis, C.S.V., eds., *Living No Longer for Ourselves: Liturgy and Justice in the Nineties* (Collegeville, Minn.: Liturgical Press, 1991); Mary E. Stamps, ed., *To Do Justice and Right upon the Earth: Papers from the Virgil Michel Symposium on Liturgy and Social Justice* (Collegeville, Minn.: Liturgical Press, 1993).

[21] Juan Luis Segundo, S.J., *A Theology for Artisans of a New Humanity*, vol. 4, *The Sacraments Today* (Maryknoll, N.Y.: Orbis Books, 1974).

Michel's life and thought, proposes a way forward. While noting that a "great strength of Michel's work is his integration of the social ministry of the church with the prayer life of the Christian," he shares Michel's frustration that despite regular participation in liturgy, many laity seemed to remain unaffected.[22] Michel felt this was due to lack of education; if the liturgy could be celebrated in such a way that its true meaning was clear, its power could not be stopped. Himes, writing fifty years after Michel, has a more critical sense of the ways the liturgy itself can bear structural injustice, excluding women from leadership, for instance.

Himes critiques Michel and those who simply reassert the "formal principle" of liturgy's connection to works of justice, suggesting that such formality keeps them from seeing the sorts of things, in the liturgy or in the community, that frustrate liturgical formation in the way Michel envisioned. As a remedy, Himes calls for work that would move beyond such assertions of "the linkage between Eucharist and social justice, and examine in an empirical way what actually happens at sacramental celebrations."[23]

I will return to Himes's empirical suggestions below. First, however, I turn to the developments among Protestants writing on worship and social ethics. It is perhaps ironic that despite the twentieth-century revival of Thomistic philosophy begun by Leo XIII and Virgil Michel's dependance on an implicit Thomistic understanding of learning through bodily practice and participation, it would fall to Protestant theologians to inspire a robust revival of a virtue-ethics approach to the questions of liturgy and social ethics.

Behind current recovery of virtue ethics in moral philosophy,[24] Christian ethics,[25] and moral theology,[26] one finds a singular character—Aristotle. Of central importance is his view of how one becomes a certain sort of person. For Aristotle, the key term is

[22] Kenneth R. Himes, "Eucharist and Justice: Assessing the Legacy of Virgil Michel," *Worship* 62 (1988) 213.

[23] Ibid., 216.

[24] Alasdair MacIntyre, *After Virtue: A Study in Moral Theory*, 2nd ed. (Notre Dame: University of Notre Dame Press, 1984).

[25] Stanley Hauerwas, *Character and the Christian Life: A Study in Theological Ethics* (Notre Dame: University of Notre Dame Press, 1985[1975]).

[26] Jean Porter, *The Recovery of Virtue* (Louisville: Westminster/John Knox, 1990).

hexis. While it can be translated "habit," it is important to note that by this Aristotle did not have in mind simple and thoughtless repetition, as the English word may suggest. Rather, *hexis* refers to a state of character, a relatively permanent disposition. Thus it serves as the central mechanism by which human beings become certain kinds of people, good and bad, by practicing virtues or vices within the bounds of historical life.[27] Such a perspective echoes throughout the next set of authors who in the late twentieth century were again reviving such a virtue-ethics program as Aristotle put forward. Aristotle cast a long shadow across Western intellectual history, decisively influencing such influential philosophers as Thomas Aquinas, G.F.W. Hegel, and Karl Marx.

Because I will not explicitly return to Aristotle, I pause here to note that his influence underlies the core agenda at work in the book as a whole, that is, an effort to put forward a sociology of morality that attends carefully to the moral ideals embedded in congregations seen as communities of character and practice, those sites most formative of our habits and virtues—in short, our moral character. I now turn to the second half of the typology that began this chapter, highlighting the way Protestants have theorized the connection between liturgy and ethics.

PROTESTANT RECOVERY OF VIRTUE ETHICS

James Gustafson began as early as the mid-1960s to recover the tradition of virtue or character ethics aimed at more carefully specifying how "the church has a function in the formation of the person."[28] Rooted in his reading of Thomas Aquinas and in his work with his mentor H. Richard Niebuhr's development of an agent-centered ethic around the metaphor of "responsibility," Gustafson's work is a critique of then-dominant ethical approaches too concerned with the context or underlying principles of ethical action.[29] He felt that for the sake of the integrity of the church, Christian ethics should take better account of "what forms the self." His concern stemmed, in

[27] Aristotle, *The Nicomachean Ethics*, trans. David Ross, rev. J. L. Ackrill and J. O. Urmson (New York: Oxford University Press, 1980) xxviii.

[28] James M. Gustafson, "Christian Faith and Moral Action," *The Christian Century* 82 (November 3, 1965)1345–1347.

[29] James M. Gustafson , "Context Versus Principles: A Misplaced Debate in Christian Ethics," *Harvard Theological Review* 58 (April 1965)171–202.

part, from the fact that "the more cultural pluralism is involved in forming selves, the more important it is for communities to see how their particular loyalties and values enter into the shaping of persons who are rightly conditioned by other loyalties and commitments."[30] Gustafson directly connected this concern for Christian formation to the issue of worship and spiritual practices that inculcate certain senses—dependance, gratitude, repentance—that give shape to the moral life. He suggested that because of its role in forming these senses, "worship and meditative prayer are fundamental requisites of the Christian moral life."[31]

Gustafson's early work on character ethics lies behind the current influence of this ethical approach in Christian ethics generally and in the discussion regarding liturgy and ethics. I will focus my discussion of character, liturgy, and ethics by taking up the work of Don E. Saliers and Stanley Hauerwas, two students of Gustafson who have become central to further developments on the question of liturgy and ethics. Saliers' work on this question began as a rejection of 1960s sociological critics who argued that the church was ethically bankrupt because its powerful rhetoric gave way to a culturally captive middle-class morality.[32] In his classic article "Liturgy and Ethics: Some New Beginnings," Saliers attempts to shift the conversation from external and causal evaluations of the relation between liturgy and ethics to a view holding that when properly seen, the pairing entails an intrinsic and conceptual connection. In short, Saliers argues that "certain affections and virtues are formed and expressed in the modalities of communal prayer and ritual action. These modalities of prayer enter into the formation of the self in community."[33] Drawing on the work of Gustafson

[30] James M. Gustafson, *Christ and the Moral Life* (New York: Harper and Row, 1968) 263n.

[31] James M. Gustafson, "Spiritual Life and Moral Life," in *Theology and Christian Ethics* (Cleveland: The Pilgrim Press, 1974) 175.

[32] See, for example, Gibson Winter, *The Suburban Captivity of the Churches: An Analysis of Protestant Responsibility in the Expanding Metropolis* (New York: Macmillan, 1962); Peter Berger, *The Noise of Solemn Assemblies: Christian Commitment and the Religious Establishment in America* (New York: Doubleday, 1961).

[33] Don E. Saliers, "Liturgy and Ethics: Some New Beginnings," *Journal of Religious Ethics* 7 (Fall 1979) 173 (subsequent references in the text by page number).

28

and Hauerwas, among others, Saliers outlines an approach to the question of liturgy's relation to ethics.

First, Saliers claims: "to worship is to find one's existence oriented in attitudes, beliefs, and intentions"(173). What one believes to be true has effects on one's actions. To confess loyalty—that is to say, Saliers argues, to worship—both forms and expresses the person's or community's orientation to the world (174). Here and elsewhere Saliers' argument suggests certain modes of investigation conducive for "testing" his claims in actual congregations. To test the claim that worship orients action, one would need to study the embodied and linguistic practices of ritual performance as insight into the character of the loyalty expressed but also attend to the type of ethical orientation expressed and its directions in embodied actions in daily life. What form do worship's orienting effects take? Many forms, Saliers answers, because although worship is normative in its orienting power, "not all who participate in its language and action are shaped by it. . . . Not all who say the words and participate in the stylized activities fully understand what it is to say and do these things and to *mean* them" (176).

Second, one's moral orientation and its directions in daily action arise, Saliers argues, from "available *mythoi*—stories and narratives of human existence in which a picture of the moral good and associated ideas are expressed" (175). Certainly these Christian *mythoi* differ according to interpretative communities, including the questions of whose interpretation and for whom within and among communities. Further, other institutional ideals and practices, along with *their* narrative traditions, already shape a community of faith through its members' participation in the world. For example, the values of "liberal individualism" pervade American culture. The mass media are driven by a utilitarian, market-based calculus, but its public face more often plays on an expanding sense of "personal autonomy" tied to an expressive style of commitment.[34]

---

[34] See Don E. Saliers, "Afterword: Liturgy and Ethics Revisited," in *Liturgy and the Moral Self: Humanity at Full Stretch before God,* ed. E. Byron Anderson and Bruce T. Morrill (Collegeville, Minn.: Liturgical Press, 1998) 216–217; also the discussion of "expressive individualism" as one of the primary moral languages in American life in Robert N. Bellah and others, *Habits of the Heart: Individualism and Commitment in American Life* (Berkeley: University of California Press, 1996 [1985]).

Attempts to understand the formative power of Christian narratives on moral action must account for the formative power of these other "secular" traditions. This is so, in part, because Christians living in a pluralistic society do some things together and do many other things with other configurations of people according to other institutionally patterned ideals, practices, rules, and regulations.[35]

Third, when Christian people engage in liturgical activities, they are, according to Saliers, "doing something, performing an act" (176). The moral orientation one inhabits consists of an embodiment of the narratives in which one has lived one's life (or which have lived in and through one). This insight has received much elaboration through recent interpreters of ritual life and the body.[36] These insights require attention to the nature of bodily inculturation, to kinesiology and physiology, to habits and bodily mastery of skills, and to the passions and dispositions and affections that are central to the power of cultural *mythoi* and ritual actions to shape human beings in certain ways, with certain effects. Here, Saliers' analogy to saying "I love you" makes the point. The words themselves and the grammatical structure are not the core of the social meaning, Saliers argues, but rather the bodily effect or enactment of the saying, a saying that carries present emotional weight of a particular sort and also the historical weight of previous actions of devotion. The three words "I love you" in that order may hypothetically be said to mean many things, but only a grounded "thick description" of the context and bodily action of the speech will illuminate the intention and meaning of the words as well as their reception and effect.

Theologian Stanley Hauerwas has increasingly focused on the description of worship practices as essential to any discussion of the church as social ethic. This fact strikes me most about Hauerwas's developing position. Although he has not always explicitly held such a view, it is the logic of his practical theological aim—"to foment a modest revolution by forcing Christians to take them-

---

[35] For example, they vote with other citizens, shop at the mall with other consumers, look at paintings with other art lovers, and work with others to pay the bills, if not fulfill their true vocation. See Gustafson, *Christ and the Moral Life*, 263.

[36] Notable here is the work of Pierre Bourdieu (see the discussion in chapter 2 below, pp. 58–65).

selves seriously as Christians"–that has pressed him further and further toward grounding his claims for the formative power of worship in congregations.[37]

Hauerwas's understanding of the church offers one angle for examining his view of how liturgy and ethics relate. First, he argues, the framing of the question is wrong. Liturgy *is* ethics; Christian ethics has no substance apart from its participation in a "storied" community–a community where "the story is not merely told but embodied in a people's habits that form and are formed in worship, governance, and morality."[38] This claim grounds his wellworn aphorism that "the church does not have a social ethic; the church is a social ethic."[39] The church's first task is to live the truth of its identity in God through Christ, thus helping the world to know it is the world.[40] Such a community is "God's gesture on behalf of the world to create a space and time in which we might have a foretaste of the Kingdom."[41]

If the church has as its first task to make the world the world by being its contrast, the church has as its essence a social and political task.[42] Worship and the things that constitute it, such as prayer, preaching, baptism, and the Eucharist, among others, fold Christians into God's life as Christ's Body. By one's participation in the Body of Christ, one's life includes baptism and Eucharist but also "immersion in the daily practices of the Christian church: prayer, worship, admonition, feeding the hungry, caring for the sick, etc." Hauerwas concludes: "By these we are transformed over time to participate in God's life. So we become full members in a city ordered to peace."[43] This participation in the body is a political reality

[37] Stanley Hauerwas, *In Good Company: The Church as Polis* (Notre Dame: University of Notre Dame Press, 1995) 12.

[38] Stanley Hauerwas, *The Peaceable Kingdom: A Primer in Christian Ethics* (Notre Dame: University of Notre Dame Press, 1983) 98.

[39] Ibid., 99.

[40] Stanley Hauerwas, *Christian Existence Today: Essays on Church, World, and Living in Between* (Durham: The Labyrinth Press, 1988) 102.

[41] Ibid., 106.

[42] Hauerwas, *In Good Company,* 249, n.12.

[43] Stanley Hauerwas and Charles Pinches, *Christians Among the Virtues: Theological Conversations with Ancient and Modern Ethics* (Notre Dame: University of Notre Dame Press, 1997) 69.

produced and maintained through sacraments as political rituals. Sacraments, writes Hauerwas, "are not just 'religious things' that Christian people do. They are the essential rituals of our politics."[44] Therefore, the "liturgy is not a motive for social action, it is not a cause to effect. Liturgy *is* social action."[45] The church in Hauerwas's vision is an alternative public, a society constituted by its own distinct practices, goods, and modes of life.[46]

Such views have contributed to the tendency of critics, including Hauerwas's teacher James Gustafson, to label him a "sectarian," especially in the sense of abdication of responsibility for participation in the difficult and complex public moral issues of today. Gustafson believes that Hauerwas's focus on explicit Christian language limits the ability of concerned Christians to be intelligible in public. He also charges that Hauerwas's position is untenable, given that the church is only one of the communities that shape the life and thought of modern Christians.[47] As a result, as Gustafson famously put it, such a position makes Hauerwas's God "the tribal God of a minority of the earth's population."[48] While any extended discussion of this debate goes far beyond the task at hand, Gustafson's broadside marks an important shift in Hauerwas's means of answering critics, a task which for the first time includes consideration of real churches.

In defending his view of liturgy *as* social action against the charge of being "sectarian" and publicly "irresponsible," Hauerwas takes on the task of attempting a careful description and interpretation of the significance of an administrative board meeting at his church at that time, Broadway United Methodist, in Notre Dame, Indiana. In so doing, he avoids speaking only about an ideal church. But rather than claim a sociological perspective, he argues that his "telling of the story" is normative in intent; it serves "not

[44] Hauerwas, *The Peaceable Kingdom*, 108.

[45] Hauerwas, *Christian Existence Today*, 107. A nearly identical phrase is found in *The Peaceable Kingdom*, 108.

[46] Hauerwas, *In Good Company*, 6–8.

[47] James M. Gustafson, "The Sectarian Temptation: Reflections on Theology, the Church, and the University," *Catholic Theological Society of America Proceedings* 40 (1985) 83–94.

[48] James M. Gustafson, "Response to Critics," *Journal of Religious Ethics* 13 (Fall 1985)196.

just as an example but as an argument for how Christian ethics ought to be done."[49] Such a telling is informed by, and attempts to test, his constructive theological and ethical positions. At stake was whether in fact his understanding that liturgy *is* social action could escape the charge of "sectarian."

Through the example of his congregation, Hauerwas aims to show both that actual churches do act the way he thinks the church "should" and that the charge of sectarian misses the sort of "responsibility for the world" that Hauerwas's view of liturgy *as* social action implies. Hauerwas describes a board meeting where two issues—repairing the leaking roof and moving to weekly Eucharist—took center stage in discussions. Given the impoverished neighborhood surrounding the church, Hauerwas interprets the commitment of large sums of money for roof repair as a theological-ethical stance to be a witness of God's presence in and for that neighborhood. Weekly Eucharist, Hauerwas argues, subsequently led the congregation to propose, not a soup kitchen for the needy, but rather an after-church lunch shared among the members and all who wanted to come from the neighborhood. Again, this action held powerful symbolic and actual power for Hauerwas in that it embodied the church's calling to be a witness to the kingdom come near in Jesus Christ, and a concrete symbol to the neighborhood that all was not lost. While their first concern was not city politics, Hauerwas notes, their commitment to be a presence in the neighborhood included concern "about what was happening in the politics of the city."[50]

Hauerwas's empirical analysis of the church permitted him to develop a theological ethic that helps people "appreciate the significance of their worship." In Broadway, he "saw a congregation formed and disciplined by the liturgy that made possible an extraordinary social witness. That congregation's life belies distinctions between theology and liturgy, ethics and liturgy. The meal they prepare every Sunday for the neighborhood is not the way they express their social ethical commitments in distinction from their liturgical life. Rather, the meal they prepare and liturgical life

---

[49] Stanley Hauerwas, *Christian Existence Today*, 113.
[50] Ibid., 122.

are for them parts of a single story. The theological task is first and foremost to help us and them understand why that is the case."[51]

Hauerwas's theological task begins, then, by the admission:

"we have not paid enough attention to how difficult it is to understand the common things we do as Christians: pray, baptize, eat meals, rejoice at the birth of a child, grieve at illness and death, reroof church buildings, and so on. If we cannot describe theologically the significance of these activities, we will distort what we do by having to resort to descriptions and explanations all too readily provided by our culture."[52]

What our culture provides us, he says, are social-scientific accounts of the life of congregations. He does not mean to "deny the value of sociological, psychological, and general social-scientific accounts of the life of congregations." Yet, he continues, "the issue is the uncritical use of the social-scientific paradigms which often, if applied rigorously and consistently, methodologically preclude the theological claims necessary for the church's intelligibility."[53] He fears that in the translation of theological claims to publicly intelligible claim, the church implicitly limits its social role to blessing society, and especially the most influential forces: political liberalism and market captialism.

Holding such a view of social science places Hauerwas in a bind. On the one hand, he seeks to provide a theological description of the moral significance of liturgical practices in the lives of ordinary congregations. Such work is essential to his claim that the church and its worship are themselves a social ethic, the very means by which the church is responsible to and for the world. Yet, on the other hand, he warns against drawing on the very resources that, with critical use, may make such a description rigorous enough to make sense of what he rightly labels difficult work: the work of understanding the common things done by Christian communities.

First, Hauerwas defeats his own aim of grounded theological work because he does not go far enough, carefully enough, in his attending to congregational life. For example, Hauerwas empha-

[51] Ibid., 125.
[52] Ibid., 123–124.
[53] Ibid., 130n.

sizes the importance of the liturgical practices of congregations generally, as well as how important eucharistic practices were at Broadway, but he does not offer any description of those practices. He asserts that such practices were done and meditates on their theological meaning at length. This approach seems to at best minimally fulfill his own call to understand everyday practices of congregations, practices that are at once theological, liturgical, and ethical, but maybe also utilitarian and self-serving, shallow, or even explicitly unjust in one way or another.[54] My advocacy of a critical yet empathetic listening and questioning of congregational life echoes what Nicholas Adams and Charles Elliott provocatively call "ethnography as dogmatics." They explicitly try to address Hauerwas's worries by arguing that speech about God's world requires description and that ethnography offers sophisticated means to develop skills at such description. "Theologians," Adams and Elliott argue, "should attempt to become better ethnographers."[55]

Second, it follows that Hauerwas's polemically driven theological framework, "liturgy as ethics," does not include a view of culture nuanced enough to capture the impact of cultural pluralism forming contemporary Christians and their congregations. Whereas Hauerwas's rhetoric draws a simple church-world distinction necessary for discussing a Christian culture and its practices contrasted with the world and its practices, actual modern people, including Hauerwas, have commitments to work, family, citizenship, and leisure, in addition to religion. All these are legitimate commitments for contemporary Christians, at least those inhabiting my case congregations.

This problem cannot be ignored, as Hauerwas does, because American society, like all societies that have passed through the painful process of modernization, is constituted by differentiated

54 Susan Ross develops these issues in relation to the question of women religious who are required to have a priest, who is always a man and thereby an outsider to their community, come to preside at celebrations that include the Eucharist. See her "Like a Fish Without a Bicycle?" *America* 181/17 (November 17, 1999)10–13; "Liturgy and Ethics: Feminist Perspectives," *Annual of the Society of Christian Ethics* 20:263–274

55 Nicholas Adams and Charles Elliott, "Ethnography Is Dogmatics: Making Description Central to Systematic Theology," *The Scottish Journal of Theology* (Autumn 2000) 339–364.

yet interrelated and interconnected spheres of activity, each with potentially significant tensions with theological commitments. While theological commitments claim a central site orienting one's relationships in other spheres, each sphere (economic, familial, political, etc.) entails a distinctive moral logic that drives toward imperialism in relation to the others. Further, the spheres are not totally distinct; in their existing forms, they often appear as interconnected hybrids in complex organizations like the congregation. Max Weber calls this the problem of modern polytheism.[56] Luther calls it the problem of idolatry.[57] Seen in theological or sociological terms, this problem results in persons and communities living with multiple moral goods, ideals, and languages, aiming action toward multiple ends, each related to the various moral worlds in which they live.[58]

AN EMPIRICAL TURN

Despite various calls for it going back two decades, empirical "testing" of claims about the intrinsic connection between liturgy and ethics still awaits serious attention in Christian ethics and moral theology.[59] On the Catholic side, such ethicists as Kenneth Himes have stated the need to move beyond assertion to examine real churches. Evidence of interest in this work by Catholics is slim thus far; one

---

[56] Max Weber, "Science as a Vocation," 129–156, and "Religious Rejections of the World and their Directions," 323–359, in H. H. Gerth and C. Wright Mills, trans. and ed., *From Max Weber: Essays in Sociology* (New York: Oxford University Press, 1946); and see also Robert N. Bellah, "Max Weber and Word-Denying Love: A Look at the Historical Sociology of Religion," *Journal of the American Academy of Religion* 67 (June 1999) 277–304.

[57] Martin Luther, "The Large Catechism," in *The Book of Concord*, ed. Theodore G. Tappert (Philadelphia: Fortress Press, 1959) 365ff.

[58] Michael Walzer, *Spheres of Justice: A Defense of Pluralism and Equality* (New York: Basic Books, 1983).

[59] As evidence for lack of attention to such study in the field of Christian ethics, one could look at the recent mapping of the field in the volume *Christian Ethics: Problems and Prospects*, ed. Lisa Sowle Cahill and James F. Childress (Cleveland: The Pilgrim Press, 1996). It contains almost no mention of worship *at all*, let along serious engagement of the question, despite its importance for James M. Gustafson, whose legacy to the field the volume honors. This lacunae was not lost on Gustafson, who in his "Afterword" notes the absence, gently scolding his former students for the neglect.

could turn to a celebration of the twenty-fifth anniversary of the Constitution on the Sacred Liturgy held at Georgetown University as an example. In preparation for this celebration, four American liturgical centers undertook a study of fifteen parishes that had implemented liturgical reforms in the wake of Vatican II. Eight scholars reviewed the data on these parishes and made presentations at a colloquium during the celebration. None considered the question of liturgy and ethics. Father Peter Henriot, S.J., was invited to attend the colloquium, listen to the major papers, and then offer remarks on the linkage of "faith with justice." He found the task difficult, given what he viewed as "a disturbing absence of attention in this colloquium to the link between liturgy and social concerns."[60]

From the perspective of the Protestants such as Hauerwas, as I noted above, the internal logic of the arguments strongly implies a need for empirical study. Robin Gill, in a powerfully argued new book entitled *Churchgoing and Christian Ethics*, critiques Hauerwas in similar ways. Because Gill's is one of the only thoroughgoing efforts to apply sociological methods and theories to character ethics, his argument deserves discussion here. He begins with an appreciative critique of Hauerwas, for Gill fundamentally works out of a virtue-ethics model as well. Yet, as Gill maps out Hauerwas's developing arguments, he balks at Hauerwas's strong rhetorical position that the church is the sole repository of Christian virtues and that the church exists as a "pure" community set over against the world. Gill singles out *Resident Aliens*, Hauerwas's most popular book, as exemplary of these problematic views. The problem is, Gill notes, Hauerwas speaks mainly of an idealized church, but by his investment in a character-ethics approach, he depends on the actual church for schooling Christians.[61]

---

[60] "Liturgy and Social Concerns," in *The Awakening Church: 25 Years of Liturgical Renewal*, ed. Lawrence J. Madden (Collegeville, Minn.: Liturgical Press, 1992)115–120. A step forward may be Mathew Jayanth's book *Eucharist and Social Ethics: Explorations Toward Understanding Social Ethics as Intrinsic to the Theology of the Eucharist* (Berkeley: Graduate Theological Union, 1997), because it includes interviews with members of various local parishes in order to see how they articulate and practice an integration of sacramental participation and sacrificial living they call "being Eucharist for others."

[61] Robin Gill, *Churchgoing and Christian Ethics* (New York: Cambridge University Press, 1999) 13ff., esp. 21.

The problem, Gill argues, is that actual church people don't look much like "resident aliens" but rather look a lot like everybody else. He makes the argument that Hauerwas's claims of Christian culture and practices forming a distinctive social ethic are quite testable. He dismisses sociologists who consider churchgoing as an epiphenomenon, instead arguing for a "cultural theory" that posits that churchgoing and especially communal worship shape and re-inforce Christian beliefs and behavior.[62] Thus, he argues, a decline in churchgoing should precede declines in Christian belief and be-havior while active churchgoing should evidence increases in Christian belief and behavior.

In the center of the book, constituting chapters 4 through 7, the reader finds detailed statistical analyses of the annual British Household Panel Survey, which includes questions about church-going as well as a variety of beliefs and behaviors. Gill's original analysis of this survey data focuses on three general areas: indica-tors of Christian beliefs (faith), indicators of seeing life as worth-while (hope), and indicators of altruism (love). He concludes that churchgoing is strongly correlated with certain values and virtues, beliefs and behaviors not unique to churchgoers but more distinc-tive of them than of non-churchgoers.[63]

Gill then asks the obvious question: How does churchgoing have such an influence? If, as Gill argues, a cultural theory of church-going states that people learn these beliefs and virtues in church, how is this so? By way of an answer, Gill engages in a long discus-sion of various worship practices central to traditional Protestant (Presbyterian, Anglican) and Roman Catholic churches. These, he argues, are the constitutive practices of "the distinctive culture of churchgoing and act as crucial carriers of Christian identity."[64] He goes to great lengths to show that they together contain the values his survey analysis found more strongly present in churchgoing people. He concludes:

"Significant traces of faith, hope, and love have been detected amongst those most exposed to the culture of churchgoing. The staple ingredients of this culture–hymns, sermons, intercessions,

[62] Ibid., 64.
[63] Ibid., 197.
[64] Ibid., 226.

public confessions and, above all, readings of Scripture and celebrations of the Eucharist–all act as carriers of this distinctive culture. Together they continue to shape lives—however imperfectly—of faithful worshipers."[65]

So, his argument here shows its resonance with a character-ethics approach: by going to church and engaging in its practices, one's habits and thus character are formed.

It is ironic, however, that in trying to escape Hauerwas's claims for an idealized church, Gill ends up with another sort of idealized church—his churchgoers don't go to any actual church but are generic Christians who go to generic churches. Depending on survey data, Gill individualizes the question of churchgoing and then makes a pseudocommunal claim about churchgoing itself, aside from the character of the particular local church. Maybe because his measures of Christian belief and behavior are so general (faith, hope, love), this fact does not matter as much as it could. Still, the fact that he brushes over denominational, cultural, racial, and other differences within and among churches limits the real resonance his churchgoers can have for the reader.[66]

Such preference for a generic-real church may be understandable given his total dependence on survey data, yet it feeds a second problem that Gill shares with Hauerwas: his conclusions still depend on a simple cultural view of church and world as distinct. Theologically speaking, Gill and Hauerwas are right. But because neither broaches the topic of cultural pluralism and the complicated, bifurcated social-structural worlds influencing and shaping Christian people and their communities, they miss the ways real communities of faith are Christian in ways that tightly interrelate with what I refer to as their congregational "communal identity." Without this more complex understanding of culture and community, character ethicists put forward a too simple linear model of

---

[65] Ibid., 229.

[66] Ibid., 211. For instance, he briefly discusses denominational differences in hymnbooks and yet seems oblivious to the fact that there are churches (for example, the fast-growing African-American "Word" churches in the United States) that not only do not have hymnbooks but do not *ever* sing hymns in the traditional sense.

formation that belies the actual process of complicated formation in the lives of particular Christian communities.

Thus, Gill's question about *how* churchgoing makes its influence on the beliefs and behavior of members is still relevant for this study to ask. Margaret Farley, who responded to Saliers' paper when it was originally given at the Society of Christian Ethics meeting in 1979, suggested such a testing of claims. Reflecting on her experience in the Roman Catholic Church, Farley commented that many Christians find the liturgy today "deadening, not enlivening; impoverishing, not enriching." She asked, "After years of efforts at liturgical renewal, how is it that we do not everywhere know new life?" She pointed out the need to "specify *how* the Christian as moral agent may be changed in ways more or less powerful, more or less truthful."[67]

In addition, Farley suggested that the answer may lie in understanding the relation between the identity of a particular community in relation to its liturgy and ethics. Although suggestive, she does not develop this addition of the element of community. Some simple points drawn out from the discussion point ahead through the next chapters to focus what issues are at stake for the concluding chapter of the book.

- Can the claims of virtue ethics regarding worship's formative power on Christian social witness be supported from empirical evidence?
- How is formation of Christians in worship and communal life more or less powerful, more or less successful?
- What is the role of community in relation to public worship and work?
- Does the church produce and sustain a distinctive public witness and if so, how?

The aim of the next chapter is to mine relevant sociological materials for help in finding answers to such questions through the case studies in part 2 below.

[67] Margaret Farley, "Beyond the Formal Principle: A Reply to Ramsey and Hauerwas," *Journal of Religious Ethics* 7:191–202.

Chapter Two

Sociologizing the Debate:
Identity, Ritual, and Public Commitment

While the social-scientific study of religion has historically expected the demise of traditional religion's public influence, leaving
religion relevant only in the private sphere of personal meaning,
some sociologists have recently engaged in both widespread re-
evaluation of the traditional sociological judgements on the issues
as well as research into the new religious presence in public life.[1]
Few studies, however, look specifically at the relationship between
congregational religious life and civic commitment.

This chapter takes up two sociological subfields—congregational
studies and sociology of practice—that serve to theoretically
ground my analyses of the three case congregations discussed in
part 2 of the book. In this chapter's first section, I assess the recent
revival in congregational studies, focusing on the church's role in
public. Such research has much to offer, for example, using

---

[1] Steven M. Tipton, "The Public Church," in Robert N. Bellah and others,
The Good Society (New York: Alfred A. Knopf, 1991); José Casanova, *Public Reli-
gions in the Modern World* (Chicago: University of Chicago Press, 1994)
179–219; Christian Smith, ed., *Disruptive Religion: The Force of Faith in Social
Movement Activism* (New York: Routledge, 1996); Peter Berger, ed., *The
Desecularization of the World: Resurgent Religion and World Politics* (Grand
Rapids: Eerdmans, 1999); Lowell W. Livezey, ed., *Public Religion and Urban
Transformation: Faith in the City,* with an epilogue by R. Stephen Warner (New
York: New York University Press, 2000); Robert Wuthnow and John H. Evans,
eds., *The Quiet Hand of God: Faith-Based Activism and the Public Role of Mainline
Protestantism* (Berkeley: University of California, 2002).

organizational theory's understanding of dominant models and metaphors of congregational identity in understanding what a congregation does and how it goes about it.

In the chapter's second section, I develop another approach for understanding the church's public role rooted in the work of Emile Durkheim. Building out of a critical engagement with Durkheim's work, I draw on Pierre Bourdieu's practice theory to develop what amounts to the sociological equivalent of character ethics. Thus I am able to make better sense of how ritual works by attending to the social conditions of ritual effectiveness. I conclude the chapter by highlighting the fruits of the theory, indicating how it plays a role in my congregational analyses and what I intend to show in the conclusion on this basis.

RELIGION AND PUBLIC LIFE: CONGREGATIONAL STUDIES
Since H. Paul Douglass in the 1930s, sociologists in the field of congregational studies have argued that congregations are largely determined by social context and social class. Douglass, a minister and influential Protestant churchman, led a massive effort to understand the changing shape of congregational life in relation to the vast changes taking place in the nation during the first decades of this century. While he studied both rural and urban shifts, Douglass was particularly influential in analyzing the problems and possibilities of the city church. In works such as *1000 City Churches and How to Study the City Church,* Douglass put the techniques of social science, especially survey and demographic research, at the service of the larger movement of social reform spawned by the Social Gospel. While he accounted the shape of an individual church mostly to its denominational structure and style—its constituencies, organization, leadership, and finance—its prospects for success were directly tied to the determinative influence of its social environment. He wrote:

"Differences in human fortunes suffered by the church's immediate constituencies and changes in these fortunes due to changes in the environment largely control the institutional destinies of each particular church. Where the environment is prosperous and progressive, the church can scarcely fail to 'succeed.' Where it is miserable and deteriorating the church can scarcely avoid failure."

His argument in the book shows in great detail how the church's fortunes dwell "in the grip of these dominant forces."[2]

Douglass's research program fell victim to the "religious depression," and only with the religious boom of the post–World War II years did another serious movement begin in congregational studies, this time dealing with the questions of suburban growth and urban decline. In the late 1950s the National Council of Churches, claiming a membership of over forty million Americans, undertook its "effective city church" project, attempting to stem the growing tide of criticism that a suburban captivity of the churches had cut off the moral voice of the church and left the city to burn with the unrest of the times. While the critics debated, congregations lived through a profound restructuring as a shift to a new generation that came of age in the 1960s took hold. This generational shift is beautifully documented in Steven Warner's *New Wine in Old Wineskins*. This study of a Mendocino, California, Presbyterian church details a shift in membership and pastoral leadership from liberal to conservative evangelical dominance, a shift that gave strong impetus to conservative churches of many types.[3] These changes inspired an inward turn, and new studies on church growth and the internal health of the congregation appeared, while the question of the congregation's relation to its community fell off the agenda.

In this context the study of David Roozen, William McKinney, and Jackson Carroll entitled *Varieties of Religious Presence: Mission in Public Life* was intended to put the question of church and public life back on the agenda of congregational studies. Given the social changes since the 1950s, the authors wonder, what public role does religion play in the early 1980s? The particular value of the approach developed in *Varieties of Religious Presence* is its long-term and in depth focus on one city—Hartford, Connecticut. The authors spend multiple chapters sketching the history of the city along with the changing role religious groups played in its civic life. This historical view not only strengthens their ability to see

---

[2] H. Paul Douglass and Edmund deS. Brunner, *The Protestant Church as a Social Institution* (New York: Harper and Brothers, 1935) 237–238.

[3] R. Stephen Warner, *New Wine in Old Wineskins: Evangelicals and Liberals in a Small-Town Church* (Berkeley: University of California Press, 1988).

with more perspective the relative position and strength of religious groups in the city today, but it also assumes that cities have collective lives, symbols, and stories that reflect and shape the city.[4]

The authors of *Varieties of Religious Presence* developed a grid of various "mission orientations" that congregations took toward the world and studied the congregations of Hartford to understand the various reasons behind the diversity of orientations. The authors draw upon the classic sociological distinction between "church" and "sect"-type religious organizations.[5] They then develop a survey with questions geared to place Hartford congregations in relation to four "mission orientations" that nuance this church-sect theory:

- "civic" and "activist" congregations are both focused on the importance of their actions for life in the world around them;
- "sanctuary" and "evangelist" congregations tend, however, to focus believers toward actions that assure their salvation.

Thus, through sending this survey to all religious leaders in all congregations in Hartford, followed up by six-day field studies in congregations thought to exemplify a particular "mission orientation," the authors come up with a descriptive map of the styles of religious influence in public life in Hartford.

In attempting to understand the congregations in relation to their environment, Roozen and his coauthors develop an approach drawing on what in organizational sociology is known as "open systems theory."[6] This allowed them to follow the congregational studies tradition begun by Douglass that takes seriously the im-

[4] Thus each chapter of my congregational case study begins with a section on the history of the congregation in relation to the city.

[5] Max Weber distinguished between a "voluntary association" *(Verein)*, a corporate group whose established order claims authority over the members only by virtue of a personal act of adherence, and a "compulsory association" *(Anstalt)*, a corporate group whose established order claims authority over every individual who conforms with certain specific criteria, such as birth in a particular territory, etc. See *The Theory of Social and Economic Organization*, ed. and trans. by Talcott Parsons (New York: The Free Press, 1947). Also, Ernst Troeltsch, *The Social Teachings of the Christian Churches* (Louisville: Westminster/John Knox, 1992) .

[6] W. Richard Scott, *Organizations: Rational, Natural, and Open Systems*, 3rd ed. (Englewood Cliffs, N.J.: Prentice-Hall, 1992).

pact of the congregation's social environment. Yet in contrast to the strong determinism of H. Paul Douglass's position, the open systems theory allows Roozen, McKinney, and Carroll to give weight to the internal congregational identity and its ability to influence its social environment. They term this an "interactionist view" and sum it up in two succinct points:

1. A congregation—its theology and ethics, its worship, its programs, its style of operation, and what it does or does not do with reference to mission—is profoundly shaped by its social context (especially the local community context) and the social class of its members.
2. A congregation, by virtue of its relationship to a religious or faith tradition, has the capacity, in a limited way, to transcend the determinative power of its context and the values and interests of its members, so that it influences them as well as being influenced by them.

Drawing on this interactionist approach, Roozen and his co-authors give various reasons why congregations adopt such different orientations to public life. First of all, they suggest that social context makes a big difference, at least insofar as congregations have a strong orientation at all. Geographic setting, as a part of social context, most often predicted the mission orientation of a given congregation.[7] According to the authors, an "everything looks bright in the suburbs" context leads to a lukewarm congregation that above all seeks not to offend but rather to maintain the status quo in public relations. In contrast, the "rough and tumble" city, with its problems and diversity, forces stronger reactions on the part of congregations. Consequently, city churches were much more likely to have strong orientations and to be activist in their orientation, compared with churches in other locales.

Second, the authors suggest that social worlds of the members strongly influence the congregational "mission orientation." For example, racial and ethnic backgrounds strongly impact congregational identity. Further, sets of moral languages, learned at work,

[7] Alan K. Mock's follow-up study of sixty-two congregations found that more than 75 percent of the activist churches were in the inner city. "Congregational Religious Styles and Orientations to Society: Exploring Our Linear Assumptions," *Review of Religious Research* 34 (September 1992) 20–33.

home, school, and church, conflict between and even *within* persons. These conflicting social worlds have the effect of pushing middle-class churches, whose members are shaped through (and who also work to shape) a variety of institutions, toward a civic orientation that allows them to work out the moral balance on any particular issue. While congregations with weaker congregational identities do not seem able to provide a religious center to adjudicate between these conflicting moral languages, those with strong identities are often able to offer some level of religious belief and action that judges, and in important ways trumps, ideals and modes of actions from other spheres, such as the marketplace, government, or judiciary.

Third, a congregation's dominant theology of how God is active in the world is also highly determinative of a congregation's mission orientation. Those who view God's work as building the kingdom of God on earth will have a strong theological motivation for seeking justice and peace in this life. Those who view God's work as bringing souls into a kingdom not of this world likely find their ultimate theological motivation in seeking the redemption of individuals out of society. Often the dominant theological views within a congregation serve to legitimate the social identity of the membership (especially in terms of class). Yet such theological traditions embodied in congregational identity can in limited ways allow congregations to transcend the strongly determinative power of their social context and the social class and status of its membership.

Whereas Roozen, McKinney, and Carroll focused the development of their mission orientations on differences of religious content, other recent work in congregational studies that show how the "cultural models" congregations use to define their identity offer powerful ways to understand their form, that is, the distinctive structuring logic running through a congregation, focusing on certain religious-institutional tasks. In an effort to understand patterns of conflict and resolution in congregations, Penny Edgell Becker's recent study of twenty-three congregations in a Chicago neighborhood found that "local religious cultures are not completely idiosyncratic, but that they come in patterns." Becker calls these patterns "congregational models." It turns out that rather than organizational size, denomination, or polity, local culture seemed to hold the key to a congregation's process of responding to conflict.

Drawing on cultural sociology[8] and new institutionalist theory,[9] Becker argues that these models "are the sets of rules within a given institutional field that determine which bundles of elements go together and, therefore, which ones are available, functional, and appropriate, yielding a stable number of organizational types."[10] In short, she argues, there is an internal and logical connection between claims about "who we are" and understandings of "how we do things here." Further, the core tasks are not separable from the identity but are constitutive of it—they are "understandings about what it means to be 'us' and not some other congregation."[11] While Becker tends to describe these sets of interconnected ideals and practices as "bundles of rules" organizing local understandings of identity and action, talk of rules derives primarily from studies of corporate and bureaucratic organizations where it makes more sense.[12] Churches, as the above discussion makes clear, focus much more on what Mary Douglas describes in terms of institutional linking of specific programs, goals, and ways of doing things to larger conceptions of the good.[13]

As Becker analyzed her data from these congregations, she looked for patterns in conceptions of their ideal as a congregation that gave, in her terms, a rule-like logic to which elements of congregational activities were of most importance. Nineteen of her

---

[8] Especially Gary Alan Fine's work, *With the Boys* (Chicago: University of Chicago Press, 1987).

[9] Paul J. DiMaggio and Walter W. Powell, "Introduction," in Walter W. Powell and Paul J. DiMaggio, eds., *The New Institutionalism in Organizational Analysis* (Chicago: University of Chicago Press, 1991) 1–40.

[10] Penny Edgell Becker, *Congregations in Conflict: Cultural Models of Local Religious Life* (New York: Cambridge University Press, 1999) 12.

[11] Becker, *Congregations in Conflict*, 181.

[12] She quotes Neil Fligstein, *The Transformation of Corporate Control* (Cambridge: Harvard University Press, 1990); and Joseph Galaskiewicz, "Making Corporate Actors Accountable," in DiMaggio and Powell, *The New Institutionalism*, 293–310.

[13] Mary Douglas, *How Institutions Think* (Syracuse: Syracuse University Press, 1986).

twenty-three congregations exhibited a predominant orientation to one of the four models she found: houses of worship, family, community, and leader (the other four were in transition from one model to another). All congregations included some focus on what Becker calls the three core tasks institutionalized in the field of American congregational religion: religious reproduction (usually worship and education), building religious community (interaction within the congregation), and witness (interaction with outsiders).[14]

The key is how each model structures the congregational action in relation to each task. *House of worship* congregations focus on worship and religious education, tending not to make significant demands on member loyalty and time, and viewing their physical presence in a community as a witness to others. *Family congregations* value worship, religious education, and social activities that provide close-knit and supportive relationships. Such caring for individual needs constitutes their social witness as well. *Community congregations* embody the close-knit focus of the family congregation but tend to place high value on expressing feelings and values through democratic processes, policies, and programs that bear witness to members' social commitments. *Leader congregations*, while upholding an attention to worship and religious education, do not place as high a commitment on intimacy and social connections and instead focus on connecting religious values to actions that serve an activist mission to engage and change the world around them.[15]

Each of these types, Becker argues, is broadly embedded within a local culture. While generally not explicit, evidence of such embedding would exist in rituals and repertoires of hymns, in planning documents and slogans, and in the preference for certain types of programs. However, they do not determine every aspect of the culture; rather, the congregational model—family, leader, etc.—marks the dominant features of the public culture. Models structure the public space, including "what issues–and whose issues–make it onto the table, as well as different repertoires of participation and contention."[16]

[14] Ibid., 14.
[15] Ibid., 12–14 and chs. 3–6.
[16] Ibid., 182.

Thus the four models can be seen as four distinct kinds of public spaces or public arenas insofar as each institutionalizes certain cultural logics, certain moral ideals and practices. Families, for instance, have a conservative, patriarchal moral logic that values doing things as they have been done, a sort of moral weighting of the memory of the living community. Community churches, however, bend over backward to accommodate diverse perspectives, embodying an expressive ethic that balances moral imperatives with caring regard for all. Leader churches, unlike community churches, depend on strong pastoral leadership to direct mission toward key goals and actions.

In sum, Becker and Roozen offer key pieces for this effort to marshal resources from the social sciences. Their use of organizational theory and of organizational mission orientations and models helpfully focuses on the identity of a congregation as a public culture in its own right. Even so, their research falls short of pursuing this question: How are individual participants motivated or, better, offered an understanding of how things really are through incorporation into an ideal vision of the world, inspiring commitment to remake the world in the image of the ideal through participation in public witness and action of whatever sort? Theologians claim that participation in worship shapes and sustains such public spiritedness. It remains for me to discuss some sociological theories regarding just this claim.

HOW RITUAL WORKS: THE SOCIAL CONDITIONS OF RITUAL EFFECTIVENESS

While various options exist, the French sociologist Emile Durkheim arguably developed the most famous position on the power of ritual to form collective identity and moral community. At the outset of my research, I placed Durkheim's theory of ritual action producing moral community as a sociological equivalent next to the theological claims above in chapter 1, claiming that participation in ritual had certain formative effects. Yet, my fieldwork undertaken in congregations led to increasing doubts that such theories would hold true, at least in an unaltered state. I spent enough time in the congregations to see that specific ritual content and style led to conflicts that threatened ritual's efficacy in creating communal identity. Such a discovery led me to ask more critically about Durkhiem's theory of ritual. Thinking through the reason it failed to help my analysis led directly to the proposal I develop to remedy Durkheim's shortcomings. I do this by foregrounding a neglected component of his thought, now known as practice theory, and now most vigorously expounded by Pierre Bourdieu.

A root problem in Durkhiem's ritual theory lies in the pervasive influence of a Kantian ethic of abstract moral obligation. The essence of ritual and its power is, Durkheim argues, simply the fact of assembly and rehearsal of "the beliefs held in common: the memories of great ancestors, the collective ideal the ancestors embody— in short, social things."[17] And in even clearer terms, Durkheim suggests

"the real function of a rite is not the specific, well-defined results it seems intended to reap and by which it is usually characterized. Instead, its real function is a general result, which can take different forms in different circumstances and yet remain always and everywhere the same . . . the true function of the cult is to arouse in the faithful a certain state of soul, of moral strength and confidence."[18]

While ritual particulars differ widely, "what matters most is that the individuals are assembled and that feelings in common are expressed through actions in common."[19] Thus Durkheim sums up his theory of ritual in *The Elementary Forms* by concluding that all the variety of ritual types he studied are at most variations on this same idea. Seen from the perspective of the faithful, rites seem to be a sort of "mystical mechanics" in which physical effects are claimed for the performance. Yet, he writes, "in the end, the point is not to exert a kind of physical constraint upon blind and, more than that, imaginary forces, but to reach, fortify, and discipline consciousness."[20]

The basic logic of Durkheim's theory of ritual echoes in his claim that rites "discipline consciousness," a claim clearly manifesting its Kantian influence.[21] Durkheim saw that collective representations de-

---

[17] Emile Durkheim, *The Elementary Forms of Religious Life,* trans. Karen E. Fields (New York: The Free Press, 1995) 352.

[18] Durkheim, *The Elementary Forms,* 390.

[19] Ibid.

[20] Ibid., 422.

[21] But Kant's influence is not all that can be said. Below I note Durkheim's more Aristotelian focus on habit and character.

rived from individual beliefs, and through ritual such idealizations of the moral authority of society acted back on individuals in the form of a categorical imperative. Durkheim's preference for moral abstraction in the form of a universal categorical imperative leads him to see rites as effective sources of the production of moral community through a social "ought" idealized, symbolized, and calling the assembled worshipers to obey. Such a bias leads Durkheim to leave aside the particulars of ritual practice in their complexity.

Such particulars are, it turns out, the crux of understanding how, when, and for whom ritual works. I now turn to an example drawn from my case study of the Catholic Shrine of the Immaculate Conception in chapter 3 in order make the case again in a grounded way while at the same time setting up communion as a key test case for the theory I develop in response to Durkheim as well as my cross-comparative analysis in the conclusion of the book. In brief, I show that for the Shrine, the specific content of the Eucharist influences the specific shape of moral acts, such as efforts to welcome and care for the needy. At the same time significant communal conflict in the congregation raises questions about the ritual's efficacy in forming moral community. This example makes it clear that in order to understand the moral implications of ritual content and conflict, one must look to the particular social conditions giving rise to the ritual practice, not simply the general function of the rite acting over against social conditions.

A Case Example: the Eucharist
In his book *The Origins of Christian Morality,* Wayne Meeks argues that the ritual of the Eucharist (the Lord's Supper, Holy Communion) worked as a fundamental social practice shaping, reinforcing, and giving meaning to the moral lives of early Christians. The logic of the meal, he argues, played off of patterns of inequity in Greco-Roman society, where meals reinforced a social hierarchy through a hierarchy of tables, each with matching quality of food and drink. Such social hierarchy strengthened the social honor of the well-placed in and through their proximity to those who had much less, thereby reconstituting the difference between them. Such was St. Paul's complaint in 1 Corinthians 11:20-21, where he reminds the Corinthian church, "When you come together, it is not

really to eat the Lord's supper. For when the time comes to eat, each of you goes ahead with your own supper, and one goes hungry and another becomes drunk." The Eucharist depended on and reversed this status hierarchy, following out the logic of the Lord whose meal it is, who took the form of a servant and died for all, even the least. Rather than reinforcing a ritual of self-serving social hierarchy, the Eucharist as a social practice depends on becoming servant to others and becoming one with the Body.[22]

The moral power of such ritual practice came through a reversal of content and its meaning in relation to traditional patterns of social interaction in the world. Further, formation in such a ritual practice implied a moral pattern of analogous actions flowing from this out into one's daily life, starting with everyday meals. Durkheim's approach, I argue, would not be tuned to see the absolutely central way the content of the Eucharist makes the ritual powerful in relation to worldly patterns of eating and also the ways in which the communal conflicts could make the formative power of the ritual ineffectual. In order to elaborate the weight of these claims and begin to suggest other ways of thinking about ritual power, I will briefly describe the ritual practice of "communion" at the Catholic Shrine of the Immaculate Conception on a particular Sunday.

The Shrine, an ox-blood red brick, gothic structure in the heart of downtown Atlanta, faces on one side the Fulton County Justice Center (with its courts and jail), and on its left, the bright red World of Coca-Cola, a museum for (or shrine to) the "world's most popular soft drink." Though historically working class, the Shrine today is largely middle-class, its membership of three hundred families working chiefly in public sector jobs, especially medicine and education. Though historically ethnic Italian, the Shrine's membership today is half white and half black, including African Americans, Africans, and Haitians. In addition, about one-third of the congregation is gay or lesbian.[23]

[22] Wayne A. Meeks, *The Origins of Christian Morality: The First Two Centuries* (New Haven: Yale University Press, 1993) 91–98.

[23] The membership in 1987 was around ninety families, mainly white members whose families had been in the church for a number of generations, and African Americans, whose families joined in part because their children at-

Entering the church through two sets of wooden doors, one sees a huge baptismal font in the middle of the open back area. The nave contains four sections of pews, two on the outside set off by huge pillars holding up the soaring ceiling, and two middle sections split by the main aisle. Carpeted steps lead up from the front pews to the raised altar area, with an ambo (reading stand or pulpit) on the left, a plain rectangular table draped in a floor-length white cloth, and two chairs for presiders on the right. Behind is the old (pre-Vatican II) altar, a huge white marble sculpture soaring up toward the brilliant blue-and-white stained-glass portrait of the Virgin Mary.

The communion portion of the liturgy at the Shrine is called the "Liturgy of the Eucharist." The Eucharist is celebrated daily, as well as twice every Sunday. On a typical Sunday the Liturgy of the Eucharist begins with the presentation of the gifts of bread and wine, carried up by lay members, received by Father Adamski, who raised them above the altar in offering before handing the offering plates to the altar server and placing the vessels of water, wine, and bread on the table. He pours just a bit of water into the wine. Then he turns to the altar server who assists him in ceremonially washing his hands. He takes the thurible from the altar server and swings it three times over the elements on the altar, smoke from the incense rising up with each swing. Father Adamski returns the censor to the altar server, turns to the altar, and begins the long Eucharistic prayer. This prayer requires several back and forth responses between priest and parish, ending with the Great Amen. All say the "Our Father" in unison followed by the sharing of the peace of Christ with one another while singing the upbeat hymn, "Weave, weave us together." The communion assistants rise and go to the altar to assist in the breaking of the bread–literally breaking round loaves into hundreds of small bite-sized pieces.

Father John invites the congregation to come forward for the meal, and people process down the central aisle, beginning with

---

tended Immaculate Conception's school. Many newer members, including younger white professionals living in urban neighborhoods, all the gay and lesbian members (attracted through the priests' openness and the AIDS outreach programs), and African American families (attracted by the inclusive community), joined during the tenure of the pastor during the time of my study, Father John Adamski.

those in the rear. They first receive a piece of bread, given with the words, "the body of Christ." Walking to either side, one meets a communion assistant with a chalice of wine. People may either dip their bread into the cup of wine, or drink from the cup, and the phrase, "this is the blood of Christ" is said. Upon returning to their seats, people kneel and pray or sing meditative communion hymns while the others continue to go forward. When all are finished, all rise for the post-communion prayer. In total, this smooth and flowing process takes a little over twenty minutes, more than one third of the service as a whole.

Evaluating Durkheim's Theory

While my description of the Shrine's eucharistic ritual is brief, it has the virtue of allowing some grounded evaluation of Durkheim's theory of ritual. In doing this, it is important to note but not overextend the powerful implications of his theory. Scholars continue to find it powerful, no doubt, because it describes the real forces embodied in common religious symbolization and its ritual enactment. Yet the generality of this theory is both its benefit and its bane.

What, then, might Durkheim's theory illuminate in this case example? The above example of the Shrine shows a contemporary Christian congregation enacting one of the central rituals of the faith—a meal centered on sacrificial enactment of the last meal Jesus shared with his disciples before he was crucified. Seen from Durkheim's theory of ritual and collective identity, through this assembling to share this meal, the congregation does the "one thing needful" (212) in order to impress the moral force of ritual on its participants. They gather around the central symbol of their faith and the source of their identity as members of the Body of Christ, the church. By this "plunge" into assembly and the emotion evoked by such a common practice (take, eat; take, drink) done together, they each find assurance that in participating in the eating and drinking, they are made one (once again). The fact of common participation, oriented around the central symbol of their faith, produces the moral authority of group identity and by real forces acts to "reach, fortify, and discipline consciousness"(422).

This Durkheimian view has two problems. In order to offer an interpretation of its general function, Durkheim would not need more ethnographic details. In his theory of ritual, the essential thing is that the congregation assembles and enacts the rite, not its particular contents. Further, he would not require interviews with participants, because the faithful most often mistakenly attribute a physical efficacy to the ritual when in fact the scientist sees that its real power is to "remake" them as a moral community, accountable to the common ideals their symbols express. Yet it was exactly through my interviews and extended observation that I began to see how communion and its style and form of enactment both acted as the positive content undergirding the Shrine's moral vision and, for some, a source of conflict over moral identity and moral action.

Durkheim's theory of ritual, by focusing on the rule-like character of ritual in making moral community, deemphasized the ideational *content* of the ritual practice itself. Such a view depends on also leaving aside the question of ritual *conflict* that results in the failure of these moral forces brought to bear on individuals through ritual practice. I will take each in turn, drawing out the example of the Eucharist at the Shine.

First, in what way did the content of the communion ritual matter? Since the Shrine has increasingly deepened its commitments to social ministry projects, including most importantly their work in hosting a lunch program and a winter homeless shelter, I expected their ritual practice to support lives that are substantively impacted by the symbols they ritually enact. Their practice of communion raises this point, one that is in danger of being overlooked exactly because it is so obvious. Along the lines of Meeks's argument, members of the Shrine believe that through the participation of the community in the ritual eating and drinking, they are stepping out of ordinary roles and distinctions and approaching the Lord's table on the basis of an identity given freely in baptism. As children of God, they now eat and drink as one body, "made" one in their eating of the One who gave his life for them. They see this divine act and its reenactment through the ritual of communion as a model and motivation for their own outpouring of food and shelter, as well as compassion and hospitality, on the many poor and needy people living on downtown streets.

Yet the import of ritual content multiplied when I realized that the Shrine suffered from conflicts related to its communal identity and communion practice. The Shrine had a deep conflict over its communal identity, embodied in the person of the priest, whose commitment to social justice had produced a fundamental shift in the parish's life. Because some held the Shrine (meaning here especially the building) to be a sacred site, they bristled when Father Adamski first began using the parish hall for a weekly dinner with men suffering from HIV/AIDS and soon thereafter as a night shelter for the homeless. Therefore some members (especially some longtimers) rejected his legitimate pastoral authority and either withdrew their support physically by leaving or symbolically by participating while withholding support for his leadership.

Surprisingly, because of his relatively conservative liturgical leadership, Father Adamski created a context for some to accept his liturgical leadership while rejecting his pastoral leadership in addressing social issues. He consciously uses what he terms a "conservative" approach, not only because he feels it is right but also because of its salutary effect on critics in the congregation and in the archdiocesan hierarchy. He has achieved this by paying attention to the upkeep and respectful renovation of the church's interior; by including the decorum involved in the ceremonial handwashing and the use of incense at the altar, cleansing himself and making holy space before approaching the altar for the beginning of the great thanksgiving; by his rubrically correct presidency during the Eucharist as a whole; and by effectively promoting a devotional atmosphere through his bearing, gesture, and tone.

Ritual as Social Practice

In speaking of affections, bearing, gesture, and tone, I have already begun to depend on another way of speaking about ritual and its power, and I now turn to an elaboration of that approach. Viewing ritual as a social practice entails understanding it as formative of a *habitus,* a bodily knowledge learned through apprenticeship in a community of practice. In building this approach to understanding how ritual works, I touch on a tradition of thinking in these terms that ironically derives from Durkheim. Elaborating this alternative tradition of thought about ritual, submerged in Durkheim as it were, undergirds the analytical framing for interpretation of worship through the rest of the book. While I begin with Durkheim, I

draw resources for this view of ritual from Marcel Mauss and especially Pierre Bourdieu, while turning these theoretical resources to
my own advantage through a return to consider the key case example of the Eucharist.[24]

Durkheim on Habit and Practice
Durkheim uses the terms "habit" and *"habitus"* in talking about
what I call here "bodily knowledge." While for a number of reasons,
including his predilection for Kantian moral thinking, Durkheim
did not place a theory of habit and bodily knowledge at the fore-
front of his sociology of religion, it was a concept he employed
throughout his career.[25] His celebrated argument for occupational
groups in part sought to teach the habits of disinterestedness and
sacrifice necessary to counterbalance the influence of individualism
in modern industrial society.[26] Further, his deep involvement in educational reforms stemmed from his conviction that schools could
serve as "an apprenticeship" in the requisite habits of moral life.

"There is a whole system of rules in the school that predetermine
the child's conduct. He must come to class regularly, he must ar-
rive at a specified time and with an appropriate bearing and atti-
tude. He must not disrupt things in class. He must have learned
his lesson, done his homework, and have done so reasonably well,
etc. There are, therefore, a host of obligations that the child is required to shoulder. Together they constitute the discipline of the
school. It is through the practice of school discipline that we can inculcate the spirit of discipline in the child."[27]

Although Durkheim uses the term "system of rules" here, what he
in fact describes is a set of practices that inculcate in the child a

---

[24] Bourdieu's work has many aspects and cannot be fully summarized here,
of course, but see especially Pierre Bourdieu and Loïc J. D. Wacquant, *An Invitation to Reflexive Sociology* (Chicago: University of Chicago Press, 1992) and
Culture and Power: The Sociology of Pierre Bourdieu (Chicago: The University of
Chicago Press, 1997).

[25] Charles Camic, "The Matter of Habit," *American Journal of Sociology* 91
(1986)1039–1087.

[26] Emile Durkheim, *The Division of Labor in Society*, trans. W. D. Halls (New
York: The Free Press, 1984) xxxi–lix.

[27] Emile Durkheim, *Moral Education*, trans. Everett Wilson and Herman
Schnurer (New York: The Free Press, 1961) 148.

certain spirit of schooling.[28] It is exactly such practice in particular social settings, with its various specific expectations in conduct, that Durkheim thought could produce a *"habitus* of moral being."[29]

Although such clear references to habit do not combine into any constructive theory, Durkheim clearly has in mind at various points just such a view of the production of habit, of "bodily knowledge." Durkheim's nephew, Marcel Mauss, picked up these notions and developed them in a nascent theory of "body techniques," which amounted to an effort to think through his ethnographic observations regarding the social particularity of given actions such as walking or marching. For instance, he noted, the English and the French military have such incompatible marching styles so as to make marching together nearly impossible.[30] In helping him to understand this, Mauss developed the notion, already present in Durkheim's earlier work, of "the social nature of the *'habitus.'"* Mauss writes that "the word translates infinitely better than *'habitude'* (habit or custom), the *'exis,'* the 'acquired ability' and 'faculty' of Aristotle."[31]

Bourdieu's Theory of Ritual Practice

Pierre Bourdieu has elaborated on Durkheim and especially Mauss, working out a sophisticated understanding of the role of *habitus* as a socially acquired ability that can aid our making sense of ritual's power. I am not really interested in Bourdieu's larger theoretical project for my purposes here.[32] Rather, I follow the lead of David

[28] However, even here Durkheim's strong normative intent—the implied Kantian "ought"—diverts his attention from what Bourdieu and others have found in terms of formations rooted in early childhood that for some "fit" the discipline required of the school and thus lead to success while others "clash" and thus lead to failure or at least a painful process of "reformation."

[29] Emile Durkheim, *The Evolution of Educational Thought* (London: Routledge and Kegan Paul, 1977 [1904–1905]) 29.

[30] While not a theoretical work, the intuitive insights of William H. McNeill develop just these points in his *Keeping Together in Time: Dance and Drill in Human History* (Cambridge, Mass.: Harvard University Press, 1995).

[31] See Marcel Mauss, "The Notion of Body Techniques," in his *Sociology and Psychology: Essays* (London: Routledge and Kegan Paul, 1979) 99ff.

[32] Debates and critiques of Bourdieu abound. Generally, see the incisive critiques developed in Paul Rabinow, *Essays on the Anthropology of Reason* (Princeton: Princeton University Press, 1996) 7–13; Richard Biernacki, *The Fabrication of*

Ford, a theologian, and Timothy Jenkins, an anthropologist, both from Cambridge University, who draw on Bourdieu for understanding the Eucharist, and rituals of congregational life generally, as ritual practice.[33] Ford is a practical theologian and Jenkins an ethnographer of ritual in daily life. From their writings I have drawn out three main components from Bourdieu's work:

1) the relation of ritual and the acquisition of *habitus;*
2) the apprenticeship within a community of practice required for its acquisition;
3) the socially informed body as the nexus of intersecting practices.

First, the relation of ritual and the acquisition of a *habitus.* Drawing on the tradition of writing on "rites of passage" rituals, Bourdieu discusses what he calls the "rites of institution" that effectively—when they work—reproduce the elite classes in France. He highlights the work undertaken by the aristocracy and the energy it must expend to convince the rising generation to accept the necessary sacrifices implied by their position, that is, "by the acquisition of durable dispositions which are a condition for the preservation of privilege."[34] He continues:

"This explains the role given to ascetic practices, even physical suffering, in all the negative rites which are destined, as Durkheim said, to produce people who are out of the ordinary, in a word, distinguished. It also explains the role of training which is universally imposed on the future members of the 'elite' (the learning of dead languages, the experience of prolonged isolation, etc.). All groups

---

Labor, Germany and Britain, 1640–1914 (Berkeley: University of California Press, 1995) 21–25; Craig Calhoun and others, eds., *Bourdieu: Critical Perspectives* (Chicago: University of Chicago Press, 1993).

[33] See Timothy Jenkins, "Fieldwork and the Perception of Everyday Life," *Man* 29 (June 1994) 433–455, and *Religion in English Everyday Life: An Ethnographic Approach* (New York: Berghahn Books, 1999); and David Ford, *Self and Salvation: Being Transformed* (New York: Cambridge University Press, 1999). Ford notes that he "longs to find a full anthropological study of Eucharistic practice along the lines suggested by Jenkins and Bourdieu." I have not provided that, but I hope that this study continues in that direction.

[34] Pierre Bourdieu, *Language and Symbolic Power* (Harvard: Harvard University Press, 1991) 122.

entrust the body, treated like a kind of memory, with their most precious possessions."[35]

While culture is in a sense arbitrary, such rites impose a cultural limit within the body "in the form of a *sense of limits*" functioning to distinguish one from another, through external signs, such as "the 'choice' of outward signs expressing social position, like clothes," but also through "incorporated signs such as manners, ways of speaking—accents—, ways of walking or standing—gait, posture, bearing—, table manners, etc. and taste."[36]

Immediately one sees that Bourdieu is trying to describe the way in which particular social space—one's social class, nationality, religious identity, gender, whatever—becomes to some extent merged with one's embodied existence. Those social distinctions, those things that make one what one is and not another, Bourdieu describes as "bodily knowledge."[37] Such situated, practical "being in the world" brings to the fore Bourdieu's notion of *habitus*, whose "capacity to construct social reality is itself socially constructed." This capacity is a product of "a socialized body, investing in its practice socially constructed organizing principles that are acquired in the course of a situated and dated social experience" (137).[38]

Bourdieu's theory of ritually produced bodily knowledge rests fundamentally, then, on the idea of *habitus*. The idea is meant to combat theories of action that view human behavior as either totally determined by social structures or the alternative view that humans are rational and voluntary actors, freely following their own carefully planed life-courses. Speaking of ritually formed bodily knowledge in terms of the *habitus* instead offers a means to speak of both constraint and freedom in action. Bourdieu therefore posits that through an open learning experience in the social world, people bear the marks of such experience as *habitus*, as a

[35] Ibid., 123. See here the similar idea of body memory in Paul Connerton, *How Societies Remember* (New York: Cambridge University Press, 1989).

[36] Ibid.

[37] Pierre Bourdieu, *Pascalian Meditations* (Stanford: Stanford University Press, 2000) 130. Additional citations in the text.

[38] Bourdieu uses the term *habitus*, consciously building on its use in Hegel, as well as Mauss. See Bourdieu, "The Genesis of the Concepts of *Habitus* and of *Field*," *Sociocriticism* 2 (1985) 15.

system of schemes of perception, appreciation, and action allowing what appear to be "spontaneously" appropriate responses to objective conditions.

Such spontaneously appropriate response, Bourdieu argues, is what should be called a "practical sense." He explains:

"The practical sense is what enables one to act as one 'should' (ôs dei, as Aristotle put it) without positing or executing a Kantian 'should', a rule of conduct. The dispositions that it actualizes–ways of being that result from a durable modification of the body through its upbringing–remain unnoticed until they appear in action, and even then, because of the self-evidence of their necessity and their immediate adaption to the situation" (139).

This exposition of practical sense shows that the action it implies, while "objective" and "necessary," does not imply any form of abstract categorical imperative, any Kantian "should." But practical sense does not imply cognitive sense either, for it is a sort of self-evidence, and because it is so, is a "necessity." That is, it is a necessity only in the sense of a "natural fit" with the requirements of the specific and particular tendencies within a particular sphere of social life.

The second of Bourdieu's ideas I wish to employ argues that the acquisition of *habitus* requires apprenticeship within a community of practice. Within a particular social sphere (sport, politics, religion, art), one can see the way groups share a basic assumption about the value of their participation and the sort of action required. Groups like an orchestra or a sports team could be seen as communities of practice, though Bourdieu does not explicitly use the term. In such a community, similarly formed people can, Bourdieu writes, "perform a practical operation of quasi-bodily anticipation of the immanent tendencies of the field and of the behaviors engendered by all isomorphic *habitus*, with which, as in well-trained team or orchestra, they are in immediate communication because they are spontaneously attuned to them" (139). This can be so because all people "learn bodily" (141).

And, argues Bourdieu, the "most serious social injunctions are addressed not to the intellect but to the body, treated as a 'memory pad'" (141). Rites of institution and the suffering they inflict on the body are "simply the limiting case of all explicit actions through which groups work to inculcate the social limits" and to "naturalize them in the form of divisions in bodies, bodily *hexis,* dispositions, which are meant to be as durable as the indelible inscriptions of tattooing, and the collective principles of vision and division" (141). While such rites of institution produce a site of durable solidarities, such *habitus* are not shielded from changes in the objective fields of which they are a part.

For example, what the longtime members of the Shrine learned within the world of pre-Vatican II devotional practice and parish life clashed badly with the changing patterns of worship and moral action inaugurated by Father Adamski, who deeply embodies the post-Vatican II agenda for liturgical reform and social justice. Such a situation produces crisis and dysfunction for those whose *habitus* was formed through a previous community of practice different from that which it now inhabits (160–161). In analyzing such a clash in French Catholic churches in the decade after Vatican II, Bourdieu outlines the components of what he calls the "social conditions for the effectiveness of ritual," requirements including most importantly the people with a disposition to recognize the ritual's power but also including a legitimate leader, situation, and liturgical form.[39]

Such clashes raise the third key point that I borrow from Bourdieu, namely, that the socially informed body is the nexus of intersecting practices. Exactly because *habitus* constitute durable dispositions, an embodiment of social modes in one's perceptions and valuations and actions, they have "degrees of integration" and suffer from an inertia leaving them prone to "perpetuate structures corresponding to their conditions of production" (160). Change can occur but always slowly, for they only do so on the basis of their previous state. *Habitus* are some balance of constancy and variation, which "varies according to the individual and his degree of flexibility or rigidity" (161). As with some older people, constancy prevails as a result of "rigid, self-enclosed, over integrated *habitus*"; with some young people, variation predominates, and *habitus* is incapable of encountering the world, of "having an integrated sense of self" (161). One might here talk about the fit of one's competence with the requirements of the objective situation. By competence, it

[39] Bourdieu, *Language and Symbolic Power,* 113.

should be noted, Bourdieu means the sense of practical sense, of "knowing one's way around," or at least, as in the case of a newcomer, having "a *habitus* that is practically compatible, or sufficiently close, and above all malleable and capable of being converted into the required habitus, in short, congruent and docile, amenable to restructuring" (100).

The Case of the Eucharist Revisited

In a fairly straightforward and brief manner now, I can revisit my case material on the Eucharist at the Shrine, aiming in the process to show the promise of Bourdieu's view of ritual. First, the problem of content: at the Shrine, the Eucharist's whole "sense," including its actions of mutual sharing of one bread and cup, as well as the scriptural stories that interpret such action, *in general* produces a people who are out of the ordinary, ritually folded into a "world" of divine inclusion where all are welcome at the table and all are fed. Such a way of "being in the world" or "being occupied by such a sacramental vision of the world" conflicts strongly with the cold meritocracy of our market-driven society. Further, by virtue of one's inclusion within a particular social location and the *habitus,* the bodily knowledge formed there, this church offers a marked identity, a people "out of the ordinary." In a world where structural inequality condemns many to the margins of society, far from the tables of plenty, such inclusion in a sacramental vision stands in distinction to the world of the market as a positive alternative and moral judgment.

The problem of attending to content, however, leads to the second problem: conflict. Even communion's ritual content, so powerfully present at the Shrine, breaks apart in its formative effect exactly because the members have not all experienced similar ritually produced "bodily knowledge." Conflicts over social ministry break ritual efficacy. Bourdieu sees that both *habitus* and its social habitat change in a variety of ways; further, the variety and malleability of bodily knowledge "varies according to the individual and his [sic] degree of flexibility or rigidity."[40] So, in my case congregations, for some the "fit" between *habitus* and habitat is more or less smooth, and things seem "as they should" (often those in

---

[40] Bourdieu, *Pascalian Meditations,* 161.

63

leadership or cooperating and supporting it); for others their "fit" is gradually molded to the current situation through the physical and emotional suffering entailed in apprenticeship (for example, new members); and for still others their "fit" is mismatched, having been formed in another time or place and is seemingly too stiff to adjust now (for example, with some longtime members).[41]

Insofar as all participate in the rites of communal life, these rites have variable effects, and only in certain circumstances and after a process of group subjection to the same objective conditions can one say that something like Durkheim's ritual force creating moral community is effective. Bourdieu explains this by reference to sports teams and orchestras, groups one might term "communities of practice" that learn together and share "isomorphic *habitus*."[42] To the extent this happened at the Shrine, it happened because of the focused work of Father Adamski over a fairly long period of time, all the while holding to his view that he could not "tell" people how their lives could be transfigured through participation in the breaking of the bread but could only show them by inviting them, by drawing them into the practices that themselves became the school of transfigured life. In such a situation, however, the ritual production of moral community and action does not result from a Kantian "social ought" brought to bear in the theory of ritual Durkheim imagines. Rather, the "should" of practical sense, inculcated through ritual practice, gives participants a disposition that without thinking recognizes the situation and responds to it with a "yes, this is who we are; this is what we should be all about here."

[41] Ann Swidler's work on "culture in action" (drawing on Bourdieu) argues that such ritual influence would be most dramatic in times of cultural upheaval, socially or personally—for example, the young or "young in the faith" who are learning the "way things are here." However, she also notes that a ritual or other cultural resource may become "more central in a given life, and become more fully invested with meaning" even during relatively calm periods through, for example, renewal movements. Ann Swidler, "Culture in Action: Symbols and Strategies," *American Sociological Review* 51 (1986) 281, and her more recent *Talk of Love: How Culture Matters* (Chicago: University of Chicago Press, 2001).

[42] Bourdieu, *Pascalian Meditations*, 139. Also see Etienne Wenger, *Communities of Practice: Learning, Meaning, and Identity* (New York: Cambridge University Press, 1998).

This language has remarkable resonance with Penny Becker's articulation of how congregational models work to structure identity and action; as she puts it, who we are and how we do things here. Indeed, what may seem a set of disparate studies now can be seen as interlocking perspectives uniquely suited for the sort of study I've undertaken. On the one hand, I draw on the power of organizational ideals embodied in mission orientations or congregational models, along with the understanding that such models imply particular modes of forming and living out of a local public culture where some things are done as a matter of course and others are not done because they are not even thought. On the other hand, I develop a theory of ritual as a social practice, rooted in the *habitus* produced in communities of character and practice. These mutually reinforcing theories serve to highlight my efforts to show how each congregation has developed and lives out its own style of faithfulness, shaped by its complex communal identity and in dynamic interrelation to its members and to the society around it. I return to these themes directly in the conclusion, putting them into play with the theological claims of chapter 1. For now, I lead the reader into the cases by way of a brief introduction to the city of Atlanta.

Part Two

Three Case Studies in Atlanta's Old Downtown

A Contextual Introduction to Atlanta

Atlanta has never been a characteristic southern city in the manner of Charleston or Savannah. From its founding in the mid-nineteenth century to Henry Grady's "Northern city in the South" to Mayor Bill Campbell's Olympic "City of Dreams," Atlanta has distinguished itself in the South for its effort to become "another New York."[1] Like many American cities, Atlanta has achieved dramatic growth since World War II while suffering a major decline of its center city area along with marked increases in crime, drugs, violence, homelessness, and poverty.[2] Again, as in many American cities, the decline of Atlanta's center city has been marked by a racial divide separating black from white and the middle-class from the poor.[3]

Civic and business leaders have long worried about the residential and economic centers of Atlanta expanding beyond downtown. An

[1] Frederick Allen, *Atlanta Rising: The Invention of an International City, 1946–1996* (Atlanta: Longstreet, 1996); Dana F. White and Timothy J. Crimmins, "How Atlanta Grew: Cool Heads, Hot Air, and Hard Work," in Andrew Marshall Hamer, ed., *Urban Atlanta: Redefining the Role of the City* (Atlanta: Georgia State University, 1980) 25–44; Charles Rutheiser, *Imagineering Atlanta: The Politics of Place in the City of Dreams* (New York: Verso, 1996).

[2] Truman Hartshorn and Keith Ihlanfeldt, *The Dynamics of Change* (Atlanta: Research Atlanta, Policy Research Center, Georgia State University, 1993); Mary Walker, *A Population Profile of the City of Atlanta: Trends, Causes, and Options* (Atlanta: Research Atlanta, Policy Research Center, Georgia State University, 1997).

[3] Clarence N. Stone, *Regime Politics: Governing Atlanta, 1946–1988* (Lawrence, Kans.: University of Kansas Press, 1989); White and Crimmins, "How Atlanta Grew"; Dana F. White, "The Black Side of Atlanta: A Geography of Expansion and Containment, 1870–1970," *The Atlanta Historical Journal* 26 (Summer-Fall 1982) 199–225.

exodus from the center city began with the "garden suburbs" in the late nineteenth century and mushroomed with the advent of the automobile age.[4] Suburban expansion was initially a white privilege, while the black population suffered under strong segregationist policies limiting residential options.[5] However, since the late 1960s minorities, including the black middle class, have left the city as well.[6] Between 1970 and 1990, 72 percent of all white married couples with children moved out of the city, and 53 percent of their black counterparts did the same.[7] The middle-class suburbanization has largely followed Atlanta's historic patterns of racial segregation, with northern areas of the city remaining primarily white, and southern areas primarily black.[8]

Atlanta's downtown has suffered the fate of most major urban centers over the last quarter century—the disintegration of communities and the built environment.[9] Vast urban restructuring has drained many of these areas of resources as both individuals and companies have left, effects both of suburbanization over the last forty years and of the process of globalization and de-industrialization of the economy.[10] Wracked by drugs, poverty, poor schools, low ac-

[4] Dana F. White, "Landscaped Atlanta: The Romantic Tradition in Cemetery, Park, and Suburban Development," *The Atlanta Historical Journal* 26 (Summer-Fall 1982) 95–112; White and Crimmins, "How Atlanta Grew"; and Howard L. Preston, *Automobile Age Atlanta* (Athens, Ga.: University of Georgia, 1979).

[5] Dana F. White, "The Black Side of Altanta"; Ronald H. Bayor, "Planning the City for Racial Segregation: The Highway-Street Pattern in Atlanta," *Journal of Urban History* 15 (November 1988) 3–21.

[6] William H Frey, "Minority Suburbanization and Continued 'White Flight' in U. S. Metropolitan Areas," *Research in Community Sociology* 4 (1994) 15–42; Lucy Soto and Matt Kempner, "The New Suburbanites," *Atlanta Journal-Constitution* (January 3, 1999) A1, 10–11.

[7] Maria Saporta, "The Middle Ground: Push for Intown Housing," *Atlanta Journal-Constitution* (September 28, 1998) E1, 7; Hartshorn and Ihlanfeldt, *The Dynamics of Change.*

[8] Hartshorn and Ihlanfeldt, *The Dynamics of Change*; Rutheiser, *Imagineering Atlanta*; Robert D. Bullard, J. Eugene Grigsby III, and Charles Lee, *Residential Apartheid: The American Legacy* (Los Angeles: Center for Afro-American Studies, UCLA 1994).

[9] John A. Jakle and David Wilson, *Derelict Landscapes: The Wasting of America's Built Environment* (New York: Rowman and Littlefield, 1992).

[10] Loïc J. D. Wacquant and William Julius Wilson, "The Cost of Racial and Class Exclusion in the Inner City," *The Annals of the AAPSS* 501 (January 1989)

cess to jobs, local government limits resulting from tax-base problems, and now questions of the so-called "end of welfare as we
know it" give reason to worry about the viability of inner cities as
places to live, work, and worship.

In response to the problems of the inner city, including significant income and wealth disparity between blacks and whites,
some academic, civic, and business leaders have called for commitment to change.[11] For example, just before Atlanta hosted the
Olympics in 1996, the CEO of Coca-Cola, Roberto C. Goizueta,
urged The Atlanta Renaissance Program, a group of Atlanta public
and private sector leaders chaired by Mayor Campbell, to look
toward the post-games era and the city Atlanta would become. He
suggested that despite the significant aims already achieved in
"hosting the world" at the Olympics, much remained to be done.
"Most critically," Goizueta suggested, "we still have work to do at
the heart of our city—downtown and the surrounding portions of
our central city."[12] The concern for a viable downtown, here shared
by the mayor and a major business leader and embodied in a specific renewal program, encapsulates the essence of Atlanta's governing regime and its long-standing interest in the well-being of
the historic downtown.[13]

Many cities have taken steps to reverse decay of the center city
through reurbanization projects, assisted by federal government
programs like empowerment zones, diversification of public housing from ghetto projects to mixed income, mixed owner-occupied
and rentals, as well as by the trendy "loftization" of old buildings
catering to live-work lifestyles and Generation X corporate workers who don't want the commute.[14]

8–25; William Julius Wilson, *When Work Disappears: The World of the New Urban
Poor* (New York: Knopf, 1997).

[11] Bob Holmes, *The Status of Black Atlanta, 1996–1997* (Atlanta: The Southern
Center for Studies in Public Policy, Clark Atlanta University, 1997); Jimmy
Carter, "Preface," in *The Atlanta Project, Because There Is Hope: Gearing Up the
Renew Urban America* (Atlanta: Carter Collaboration Center, 1993).

[12] Maria Saporta, "Let's Keep Goizueta's Dream for Atlanta Alive," *Atlanta
Journal-Constitution* (September 28, 1998) E7.

[13] Stone, *Regime Politics*; Rutheiser, *Imagineering Atlanta*.

[14] Richard Moe and Carter Wilkie, *Changing Places: Rebuilding Community in
the Age of Sprawl* (New York: Henry Holt, 1997).

Atlanta, too, has gained from such trends. Its center city has undergone a significant turnaround during the past eight years. This center-city renewal movement was linked to but certainly not only derivative of, the 1996 Olympics in Atlanta. In addition to the Olympics, this pattern of renewal ongoing throughout this decade mirrors patterns nationally (both big-city politics and a number of churches have responded to the decline and devastation of the inner city over the past twenty-five years, with refocused energy on its plight).[15] For example, although some of the worst poverty-and drug-stricken neighborhoods lie just outside the downtown business district, various programs are combining federal and local government assistance aimed at attracting middle-class families back into the city. Perhaps most dramatic is the Atlanta Neighborhood Development Partnership's work in response to Mayor Campbell's Renaissance Program estimates that the city needs between fifteen and twenty thousand new housing units in order to attract middle-class families back to the city. The Neighborhood Development Partnership has already done significant work along the Sweet Auburn corridor and in the Martin Luther King, Jr. Historic District and plans to work in neighborhoods around the center city: Peoplestown, Old Fourth Ward, Mechanicsville, and the Atlanta University corridor.[16]

Little research has been done to determine the ways that historic downtown churches contribute to the renewal of Atlanta's urban landscape. Clarence Stone's classic study notes the necessary participation of private interests, including churches and church leaders, along with formal governmental leaders, in what he calls "civic cooperation," an informal mode of cooperation in effecting change in the city.[17] Yet Stone intentionally focuses on the business

[15] Sallye Salter, "Shaping a New Atlanta: The Suburbs Are No Longer Monopolizing Developers' Dollars as the City's Core Gets Renewed Respect," *Atlanta Journal-Constitution* (February 28, 1999) Q1–5; Patti Puckett, "Rebuilding God's Houses: Bucking U.S. Trend, Intown Churches Spend $30 Million to Spruce Up Sites," *Atlanta Journal-Constitution* (October 21, 1995) F6.

[16] Maria Saporta, "The Middle Ground: Effort Underway to Encourage Building of Homes for Those Who Are Neither Rich Nor Poor," *Atlanta Journal-Constitution* (September 28, 1998) E1; Cathrine Fox, "Designing a Community: Resident of Old Fourth Ward Brings Redevelopment, Recognition to Area," *Atlanta Journal-Constitution* (September 24, 2000) L1, 4.

[17] Stone, *Regime Politics*, 5.

sector in relationship to formal governmental structures, only mentioning the church's role in a few asides on the civil rights movement and black voter mobilization.[18] Nonetheless, a number of prominent, middle-class, downtown churches built during Atlanta's earliest days continue to thrive, based in part on their public-spirited work in response to the city's needs and problems.

MARTA map showing Atlanta's Central Business District

Rather than defining boundaries for the downtown area myself, I use as a working definition of downtown Atlanta the "Central Business District" circle on every MARTA system map, which, as if magnified under a zoom lens, shows up close the streets and key buildings within what was the 1996 Olympic event zone. The

18 Ibid., 52; 166.

73

downtown, defined this way, extends from North Avenue on the north to Boulevard Avenue on the east to Turner Stadium on the south and Clark-Atlanta University on the west (see map on page 73). This area was both the focus of the Olympic events during the summer of 1996 and as a direct result, the focus of major revitalization efforts since.

The cases I've chosen are intentionally located within this zone. The Shrine of the Immaculate Conception and Central Presbyterian are on what is known as Capitol Hill, while Big Bethel African Methodist Episcopal is located at the heart of the Sweet Auburn district five blocks to the north. Each represents a peculiar sort of congregation, that of the "old First Church," but with the caveat that they are still vibrant ministries. None of them is the largest or the most prominent of their denomination in the city. Yet each retains a historic authority not unlike a cathedral, because it is the "mother church" for its denomination in the city.

The cases are distinct in one additional way. They are all "exemplary," in the sense that I explicitly chose congregations with "strong" ritual enactments tied to "strong" ethical engagements—in other words, cases that embody significant logical integrity between ideals and practice.[19] The notions of moral character implicit in the paradigm out of which my central questions come suggest that practices both embody particular understandings of the world and constitute these in the lives of those who engage such practices. It is to these case studies that I now turn.

[19] By "strong" I mean that it is very important to participants, is carefully planned, is emotionally powerful for participants, and is integral to communal and individual identities.

Chapter Three

"People Living Church":
The Catholic Shrine of the Immaculate Conception

OPENING SCENES

That morning I went down to the Shrine at 9:30 for the second of a
two-part adult education event on the death penalty. There were
about fourteen people gathered around in a circle at the west end
of the parish hall. Andy, a mid-fifties, grayish-white-haired man,
soft spoken and of medium build, led the session on behalf of the
Life Issues Committee. He passed around some materials and announced the plan for the session. Since the first session introduced
participants to the broader issues surrounding the death penalty
debates, today he intended to personalize those debates by sharing
the voices and stories of death row inmates.

The first fifteen minutes of his presentation were almost impossible to hear because of the racket that Lois was making at the
other end of the parish hall. A mentally ill homeless woman who
had adopted the Shrine, Lois was coughing and talking loudly
with two of her homeless friends. Andy later laughed and said,
"Lois offered a competing session."

Lois had her trademark outfit on—a coat with two bags slung
over her shoulders so that their long straps produce a grand "X"
across her back and front. She had short hair and a small, wrinkled
face, no teeth, and a gleam in her eye warning others that she was
capable of more than they might believe on first glance. Lois and her
friends were drinking coffee around one of the rectangular tables.

Scattered nearby on the floor were overstuffed grocery bags. The parish hall—a full-sized basement with a kitchen, a great room, and bathrooms—doubled as a soup kitchen every Saturday and as a nightly shelter for the homeless from October through the end of March. Some who spent the night also came Sunday morning for hot coffee and a roll. As one member remarked, "If we welcome [the homeless] on other days, then we *have* to welcome them on Sunday."

After the death penalty discussion was over, I went upstairs for Mass. I was near the end of my four-month research period at the Shrine, and so rather than attending to the whole of the Sunday liturgy, I now turned my attention to the impromptu mini-dramas that were occurring alongside the official performance of the liturgy.

The first thing to strike me that morning took place in the second half of the service, the Liturgy of the Eucharist. Just after the procession with the bread and wine, Father Mellott took the censer from the altar server, filled it with incense, and swung it gently forward and backward over the bread and wine.[1] As the smoke rose upward toward the sunlight filtering in through the stained-glass image of the Virgin Mary, he walked all the way around the altar, repeating the gentle back-and-forth motion. Finally he moved down into the congregation, repeating the same action. Lois was sitting in the third pew on the left side of the main aisle. She had seemed distracted and was looking down at one of her grocery bags. Yet when Father Mellott moved toward the congregation, Lois was the first to stand up (the "ritually correct" action) and turned to face him. She stood slightly bent forward, with her face outstretched, as if straining to see something far off. She had no teeth, giving her face a scowling look, but it was not beyond her to smile and laugh when something struck her as pleasant. When Father Mellott passed her with the censer, she gracefully bent a bit farther forward and made the sign of the cross over herself.

Just a few minutes later, during the communion, the congregation was singing David Haas's lovely "Table Song," with its chorus "We are the body of Christ; broken and poured out, promise of life from death; we are the body of Christ." Serving communion began with the last rows and moved forward. Lois, sitting near the front,

---

[1] Father David Mellott, a fellow Emory doctoral student in religion, was guest priest on this particular Sunday and frequently worships at the Shrine.

was pacing up and down in her pew, singing a rather off-key version of the hymn at the top of her lungs. As I moved out into the main aisle to go down for communion, Betti, a member of the Outreach Committee and head of Atlanta's Catholic Charities organization, moved out of her pew and walked down the aisle just in front of me, singing the hymn, beaming with delight as she looked at Lois. During my interview with Betti, she used the example of Lois to speak about what kind of parish the Shrine was. At the Shrine, Betti said,

"there is no pretense. There's no folks 'pretending' when everyone knows you. It's a flexible enough group of people so that, I mean, like Lois can come in there and act out and it's *okay* for Lois to be in there and acting out. I mean, you get slightly annoyed, but it's Lois. Lois is part of the congregation."

Nearly everyone I talked to at the Shrine mentioned Lois. The pastor, Father John Adamski, and Brad, a pastoral council member, worked with her in an effort to understand her situation, history, and the possibilities of helping her to a life beyond the street. Others simply knew her from her faithful presence at Mass on weekdays at 12:10 or on Sunday mornings, as she rarely missed a service. Her complicated presence in the life of the parish symbolized two central and interdependent aspects of the Shrine. From one angle, Lois symbolized the true Pauline "body of Christ" (1 Corinthians 12), a community based on diversity and a difficult but cherished openness brought about, in the words of Father Adamski, by a dependence on God's transforming power and not on worldly divisions. Lois, members reminded themselves, shared a common baptism and eucharistic meal with all gathered and thus was central to the living body of Christ. She accordingly received equal claim to basic human dignity as a beloved child of God.

From another angle, Lois symbolized the biblical "least of these" Jesus speaks of in Matthew 25. By her presence she played a priestly role, acting as an icon of Jesus by bringing to the center of the community a gut-level awareness of those many hungry and homeless in the downtown area, in their sister parish in Haiti, and around the world, all of whom depended on the material and spiritual support of the Shrine and other congregations like it. Yet exactly because of her regular tirades and episodes before, during, and after Mass, it was difficult to romanticize the work of social justice. As one member commented, "Well, [Lois is] one of God's creatures, too, but when she really gets cursing, you've got to take her out and get her some help." A diverse community brought together and "made" one body, one body turned toward participation in God's work in the world—these two aspects, symbolized in Lois's presence, meaningfully grounded the parish's 150th anniversary slogan, "People Living Church."

HISTORY OF IMMACULATE CONCEPTION, 1845–1999

Immaculate Conception Church, like the city of Atlanta itself, was not a child of the agrarian South. During the decade after chief engineer Stephen Long drove the stake for the terminus of the Western and Atlantic Railroad in what is now the heart of the city's

A view of the Catholic Shrine of the Immaculate Conception

downtown, Irish railroad workers were the majority of the small Catholic population. The Catholic presence in Georgia dates from in the late eighteenth century as English Catholics from Maryland settled in Locust Grove, Georgia, but by the late 1840s the state had four thousand Catholics and parishes in Savannah, Augusta, Macon, Columbus, and soon in Atlanta.[2] While of Irish descent, many of the new Catholic immigrants to Atlanta came from other southern cities, often following the work on the railroad.

In their first years in the new city, members met together in homes for Mass whenever a missionary priest could come up from Augusta and Macon. The first of these was held in 1845. These early Irish banded together and after only a few years as a mission site, purchased land for three hundred dollars one block down from city hall. They built and dedicated a small wooden church in 1848, making Immaculate Conception one of the first churches in the city. Its first pastor, Father Jeremiah O'Neill, had grown up in the Locust Grove Catholic community and in 1850 was assigned to develop the "Atlanta Mission."[3] At this point the city had merely 2,570 residents, and records show that the newly dedicated Immaculate Conception Church had between one and two hundred members.[4]

The location in the central city proved profoundly influential in the congregation's life and mission over its more than one hundred-fifty-year history.[5] The first and arguably most influential of these pivotal moments occurred during the Civil War. In 1861 an Irish priest named Father Thomas O'Reilly was assigned to the parish. He served as a confederate chaplain during the first stages of the Civil War and then opened his church as a hospital during the

---

[2] The first bishop, a 35-year-old native of Cork, Ireland, John England, was assigned to the newly created diocese of the Carolinas and Georgia in 1820. See Thea Jarvis, "Diocese's Growth: A Faith-Torch Passed," *Georgia Bulletin* (May 2, 1988) 1.

[3] Monsignor Noel G. Burtenshaw, "A History of Immaculate Conception Church," in *Shrine of the Immaculate Conception Dedication Program,* May 25, 1984, n.p. (A program on the occasion of dedicating the renovated church after its devastating 1982 fire.)

[4] Harvey K. Newman, "Some Reflections on Religion in Nineteenth-Century Atlanta: A Research Note," *The Atlanta Historical Journal* 27 (Fall 1983) 50.

[5] The most important resource for the first hundred years of the parish history is Van Buren Colley, *History of the Diocesan Shrine of the Immaculate Conception* (Atlanta: Foote and Davies Printing, 1955).

Battle of Atlanta in the summer of 1864. After the federal troops won victory, they forcibly evacuated much of the city's population and thus Father O'Reilly's parishioners. However, he soon filled the pews with "blue coats" during the three-month occupation. When time came for the federal troops to march south in November of that year, General Sherman ordered the city of Atlanta burned in order to assure that it would not return to its status as a major supply center for the Confederacy. However, Father O'Reilly spoke with Sherman, a Catholic himself, and warned that "if you burn the Catholic Church, all Catholics in the ranks of the Union Army will mutiny."[6] Sherman agreed, and so all the buildings adjacent to it were saved, including City Hall, Central Presbyterian, Second Baptist, and a number of homes and businesses.

As Atlanta's citizens returned to rebuild their homes and community, the members of Immaculate Conception also looked toward a new day for their parish. The old building, while surviving the fire, sustained gunfire during the battle and showed bloodstains on the wooden floor from its use as a hospital.[7] So, as a tribute to their faith and to the new spirit growing in the city generally, Father O'Reilly and the parish set about drawing up plans to build a new church building.

Drawing on Atlanta's leading architect, W. H. Parkins, the church laid out grand plans for their new church home. At this time the membership was likely the largest of any in the city, and they seemed to want to capitalize on this in producing a grand and spirited beginning to the building process.[8] The cornerstone was laid in

---

[6] Burtenshaw, "A History of Immaculate Conception Church," n.p.

[7] Because General Sherman's headquarters were in the John Neal house just down the street from Immaculate Conception, and the Union troops were camped out on the public square surrounding City Hall, all the nearby churches were used—St. Philips Episcopal as a horse stable, Central Presbyterian as a slaughterhouse, Trinity Methodist as a storehouse, and Immaculate Conception, a hospital. Only Second Baptist was spared such mundane use and could host the Christmas Day service in 1864 as Sherman and his troops left the smoldering city on their march to the sea. See the map and discussion in Colley, *History of the Diocesan Shrine of the Immaculate Conception*, 21–23.

[8] Newman, "Some Reflections on Religion in Nineteenth-Century Atlanta," estimates that in 1897, the earliest year for which we have records, Immaculate Conception's membership was around 400, with Wesley Chapel and Trinity Methodist churches next largest at 337 and 257, respectively.

style in 1869, including a procession through the streets of the city led by the firemen and the Gate City Silver Marching Band. The construction work was completed in 1873 to the acclaim of the city, and the parish welcomed the bishop from his offices in Savannah to celebrate the Mass. The local newspaper account described the dedication ceremonies at great length and commented that "the church is one of the handsomest in the South and is an ornament to our city."[9] Father O'Reilly, in the meantime, set about starting a school and did so with the help of the Sisters of Mercy in 1866. While struggling with poor health, he hoped to live long enough to say Mass in the new church. Unfortunately, his illness worsened, and after a prolonged battle he died in 1872 at the young age of forty-one. The whole city mourned his passing, both as a hero of the war and a faithful servant to the Lord. He was buried in a crypt under the altar of the new church, and his remains rest there to this day.

As Atlanta's population began to spread out along newly laid trolley lines in the 1890s, the Shrine faced a second pivotal moment in its history. Between 1890 and 1941, four new parishes were started to the north and east of the Shrine. These new parishes reflected the shifting population of the city out of the downtown area and into new suburbs, a trend that has seen only some modest reversal in the late 1990s. Although the parish had good pastoral leadership during these years, including Father Walsh, who led a fiftieth anniversary celebration of the new church's dedication, the parish was hard hit by the migration of families out of the downtown area. In this weakened position, Immaculate Conception was hardly prepared for the depression. Under the leadership of Father Joseph Moylan, the church struggled to provide for those in need, both within and outside their walls. In a concrete manifestation of such caring, the church founded a number of institutions. In 1888 the Sisters of Mercy, who had come at the behest of Father O'Reilly twenty years earlier, founded an infirmary, which later became St. Joseph's Hospital. Later, under Father Joseph Smith, the church founded Our Lady of Perpetual Help Free Cancer Home, set up to aid those who were terminally ill.

The World War II era brought unprecedented growth and change to Atlanta. The new interstate highway system both allowed the

---

[9] Colley, *History of the Diocesan Shrine of the Immaculate Conception*, 41.

city's growth ever farther out from the center city and took out large tracts of city housing as it was built. During these years the Shrine continued to struggle with a population of around a hundred families. The declining parish membership at the Shrine, combined with the rapid expansion of business and government in the downtown area, led then auxiliary bishop Francis Hyland to favor selling Immaculate Conception. Instead, Bishop Gerald O'Hara gave Monsignor James Grady, a native of Massachusetts, and an energetic young assistant, Father Donald Kiernan, also a transplant from that New England state, the mission to "restore and preserve" the church.

A fund-raising effort was undertaken, leading to a $100,000 renovation and rededication of Immaculate Conception as a shrine. This renovation and dedication were timed to take place in the Marian year of 1954, the one-hundredth anniversary of the definition of the dogma of the Immaculate Conception of Mary. The work restored the church building inside and out, including the woodwork, organ, and heating system, windows, and a new baptismal font donated the men's Holy Name Society. A grand rededication ceremony was presided over by Archbishop O'Hara. The cost, while great, was substantially reduced due to the volunteer labor of parishioners and remarkable fund-raising efforts that raised over $100,000.

According to Van Buren Colley, parish historian during this era, the restoration under Monsignor Grady "saved the Shrine, but the parish struggled with less than a hundred Catholic families, small for so great a Church."[10] In response to this continuing struggle in the center of the fast-growing Atlanta area, the Franciscan Fathers, renowned for their custodial ministry at Marian shrines worldwide, were appointed by the bishop to care for the parish in 1958. Their mission, according to the pastor during the late 1960s, was to make the Shrine "a place of prayer and devotion to which the 'sons and daughters of Immaculate Conception' love to return to refresh themselves with hallowed memories of yesteryears."[11]

Such a devotional and custodial pastoral approach dominated throughout the next decade as parish activities slowly contracted.

[10] Ibid.
[11] Van Buren Colley, *Shrine of the Immaculate Conception, Centennial Anniversary 1869–1969*, one-hundredth anniversary brochure, n.p.

By 1970, for instance, the parochial school begun by the church over a hundred years before had to close for lack of children in the parish.[12] For the same reason, the Boy Scout troop also ceased to exist. Still, due to the presence of the school through the 1950s and early 1960s, a number of African Americans had joined the still strongly Euro-American (Irish and Italian) parish.[13] This African American presence slowly grew to be roughly 40 percent of the membership by the mid-eighties but not as a result of civil rights activism or intentional outreach. While some of the Franciscan priests are remembered fondly for their pastoral work or personal warmth, a longtime member describes the period as "drifting" with no particular mission or goal other than self-preservation. Such self-preservation, however, required constant effort on the part of the membership, and monthly Holy Name Society breakfasts (with the Altar Society cooking!), bake sales, raffles, and other fund-raising activities doubled as providing important social time for the Shrine family as well as desperately needed funds for ongoing operations.

The pattern of self-preservation changed by force of external events in the early 1980s. First, the sudden rise in homelessness led the neighboring church, Central Presbyterian, to begin a night shelter. During the same period, while working at the Central Shelter, the Shrine pastor and a lay member (Father Thomas Giblin and Buck Griffin) conceived a plan to open a Saturday meal program for the hungry. They called it St. Francis' Table, and it has operated weekly since its inception in 1982.[14]

Second, just months after the genesis of St. Francis' Table, a devastating fire caused by an electrical short in the organ burned the

[12] The year 1960, ironically, marks the beginning of the rapid growth of the Roman Catholic Church in northern Georgia. There were 31,000 Catholics in 1960; 53,000 in 1970; 100,000 in 1980; 160,000 in 1990; and over 300,000 by the late 1990s, a phenomenal rate of growth driven by the general economic growth of the metro region during the same period. See Clint Williams, "Catholic Schools are in demand; Shift in metro demographics also has parishes 'just exploding'," *Atlanta Journal-Constitution* (November 7, 1999) A1.

[13] See Toinette Maria Eugene, *Black Catholic Belonging: A Critical Assessment of Socialization and Achievement Patterns For Families Black and Catholic* (Berkeley: Graduate Theological Union, 1983).

[14] Cathy S. Dolman, "St. Francis Honored by Catholics, Soup Kitchen illustrates his love, followers say," *Atlanta Journal and Constitution* (October 5, 1985) B4.

church badly. The sanctuary needed almost total renovation. After again entertaining the prospect of selling out to expanding state government offices, the parish plunged into a restoration process financed by fire insurance, spending nearly four million dollars in the effort. After sharing worship space for two years with Central Presbyterian next door, the Shrine was rededicated with great acclaim from civic leaders, preservationists, and parishioners, earning the accolade "renovation of the year" in the city of Atlanta.

The renovated building, while a source of great pride, also placed unprecedented financial burdens on what the rededication brochure called a congregation "consisting mainly of elderly people" who have "a sentimental rather than geographic attachment to the church." The insurance bill alone had tripled from $6,000 to $19,000 per year. According to Flora Graham, treasurer of the Altar Society, they had worked hard on their annual fund-raising drive, including a big breakfast, but only "raised about seven thousand dollars. It's not much." She continued, "I've been with the church more than forty years. We've worked on all kinds of fund-raising drives. We've always been very few, and the responsibility is great." While appeals went out for donations to the "mother church of Catholicism in northern Georgia," the pastor, Father Louth, noted that "people have moved out of the city gradually over the years. Nobody comes down here in the evenings. We're trying to build the church back up."[15]

By the mid-1980s, rumors circulated that the Franciscans were leaving the parish and that the Archdiocese of Atlanta would assign a priest to the church. Indeed, it was no surprise, then, when in 1987 the Franciscans announced their departure after thirty years at the Shrine, "citing a declining church membership and a need to serve elsewhere." The chancellor of the Archdiocese of Atlanta, Father Peter Ludden, recommended that while the ministries of the parish, such as St. Francis' Table, deserved to continue, "an enterprising pastor" might wish to consider opening the church to historical tours "as a way to make it better known and draw greater support from tourists."[16]

[15] Debbie Newby, "Fund-raising has new meaning at Immaculate Conception," *Atlanta Journal and Constitution* (August 24, 1985) B5.

[16] Gayle White, "Order gives up Atlanta Parish after 30 years," *Atlanta Journal and Constitution* (March 14, 1987) D2.

The new diocesan priest, Father John Adamski, spent his first year at the parish in a flurry of activity. However, despite his "enterprising" spirit, he had ideas for the revival of the parish other than putting it on the circuit of historical tours. Having been pastor of St. Anthony's Parish in the nearby West End neighborhood, Father Adamski knew well the challenges of parish work in downtown Atlanta. Further, he was just returning from a year sabbatical in New York City, where, through a series of coincidences, he had become involved in chaplaincy to men with AIDS.

A strong personality and savvy manager (he earned an MBA from Emory University in 1982), Father Adamski restructured the administrative and financial processes of the parish, making them accountable to him and to the parish as a whole. He facilitated the start of a weekly dinner for people with AIDS, the first of its kind in the city, and an important means of evangelism, leading in the course of a few years to a large gay and lesbian population among the membership. He worked with Central Presbyterian to open the parish hall nightly throughout the winter as an emergency homeless shelter. He presided over basic pastoral developments focused on encouraging deeper rootedness in the liturgical year, the sacraments, and thereby in the life of Jesus. A year before his departure, he helped the parish to celebrate its 150th anniversary with a year focused around the theme "People Living Church."

With Father Adamski's departure in June 1999, another chapter in the parish history begins. Its current life and prospects for the future, however, are deeply tied to the living memory of its long history. The historical sketch above provides some orientation to the milestones shaping the present community making up the Shrine of the Immaculate Conception. It is my task in the following sections to evoke a fuller picture of their public worship and public work, their rootedness in their sense of identity as a congregation, and the meaning of their commitments in their lives.

COMMUNAL IDENTITY

The location of the Shrine does not immediately give a clear impression of who would make up its membership. An ox-blood brick, gothic structure located in downtown Atlanta, Immaculate Conception is the oldest Roman Catholic church in Atlanta and one of the oldest standing buildings in the city. It faces in turn on its various sides the golden-domed Georgia state capitol building, the modern, reflective-glass Fulton County Justice Center, and the gaudy red neon World of Coca Cola, a museum dedicated to the history of the "world's most popular soft drink."

On any given Sunday morning, I found the diverse congregation to include young and old, singles and couples, both gay and straight, some with children and some without, able-bodied and physically or mentally challenged, well-off and homeless, highly educated and those with very little formal education. The majority, I learned, were college-educated, middle-class professionals in public and private-sector jobs.[17] While the majority were white, about 40 percent were black, and a few were Asian or Hispanic. The majority were straight, but nearly a third were gay or lesbian. While some traced family histories back to the beginning of the parish, many joined during the tenure of the current pastor, Father Adamski. While a good number of newer members lived in nearby neighborhoods in the process of gentrification, the majority lived scattered throughout all four quadrants of the city, both inside the "perimeter" and outside, with some driving up to forty minutes to get to Mass on Sunday morning.

The demographic realities of the Shrine's membership quickly taught me that the question is not congregational identity but rather identities. In both informal conversation and formal interviews, I asked people to share their view of the Shrine as a whole: What image would they pick to describe it? Why did they join? What do they like about it? The answers were both quick, animated, and varied. According to members, the parish was welcoming, diverse, open, committed to outreach or to social justice, relevant, or responsible.

Most remarkable, perhaps, in offering insight into their communal identity was the way the parish council described the church in a letter to the (as yet unknown) new priest as they anxiously faced the departure of Father Adamski. At a pastoral council meeting, Rich, a balding, middle-aged man who drafted the letter, intro-

[17] Some members I talked to held middle-management jobs with private companies in computer systems, in retail sales, and in finance. Most others held jobs in primary, secondary, and college-level teaching, in public-sector jobs with the IRS or the US Postal Service, or medical and social services jobs.

duced it and asked that all read it before the discussion. The others encouraged him to read the letter out loud to them and he did. After an introductory paragraph noting their anticipation of the new priest's arrival, the letter turned to a description of the Shrine:

"The Shrine strives to be a welcoming community. We work hard to make all people feel at home here. Our parish mission statement reflects that view: We are a diverse group of people working together in Christ's name to do Christ's work. We believe you will find an incredible array of talented people from all walks of life, all races, genders, economic levels, and sexual orientations ready to welcome you and worship together. It is especially at our liturgies, when we come together, that we welcome all and strengthen our community. Inclusive liturgy, with diverse lectors, Eucharistic ministers, altar servers, etc. show all that we seek to serve God by serving our neighbor. We come to the Shrine with a sense of mission to be the most loving, supportive community of Christians possible.

"We believe you will find the various ministries run by a dedicated set of volunteers. We encourage participation by our parishioners and are blessed with wide participation. We honor every person in our parish and seek to make sure every person sees him or herself in the visible ministries and leadership roles. Our members come from all over the metro area. Some have long historical ties to the Shrine from the days when we had a parish school. Many are new to Atlanta and find in the Shrine an accepting community of people. This may well be the most diverse group of people worshiping together in the Atlanta metro area. That diversity is the strength of the Shrine. It is what makes us unique. Since we are not like most parishes with a surrounding neighborhood that provides a natural source of membership, we have tried to make our parish a magnet for those seeking to worship in a diverse environment.

"Our parish ministries reflect that diversity. Our night shelter, St. Francis' Table, and our food pantry reach out to those around us in need of shelter and food. Our relationship with The Edgewood, a home for people with HIV/AIDS, continues a long tradition of service to those living with that disease. Our Bible study and Sunday School classes reach out to those in our parish seeking a greater knowledge of their faith. Our relationship with our sister parish in Haiti reminds us of our responsibility to the greater world community. We have been actively encouraging greater involvement with our Outreach Committee and are encouraging greater understanding of each other with various 'inreach' activities such as the Shrine Shepherds, the gay and lesbian discussion groups and pot lucks, and our welcome tables on Sundays. These are all activities we have put a lot of energy into and are working to make a success. The thread that binds them all together is the belief that our parish should be part of the larger community and should seek ways to minister to those in need."

People were clearly moved by the letter and broke out in spontaneous applause. While Rich asked them for revisions they felt were needed, none were offered. They talked through the process of assigning new priests in the archdiocese and agreed that as soon as they learned the identity of the new priest, they should send the letter "sharing the core of who the Shrine is and what they are committed to in a tone of welcome and willingness to work with the new priest and his ways of working, his plans."

After the meeting I lingered and talked briefly with Father Adamski. "That was a powerful letter, don't you think?" I said. And in his characteristic way, he spoke volumes with his facial expression—a sideways smirk, a roll of his eyes, and then finally, the comment, "Pretty idealistic." Later I thought to myself that he was exactly right, but not simply in the way he thought. As much as one could point to ways the Shrine did not live up to this image of an inclusive and committed community (Father Adamski's point), they believed themselves to be that community, and their actions were given shape in relation to such a vision of their life together.

Styles and Models of Congregational Identity
This vision of the Shrine's life, eloquently unfolded in Rich's letter, takes on further substance as I move to discuss the role of a dominant model of communal identity in the Shrine's life. Overall, the response to my questions in formal and informal interviewing showed that despite diversity of terms chosen by individuals to describe the Shrine, some patterns existed at the communal level. The shifting ideals orienting the Shrine's communal life came into focus as I interviewed Flora, a second-generation Italian American, a lifelong Catholic, and a Shrine member for more than fifty years.

After spending over an hour talking about the parish's history and "how things used to be," I asked her, "So what's changed?" Her abrupt answer jumped out of her mouth even before I finished my question. "Well," she said, "it's less family and more service-oriented." It was this shift, consolidated in my mind as I listened, that gave me a means of understanding much of the current identity of the Shrine as the members see it.

Flora's remark gives a clue to both the past and the current dominant identity of the Shrine, but it also raises the question of the change. Penny Becker, in her book *Congregations in Conflict*, found that four churches in her study did not have one clear identity but were in the (painful) process of shifting from one to another.[18] Each of these churches stood out in her study because of the qualitatively different level of conflict in comparison with the others. In each case the issues were brought to a head by a new minister who brought a new vision for the parish.[19] And in each, people left the church as a result of the conflict—either the minister with some who supported him or her or those who opposed the minister. The clash over cultural models highlights their structuring effect on the cultural and moral logic of the parish leadership, public ideals, activities, and moral commitments of a congregation. The models represent fundamentally different ways of doing things, so different in fact that they often lead to intractable disputes. Flora intuitively understood that this is what occurred upon the arrival of the pastor at the time of my study, Father Adamski.

Prior to Father Adamski's arrival, the parish was near exhaustion after its heroic struggle to maintain itself during the century-long decline of the downtown area. For decades the membership

[18] Penny Edgell Becker, *Congregations in Conflict: Cultural Models of Local Religious Life* (New York: Cambridge University Press, 1999) 149–171, indicates that the conflict very often falls along the lines of longer-term members and newcomers, as was the case at the Shrine.

[19] This is often the case in churches with a hierarchical polity, because the parish has little or no control over who the new pastor will be. This anxiety, combined with a recognition that with an episcopal polity the pastoral leader has significant structural authority, led the Shrine's pastoral council to develop and send the letter discussed above, in a sense "staking their ground" in advance, with hopes that the new priest would respect who they were and how they did things.

hovered just below a hundred families and at numerous points faced serious prospects of closure. The Shrine was run by Franciscan priests from the mid-1950s until 1987, when Father Adamski began, an era during which the church's mission was described by one lifelong member as a period of "drift." Yet, due in part to a core group of hardworking and committed members and the cachet of its historical importance as the mother church of Catholicism in northern Georgia, the Shrine survived. Most of the people I spoke to from this era described the church as family. When asked what stood out over the years of her membership, an older member said, "I guess it's the familiness, the closeness, of the church. Growing up, there were two strikes against us—we were Yankees and Catholics." The memories of discrimination and attacks by the Ku Klux Klan reinforced the "community with a community" characteristic of American Catholicism during this era.[20]

Programs of this period fit the "family" model: they were almost exclusively inner-directed religious and social in nature.[21] The programs and groups included the traditional Holy Name Society for men and the Altar Society for women; Boy Scouts; devotions to the Blessed Sacrament and Mary through praying the rosary; monthly "family breakfasts" in the parish hall; and regular fund-raising events, such as bake sales and raffles. Flora's preparation notes for leading the Altar Society meeting on Sunday, September 17, 1967, tell the story of the moral commitment required of the church "family":

New Business: *Our* Cake Sale, Sun. Sept. 2;
Why? (Resumé of expected bills—Mary Perry);
Sign list—Make ahead, freeze, desperate for cakes;
Up to *us*—get word around.

In my interview with her, she recounted the way the bake sales made up the gap between giving and the basic budget, while also often providing the needed money for repairs or special projects. Devoted family members tended to the survival of the parish, car-

[20] See Michael J. McNally, "A Peculiar Institution: A History of Catholic Parish Life in the Southeast (1850–1980)," in Jay P. Dolan, ed., *The American Catholic Parish: A History from 1850 to the Present*, vol. 1 (New York: Paulist Press, 1987); Charles R. Morris, *American Catholic: The Saints and Sinners Who Built America's Most Powerful Church* (New York: Times Books, 1997).
[21] Ibid., 80f.

ing for the building as their "spiritual home" and caring for one another through good times and bad.

Upon Father Adamski's arrival, change from a "family" church to a "leader" church happened quickly. So quickly, in fact, that within a year, some people had left the church, and a petition was circulating among longtime members asking the archbishop to remove him. In my first interview with him, Father Adamski said that when the Franciscans left in 1987, he thought the parish would close. It had an "ethos focused on the past, almost as a museum." He came with a vision to turn the parish toward the present and the needs of the community around the church. In the homily on the feast of the Pentecost, he offered one version of his basic theme:

"So, Church, we need to be real clear that we don't have to go looking—'Where is the Spirit?' 'What is the Spirit doing?' The Spirit is breathing in us today, praise God. You and I are not here about history, we're not here about two thousand years ago Pentecost. We're here because the Spirit is working in us so that we might build God's kingdom now."

Father Adamski took up this vision and never put it down. As a result, some longtime members, many of whom lived closer to other churches, simply gave up and left. However, many new members joined, a fact he accounts to the Shrine's "social outreach and people choosing to belong to such a parish." Indeed, I talked with one young computer engineer over a cup of coffee one Sunday morning. He had recently moved to Atlanta from Minneapolis. He had been active in the social justice ministries in his former parish and noted that "when I came to Atlanta, I looked around for a church with a social justice commitment; that's why I chose to come here."

Members of "leader" congregations find their membership important, in part "because it expresses specific social, political, and religious values." These are not, however, simply their own values but values seen to be embodied in the larger tradition or vision of the ideal. These programs often make the pastor a civic leader as well and give the congregation a reputation as a leader, reinforcing the understanding of congregational identity held by members. In fact, the Shrine was honored by the Christian Council of Metropolitan Atlanta in 1995 with the Christian Council Award for Exemplary Congregation Community Outreach.

A group of newer members told me that they visited many churches that felt "stale." The Shrine attracted them because it was more than just a warm and welcoming community. They also wanted "a level of commitment to those in need—not just paying for it so that they don't have to see it but actually doing the work." Over Father Adamski's tenure, the Shrine programs and activities included a homeless shelter; a soup kitchen; a weekly dinner for people with AIDS; work with a sister parish in Haiti; signing petitions against the death penalty; participation in the yearly gay pride parade; political organizing in ABLE (Atlantans Building Leadership for Empowerment), and others. Moral commitment to parish life is measured by commitment to a difficult openness that builds a diverse community and to "kingdom-building" work in people's lives and together as a parish.

It should not be surprising, however, that the complexity of parish life at the Shrine was not fully illuminated by the "cultural models," in which a dominant model is assigned to each congregation on the basis of terms member use to describe themselves. These "typological" approaches entail a necessarily reductionist effect because they focus on what differentiates one type from the others, thus de-emphasizing some key aspects of parish life. For example, Father Adamski focused very diligently on developing "community" within the parish and across its diverse membership, a characteristic of "community" congregations more than of "leader" types. Ritually, he instituted such innovations as congregation joining hands while the Our Father was sung; singing "Weave, weave, weave us together"[22] just after the sign of peace

---

[22] Father Adamski picked up this song from an ecumenical worship service done for the 1992 Democratic National Convention, held in Atlanta, used it at the Shrine, and "it became sort of a theme song for us." The original words and music are copyright © 1979 by Rosemary Crow. Its text, as used at the Shrine, is as follows:

Chorus:
Weave, weave, weave us together,
Weave us together in unity and love. *(Repeat)*

We are many textures, we are many colors,
Each one different from the others.
But we are entwined with one another in one great tapestry. *(Chorus)*

A moment ago still we did not know
Our unity, only diversity.
Now the Christ in me greets the Christ in thee in one great family. *(Chorus)*

was shared and people moved about, greeting, hugging, and shaking hands with one another; lastly, a lay-religious team leading the Rite of Christian Initiation of Adults, a rite mandated in 1988 for initiating new members into the Roman Catholic community through a process marked by liturgical rites celebrated in the presence of the whole community. Programmatically, the Shrine members attempted to build community by staffing a welcome table in the rear and wearing name tags; the "Snak and Yak" coffee hour after Masses; the "Shrine Shepherd" program, in which lay members took responsibility for a group of members and kept in regular touch; the "in-reach" survey, which attempted to connect members with similar social interests; and finally the RENEW 2000 faith-sharing groups.

Liturgical renewal, including increased participation by the laity, was a second area that was central to the parish and typical of "community" churches but not highlighted through a focus on Becker's "leader model" as most dominant at the Shrine. Father Adamski carefully worked to deepen the liturgical life of the Shrine and to develop some particular ways that manifested who he wanted the parish to be and what he wanted them to do as a result. The liturgical reform represented one aspect of the "whole cloth" vision he had of what it means to "be church,"something that he articulated most clearly in his homilies but also in various meetings and in response to my questions.

These hard efforts at reform of the liturgical life of the parish, about which I will say more below in the worship section, are not characteristic of the "leader" congregations, even though Becker admits that such congregations often combine a strong commitment to outreach with a strong emphasis on worship. She writes that they have "well-planned and well-executed worship services, paying a great deal of attention to having good liturgy and music," a comment that has a performance/audience overtone quite different from the highly participatory nature of liturgy at the Shrine.[23] Yet these summary comments do not do justice to the way Father Adamski used his pastoral authority to institute substantial liturgical shifts of emphasis in the parish's practice, all with an aim of

23 Ibid., 146.

doing liturgy in such a way as to draw people more deeply into an encounter with God and to change their own lives and the life of the community. It is to worship and the particulars of such pastoral intentions that I now turn.

PUBLIC WORSHIP

The liturgical space of the Shrine revolved around two main focal points, each in its turn drawing into its orbit all who gathered. The first, and on one level the most important, was the altar. From the base of the center aisle, carpeted stairs rose five steps up to a simple rectangular altar draped with a floor-length cloth the color of the liturgical season. Some ten feet behind, the old snow-white marble altar soared upward toward the brilliant blue and white stained-glass portrait of Mary. Parishioners came to the base of the steps to receive Christ's Body and Blood in the Eucharist, a most holy moment in the liturgical ebb and flow.[24]

At the other end of the center aisle was a large baptismal font, marking both the transition from the downtown streets into the ritual space and the transition of each Catholic from the world into the Body of Christ, the church. The eight-sided font, made of rich natural wood and cream-colored tile, included both a pool for baptism and an elevated basin with water flowing over into the pool. The pool was four feet square, with water two feet deep, allowing baptism by immersion. The small elevated basin offered easy access for members who, in remembrance of their baptism, dipped the tip of their hand in the water and made the sign of the cross upon themselves. Upon entering and leaving, members approached the font, dipped a hand or finger in the holy water, signed themselves, and in so doing recreated the font's role in constituting the community as one in Christ.

The font offered a way to illuminate both the liturgical reforms undertaken by Father Adamski and their intended formative power. Father Adamski, a diocesan priest, went through seminary during and after the Second Vatican Council, a watershed for liturgical reform in the Roman Catholic Church. His enthusiasm for

---

[24] While the Eucharist is very important at the Shrine, I have abbreviated the description here, given the more extended discussion provided previously in chapter 2.

embodying these reforms in his parish work was reflected in his day-to-day manner of presiding at the liturgy—at the blessing, for instance, his long arms extended straight out, fingers spread wide, he seemed literally to extend the blessing to every corner of the room. Yet, he would say, it was not his presence but the rites themselves that he wanted to be powerful and effective.

FIGURE 3.1—
A STANDARD ORDER OF SERVICE FOR THE SHRINE

Elapsed Time	Order of Service
	Introductory Rite
0:00	Organ Prelude
0:04	Tolling of the Hour
0:05	Processional
0:06	Greeting
0:07	Rite of Sprinkling/Penitential Rite
0:10	Kyrie-Gloria
0:11	Opening Prayer
	Liturgy of the Word
0:12	First Reading (Old Testament but Acts during Lent)
0:16	Responsorial Psalm
0:19	Second Reading (usually an Epistle)
0:21	Gospel Acclamation
0:22	Gospel Reading
0:24	Homily
0:31	Profession of Faith
0:33	General Intercessions
	Liturgy of the Eucharist
0:36	Preparation of Altar and Gifts/Preparation Hymn
0:41	Eucharistic Prayer
0:49	Lord's Prayer
0:51	The Peace
0:53	Sharing Holy Communion/Communion Hymns
1:03	Post-Communion Prayer
	Concluding Rite
1:04	Announcements
1:07	Blessing
1:08	Dismissal
1:09	Recessional Hymn

Further, Father Adamski did not want the responsibility or credit for making happen whatever went well. For instance, he felt that the old font, located near the front of the church, and the accompanying seasonal decoration around the font (the Advent wreath, for instance) took attention away from the main actions of reading Scripture, preaching, and presiding at the meal. Nevertheless, in recounting the decision to remove the old font and replace it with a large pool-style font near the rear entrance, he shared the credit with the parish: "We put it in six years ago and it's the best thing we've done since I've been here."[25] There are layers of meaning to claim about the importance of the font, including its new centrality in the daily and weekly comings and goings of parishioners, its offering of a space from which to anchor the renewed rites of baptism and confirmation, another Vatican II reform, and its offering of a visual focal point for seasonal displays, such as the Advent wreath or other seasonal and symbolic art, as the first thing seen by entering worshipers.

Most important to highlight here, however, were Father Adamski's claims that the rites themselves are powerful enough to draw people into deeper communion with God, an experience that can transform people and make not only a personal but a social difference. This vision, deeply influenced by strong ideas about worship, is at root a theological vision about the divine transformation of the people of God in worship, so that they become disciples of Jesus, builders of the kingdom in the world and in their lives. I described one version of this vision in my notes on Father Adamski's homily on the feast of the Transfiguration, a homily that responded to the text from Matthew 17 in which Jesus is joined by Elijah and Moses in a blinding mountaintop vision of glory witnessed by the disciples Peter, James, and John:

"We must not cut short the journey to Jerusalem by trying to prematurely stay in the glory on the mountaintop; its point is to fill us

[25] He neglected to mention, and I did not know at the time, that the old font was a gift of the Holy Name Society for the 1954 renovation, when Immaculate Conception was designated a shrine. No older members mentioned this as an issue, but those who would have been upset by this action would likely have already left the parish some years before (the font was installed in 1994, more than six years after Father Adamski became pastor).

with a vision of that Glory, of God's kingdom, and to give us a model, from Jesus' life, of discipleship so that we can engage in many acts of blessing, transfiguring the systems of the world right now. This goes on in providing a place for the homeless with the night shelter, feeding the hungry through the work of St. Francis' Table, through collecting powered milk for Our Lady of Perpetual Help in Haiti. According to the world, we have nothing in common with that parish in Haiti, but according to God's vision, we are sisters and brothers, members of the same body, and belong to each other. Our work with them transfigures the circumstances of poverty and malnutrition. This story of the Transfiguration is not just a story of long ago, but, we believe, a story about how God works, how Jesus is present to us today in the Eucharist, that we might experience a taste of that glory and so be encouraged to join in the work of discipleship, of being a blessing to many."

Father Adamski not only preached this message, but he also attempted to embody it in the liturgical life of the parish. His most focused effort in this regard took place in an attempt to recover and revive the parish's celebrations during Holy Week, and especially the Triduum, the three-day liturgy stretching from Holy (or Maundy) Thursday through Good Friday to its conclusion in the Great Vigil of Easter on Saturday night. The Triduum, the symbolic heart of the worshiping community at the Shrine, was the life-blood of the parish during the rest of the year. This powerful, emotional, and dramatic three-day liturgy after weeks of spare Lenten liturgies drew together and constituted the parish both as a distinctive community of people and as the theological "Body of Christ," having died and risen with Jesus through the waters of baptism. One member described its meaning: "The Triduum is for us, for me, the culmination, its everything that we believe in, its our whole faith crammed into three days."

Some weeks beforehand, I asked Father Adamski what he expected and hoped for during the upcoming Holy Week liturgies. He said, first, he hoped everything that needed to get done would and that "things come off well." After the logistical worry, his greatest hope was "to make the traditions accessible to people so as to draw people in, to be influenced by the rites." I asked why this concern, and he said that attendance historically had not been that great, but it had been getting better the last two or three years. I asked what accounted for the recent growth in attendance. He said, "It takes time to draw people in, for them to get used to the rites, to expect and look forward to them."

Two key moments in the Holy Thursday liturgy illustrated Father Adamski's concern for rites that draw people in, that give a glimpse of the kingdom that leads to a discipleship "transfiguring the systems of the world." One key moment opened the liturgy. No formal processional had taken place in liturgy over the past six weeks of the Lenten season. On that day, however, a grand processional took place, including altar servers, acolytes, ushers, the deacon, and the priest, but also many lay members carrying every item needed for the liturgy over the next three days. My notes pick up the scene as people ascended from the basement parish hall, where a traditional Passover dinner of lamb and bitter herbs had just been served:

"We finished the meal and went upstairs to the church to find a bustle of activity—people were coming in, some sitting in the pews, some milling around in the rear with bags of bells, handing them out to one and all, some with banners waiting for the processional. About 7:10, after much conversation between Father John and the other processional members, including much pointing toward the altar and around the church, the procession was ready. As if he almost forgot, Father Adamski turned at the last moment and took a spoonful of incense and sprinkled it into the thurible, and smoke immediately rose up. Jeffrey, the music minister, struck up a strong prelude on the organ, leading us into the singing of the great hymn 'Lift High the Cross,' and those around us sang out with uncommon gusto. The procession was headed by the white-robed acolyte swinging the thurible, followed by an acolyte carrying the cross, then the banners—four of them, each a pole with four branches like an 'X' on top of the pole, each draped with long strips of colored cloth, giving the effect of cascades of color hanging down and flowing as the bearers slowly twirled the pole and walked forward—first green, then red, then violet, then white. Following was everything needed for the liturgy over the next three days: the Lectionary; the three vessels of oil; the new paschal candle (carried by Brad over his head, both arms stretched up toward the ceiling as if to hold the candle as high as possible); the Easter altar linens and vestments; bread and wine for Eucharist; an icon; a towel, bowl, and pitcher; and finally a branch of a redbud tree just beginning to bloom. Last came the assisting minister, Deacon Bill, and Father John. The procession was carried out by women and men, young and old, black and white, walking and wheelchair bound, gay and straight, member and catechumen, clergy and lay. Everything was set down either on the altar (wine, bread) or on the two tables prepared just in front of the left and right corners of the altar (left, holy oils; right, things needed for worship). It was colorful, joyful, and done with a deliberate step, savoring the glory of the first procession since the beginning of February two months ago."

When the Worship committee met a week later to evaluate the Holy Week services, Father Adamski was particularly proud of how the procession had come off. It was to him an embodiment of who the Shrine was and at the same time a vision of what the church should be. Brad, who had carried the paschal candle, had this to say: "Here we were, multicultural, with homosexuals and heterosexuals, and in the eyes of a lot of people that was not acceptable—that's not what the Catholic church is all about, and that's what I don't believe in, you know. I think that church is church and community is community, and it takes the whole group, no exclusion." The symbolic strength of the procession lay in its representation both of the difficult and real achievement of community across differences at the Shrine. They talked about community in terms of tolerance of individual difference *and* of all people being God's creatures. It was visually powerful, dramatic even, and worked to serve Father Adamski's ideal that these rites would be attractive, that they would draw people into an encounter with God and leave them changed in such a way that they in turn would change the world.

A second key moment took place just after the reading of the traditional Holy Thursday gospel from John 13, where Jesus kneels to wash his disciple's feet, saying, "A new commandment I give to you that you love one another; even as I have loved you, that you also love one another. By this all people will know that you are my disciples, if you have love for one another." In his homily Deacon

Bill encouraged the parishioners to help one another in simple, everyday ways so that through these things they might "develop strength as disciples, a strength that will allow us to face temptation and have the grace to do the right thing. . . . Washing one another's feet may be a small thing, but do it as one way to live in the identity given us by Jesus, that of servant and disciple." My notes describe my participation in what came next:

"The foot-washing began simply by the worship leaders spreading out to the eight locations in the front and in the rear where chairs, basins, pitchers, and towels were set for this purpose. A hymn/chant, 'Jesus took a towel,' began, and the people around me began to take off their shoes and socks in the pew. I watched for a bit, wanting to see what would happen. None of the lines of people overflowed with people, and the ushers watched over it all to assure that no stations were empty while others had a line. In each case the minister or worship assistant simply provided assistance to the parishioners who washed each other's feet, two by two. On one occasion, when a family came together to wash, the mother and small daughter sat down in the chair, and Father John, who facilitated that station, washed their feet. The rite had a flowing feeling, partly because of the chordal progression of the song, influenced by the African American spiritual tradition, and partly because the water was warm and the bowls and pitchers of white china were beautiful, partly because of the gentleness of the action. I put my feet in the bowl. The woman washing my feet took the pitcher and poured an ample amount of water over my feet and then, kneeling before me, took one foot in her one hand and scooped water onto my foot as she gently 'washed' or 'scrubbed' my foot, almost as if the water was lotion and a simple, gentle rubbing of the water over the foot accomplished the cleansing needed. This was repeated with the other foot. Then she took the towel I'd brought and held it open for me to place my feet into. She dried off my feet and then spread the towel on the floor for me to step on. All this done with no words other than the singing of the chant/hymn. As I stood, the worship assistant took the bowl, emptied the water into a nearby five-gallon, white plastic food-service bucket and replaced the bowl at the base of the chair. Most if not every single person present participated. It is not required that the community wash each other's feet as we did, but it is suggested and it brings home the reality of the assembly as the Body of Christ together, taking on Christ's life and ministry of servanthood in the world, as in the message of Deacon Payne's homily."

Again, as with the procession, the foot-washing enacted strong symbolism of the real communal ties many feel at the Shrine, a fact represented by the washing of each other's feet (while at the Cathedral of Christ the King, just a few miles north on Peachtree, Archbishop Donahue washed the feet of twelve pre-selected men from the parish, thus symbolically enacting something altogether different). Yet the washing of each other's feet also embodied the claim made about members of the parish community also being members of the Body of Christ, disciples of Jesus. The foot-washing teaches through the ritual action a way of servanthood meant to impact their lives in the world. As one member, Susan, told me, "I mean, its so servile, and that total reversal of power creates new patterns of relationships." She had been so moved by the ritual that she had actually proposed a new model for management relations at her corporate office on the basis of the foot-washing.

Lois's impact on the community's sense of identity symbolized a certain commitment to caring across differences, a difficult and varied unity among diversity. This communal ideal undergirded and in some significant way authorized the foot-washing rite as such an experientially, emotionally powerful rite for those who participated. This, then, led to other action as a church and individually, such as Susan attempted at her work. I will return to these connections in the conclusion in an effort to speak to the ways these strong rites can and at times do influence the world in ways Father Adamski evoked in his vision for liturgical life and discipleship. Now I must turn to an all too brief account of the various social-ethical ministries of the Shrine.

PUBLIC WORK

Masses on holy days and Sundays were not the only important liturgies impacting the social vision of the Shrine. There were more fluid, less formal "liturgies," celebrated around other tables, where such a vision was expressed and enacted. For example, Walter, a second-generation custodian at the Shrine, led the church's effort to feed the homeless, coordinating volunteers and cooking for more than five hundred men, women, and children every week since 1982.[26] Often between the two Masses on Sunday mornings, I would find Walter and various Shrine members talking around the table in the kitchen downstairs, drinking coffee and eating cream donuts or sausage biscuits. This kitchen crowd, whose number at one time or another made up a large percentage of the congregation, volunteered together for St. Francis' Table, for the night shelter, and for AIDS ministries. Through this work of presiding at the tables of service, they connected to the parish identity, to the character of the community, and doing so made up the ties that bind liturgy and social ethics.

I call these gatherings "liturgies," because in the literal sense of the term, liturgy is a public service, a public work, and also because of the centrality of these gatherings in doing the work of building a camaraderie that both comes out of and impacts participation in the main liturgy. Attempting to make such connections, one kitchen regular remarked, "It's not so much liturgy, okay? What's important is community, it's sharing your life that matters, it's what comes out of the Mass." It is what comes out of the Mass—their connection to one another, their commitments to the idea of the parish as diverse, socially responsible, and so on—that, through working together over time, folded them into a solidarity, into some common commitments to the work of serving the needs of the city.

Journalists and outsiders who have visited the Shrine have noted three main ministries through which the Shrine served the needs of the city. While these were core to the people's sense of identity as a congregation, they were also interestingly marginal to the actual lives of many members. Each of the three, which I will briefly describe below, at one time actively required the involvement of large numbers of members. One of these ministries, however, ceased in 1995 due to waning participation, while the others have been largely, though not wholly, taken over by legions of volunteers from local campus ministries, from suburban parishes and parochial schools, and from churches of other denominations. Efforts on the part of Father Adamski to jumpstart other social minis-

---

[26] Mr. Moore died in August 1999, yet the weekly ministry goes on as he would have wanted.

tries and an outreach committee to coordinate all these efforts were mixed. I will return to these issues after noting the basic contours of the outreach programs that made the reputation for the Shrine in the city.

Each of the three main programs the Shrine is most recognized for bears the shape of Father Adamski's phrase of self-understanding: to be "acting in the manner of Christ" in offering hospitality and dignity through the provision of basic needs. However, the first of the three programs began five years before his arrival. St. Francis' Table began in 1982, an idea conceived by Father Thomas Giblin, O.F.M., and lay member Buck Griffin while volunteering at Central Presbyterian's emergency night shelter for the homeless (Central directly abuts the Shrine on its eastern side). Father Giblin and Mr. Griffin realized that on Saturday no other organizations in the downtown area were providing services and food. Started with the assistance of Walter Moore, this table ministry has been open continuously every single Saturday since then, including two years when they were forced to move to nearby Trinity United Methodist Church while the Shrine was rebuilt after a devastating fire. As one participant put it, "Prayer takes the form of feeding others. We in turn are nourished in spirit."

The second ministry began in 1987 with the institution of Tuesday Nights at the Shrine, evening sit-down dinners for people with AIDS and their friends and families. At the time it was the only program of its kind in the city. According to Brad, the program's cook and kitchen coordinator, "It was a sit-down candlelight dinner—with *real* plates."[27] The Shrine music minister, also director of the

[27] The real plates mattered in terms of attempting to make the dinner a meal of dignity, one that reflected their intention to do things "in the manner of Christ," whose giving of himself in the Eucharist formed a moral paradigm for social ministry at the Shrine. The plates also mattered quite profoundly for those members who early on rejected Father Adamski's focus on social ministry. He recalled that "the congregation wasn't too excited about this in the beginning, it was all 'Ooh, ooh, we're going to eat off these dishes?' because it was dishes, glasses, silverware, it was not throwaway stuff, so, yeah, that was not a happy thing, but the people who were complaining were here on Sundays. This was on Tuesdays, they never sort of saw much, they knew that it was happening because I made it clear, but the communities didn't intersect in the beginning."

Atlanta Gay Men's Chorus, brought the chorus to perform. The program was not welcomed by all, to be sure. Brad painted a picture of the times: "A lot of the members left because of it. At that time, 1987, at that point in time it was still space suits, masks, gloves, fear of breathing on each other, and I think that took a lot of guts on Adamski's part, and you know he's never gutless." As the population with AIDS changed and the need for the program diminished (other programs started up to fill this role in the community), the Tuesday night dinners ended in 1995, and volunteer efforts shifted to participation in such programs as Project Open Hand, which delivered meals to people with AIDS and provided a monthly meal at the Edgewood, a residence for people with AIDS.

The third main ministry of the Shrine, like St. Francis' Table before it, grew out of the night shelter for the homeless in next-door Central Presbyterian Church. Central Night Shelter, opened in 1981, originally took in over two hundred men a night, offering hot tea and a spot on the floor. During a renovation at Central in the late 1980s, the shelter moved into the Shrine. When the shelter moved back into the Central facilities in 1992, the Shrine joined the Central Night Shelter, opening its parish hall so that together they offer ninety men a cot, a shower, a hot meal, TV to watch, and weekly foot exams by volunteer doctors. Begun in response to a homeless person freezing to death just beyond the church steps, the shelter was now open every night of the winter, November 1 to March 31. Mark and Katie, members of the Shrine, ran Central Night Shelter since its beginning, thus providing the only free shelter in the city, and all with volunteer effort. According to Katie, "If hospitality and respect are the tone, breaking down barriers is one of the central missions. Finding out that these are real people. They have the same dreams, hopes, weaknesses, and faults that we have. We need to break down prejudices, the myths, the misunderstandings." While much of the staffing came from other Catholic parishes, campus ministries, and other churches, the Shrine members officially staffed one night a month; some volunteered much more. One Shrine member, Chris, who volunteered once a month for six winters, said, "I was drawn to the Shrine for its outreach ministries and people like Mark and Katie, people who are committed to the poor, to social justice, to outreach ministry."

To be sure, there were many other outreach ministries beyond those three major ones. More occasional involvements included participation in marches (the Atlanta Gay Pride Parade, the Hunger Walk, the annual Walk for Life); tutoring in the nearby housing project, Capital Homes; and partnership with a Haitian sister parish, Our Lady of Perpetual Help. Such commitments led to widespread recognition of the Shrine as a leader in social ministry. For members of the Shrine, such recognition and the ministries that corresponded to it were at the core of the parish's image as a "leader" congregation, a responsible congregation, a place, as Father Adamski put it, where "hundreds of volunteers from all over the city join in service to others."

Most journalistic accounts of the Shrine do not make it past this outward image, one that is indeed important to members but is not the whole story. My presence in the congregation, asking about the relation between liturgy and ethics, attending planning meetings, talking with individuals, regularly elicited joking and at the same time introspective reflections on the gap between ideals and commitments on the one hand and actual follow-through on the other. Father Adamski admitted that organizing efforts for deeper commitments among the congregation as a whole were tough going. Again and again in planning meetings, the problem of busy schedules and/or a lack of time came to the fore. As Father Adamski looked forward to the summer of 1999, when he anticipated leaving the Shrine, he decided to work toward formalizing some of the scattered outreach efforts by starting an Outreach Committee. This committee, I would argue, was as important a gauge of the social-ethical commitments of the Shrine as were the three main outreach programs discussed above.

On only my second Sunday worshiping at the Shrine, I got into a conversation with Laurie, the rectory manager for the Shrine and an Outreach Committee member. She warned me that not many people were really active in social outreach: "It is hard to encourage the congregation to be active beyond one-time actions like collecting dry milk to send to our sister parish in Haiti or doing a Habitat project." Indeed, Father Adamski confided that his greatest regret in his outreach work at the Shrine was the lukewarm commitment members made to the city-wide, church-based organizing project ABLE (Atlantans Building Leadership for Empowerment). While a few political issues were addressed, these were occasional protests organized primarily by Father Adamski in conjunction with the ministers at nearby Central Presbyterian and Trinity United Methodist.

To try to get closer to this dynamic of social commitment struggling toward but not quite reaching sustained social-political analysis and action required by longer-term projects such as ABLE or adopting a Kosavar refugee family (another possibility discussed by the Outreach Committee), I will return to the example of the Shrine Outreach Committee's Easter season project on the death penalty (see my opening vignette about Lois, pp. 75–78). During the March planning meeting, the Outreach Committee chairwoman, Susan, talked some about long-range planning, but at Father Adamski's encouragement, came back to discussion of "What next?" Shuffling through a pile of mail in front of him, Father Adamski said that various things had come to him in the mail. One in particular, a petition campaign to put a moratorium on the death penalty, according to Father Adamski, "is something that the Pope has been speaking about and would give us an opportunity to tie in some education on the church's social teaching so that people know what stands the Catholic church has taken on some of these issues." Given the Christian Council of Atlanta's (CCA) upcoming April breakfast with Sister Helen Prejean, author of *Dead Man Walking*, this idea seemed to be just the right one. Taking into consideration Father Adamski's view that many in the pews would be supporters of the death penalty and would therefore need attention in liturgy and adult education before any "action" took place, the group enthusiastically planned a five-part process. Week by week the program would include viewing the video of *Dead Man Walking* with discussion; the following two Sundays would feature 10:00 a.m adult education classes on the topic; throughout the issue would be mentioned in the prayers and homilies; and finally attendance at the CCA prayer breakfast with Sister Prejean would be encouraged. With Father Adamski agreeing to take care of details in conversation with the Life Concerns Committee, under whose purview the issue fell, the meeting adjourned.

The events went off well, one by one. The first Sunday, around forty people ate lunch together and viewed the video *Dead Man*

Walking. The second Sunday, Father Adamski preached powerfully about how "faith in God should shape our attitudes toward one very significant issue in our society: the death penalty." He challenged those who might view the death penalty as acceptable: "We come together today as God's people to affirm that our faith is in *God's* ways. And the Easter challenge, if you will, is that whenever our attitudes are not transformed by God's power, then we have not fully entered into the meaning of Jesus's victory over sin and death." That same Sunday the first adult education event was led by Ron, a member of the Life Issues Committee, a Pax Christi activist, and a death-row lay minister. He outlined the empirical arguments against the death penalty but said that despite these, the vast majority of the American people said they support it. He led a skillful discussion to get at the attitudes that each of us harbors, giving rise to the urge for vengeance.

The second adult education event, led by Andy, another Life Issues Committee member and death-row lay minister, gave an extended introduction to a Georgia death-row inmate named Ron, whom Andy visited each month. This personal introduction to an inmate led to a discussion of how to come to a position of opposition to the death penalty. Ken, a new Catholic, summed up his own transformation on the issue over the past weeks in this way: "I remember when Tip O'Neill came out with his book *All Politics Is Local*. I think that a good paraphrase might be *All Religion Is Personal*. It's not the institution that does things, it's people."

The April Outreach meeting fell on the Monday after the last adult education event and after the breakfast with Sister Prejean but in time to finalize plans for a final event that would, in the words of Outreach Committee chair, Susan, "take action on our faith, provide ways to take action." She reported that the events were well attended and that there were about forty people "psyched" to do something. Betti warned that it must be an individual action, not a corporate action, for a response on this issue is "a matter of the heart." Susan suggested that indeed individual events had worked in the past—they could have an anti-death penalty petition to sign or an opportunity to write a letter to a death-row inmate. My field notes carry the back and forth discussion of ideas forward, a most extraordinary set of exchanges:

"Larry then jumped in, sort of struggling for words, 'What does one—it feels so final— this person is going to die. What does one write?' To which Andy said, 'Friendly stuff, like a pen pal. Each person is an individual—just get to know them.' But, he continued, 'You have to keep in mind that some can't write, some are retarded, and it's rare that they can keep up an active pen-pal relationship.' Paul wondered aloud if the parish could 'adopt' a death-row prisoner. Betti jumped in and said, 'I have a problem with that. First, security makes it unfeasible. It is a difficult six-month process to be allowed permission to visit, and only a few are granted the right per inmate. Second, a "parish" can't establish a relationship with an "individual."' She suggested we could *pray* for people as a parish, just like we have our prayer intentions. Andy suggested that the people he and Ron currently visit and write to could be prayed for. Larry suggested 'an angel tree like we had at Christmas.' They had a tree with the names of needy kids and a brief story about them on a tree, and you could take one and get a gift for them. He said, 'For the death-row inmates, we could have a name and a story to take home, you know, keep on the refrigerator, to keep in prayer, and have a point person to give updates on the person's status on death row as it changes. It would be good to have specific names to pray for, not like when we pray for our sister parish in Haiti.' Father Adamski jumped in and said, 'Oh, Father Roberto wants to change that. He wants us to visit, to meet them. He'd have lots of names for us.' Ron came in at this point and pressed for doing more than the 'angel tree' idea; he raised signing the moratorium on the death penalty and having an opportunity to write and visit death-row inmates. Larry led the discussion and kept raising the point that without a name and a brief story and a nice quote, it wouldn't 'touch people's hearts.' He said, 'We need a personal story; just a name is boring, a story makes it more personal.' Ultimately, a compromise action plan was worked out, and Larry agreed to help organize it along with Father Adamski and the Life Committee members."

The next Sunday the final event took place. Just before the final blessing of the Mass, the parish said together "A Prayer to Abolish the Death Penalty," written by Sister Prejean and inserted into the bulletins on attractive three-by-five cards. At each Mass an

Outreach Committee member announced the success of the series of events related to the death penalty and invited members to stop by the tables in the rear of the church, where they could sign a petition against the death penalty and pick up a flyer with the name and story of the two death-row inmates whom Shrine members visited. Shrine members could pray for them, write them, or learn how to become a visitor to Georgia's death row. The parish would continue to pray for the inmates, and the congregation would receive regular updates on the inmates' lives and changes in their status. About half the congregation took part, coming to the tables to sign the petitions or to pick up the colorful flyers with vignettes about the two death-row inmates visited by Ron and Andy.

Ironically, as they struggled to reach out in effective ways, acting on their values, the Shrine Outreach Committee was at the same time living Christian community in a way that itself spoke boldly to the world's concern for unity within diversity, for the oneness experienced by this community of people as the Body of Christ but absent in so many other places in the world. It is striking that they struggled in this way, and as I will discuss further in chapter 6, their identity both led to this struggle and hid it from view by virtue of its "naturalness."

Chapter Four

"Jesus Saves":
Big Bethel African Methodist Episcopal Church

OPENING SCENES

I took the MARTA train downtown and walked the few blocks to Big Bethel through the early morning chill. As I hurried down Butler Street, I could see the looming steeple of the church bearing the famous neon blue "Jesus Saves" sign. I was headed to a "Love Feast," a traditional Methodist ritual that John Wesley learned from Moravians on his boat trip across the Atlantic some two centuries earlier. Big Bethel holds the "Love Feast Prayer Service" at 7:30 a.m. on the Saturday before the first Sunday of the month, the Sunday when they celebrate holy communion. I walked through the side doors of the imposing granite building and down into the fellowship hall, where chairs were set up in six rows of five on both sides of the middle aisle, for a total of sixty chairs. I found a chair near the rear and waited, noting that in front a table was set up, draped in white linen cloth covering trays.

People of all ages streamed in steadily, and when the prayer service began, there were nearly forty people, giving the space a cozy, well-filled feel. For the most part, people wore sweat suits, casual clothing such as jeans and sweaters, and only a few people wore dress clothes. The service was coordinated by the Married Couples' Ministry and consisted of an opening hymn ("Blessed Assurance"), an invocation prayer ("Dear heavenly Father, we just thank you that you allowed us to gather in your house once again . . ."), a Scripture reading, and then alternating prayers and hymns. Jacques, the energetic music minister, was there to play the old upright piano in the corner. Each section of prayers had three parts, each prayed by a member in his or her own style, from the heart, and regarding a given topic. For instance, the various sections focused prayer on spiritual maturity and Christian discipleship, on national and local government, schools and school officials and teachers, and on the hungry and homeless everywhere. While some prayers were quiet meditations guiding us in our "supplication before the Lord," others built a crescendo plea, boldly approaching "the throne of grace."

As this pattern of prayer and hymn singing continued (we always sang two verses of hymns, never more), people streamed in, and before long the place was packed with nearly a hundred people, including at least ten children of varying ages. As the prayers concluded, Reverend James Davis moved to the front of the room, offered some words of greeting, and asked how many had not been to a Love Feast before. About ten people raised their hands. To this, he and other regulars said, "Praise God!" He noted that it was important for members to keep reaching out, to keep getting to know others. As if to make his point, he asked, "All right, somebody raise their hand if they know every person in the room." No one did. Then he said, "Somebody raise their hand if you see three people you don't know." Nearly all raised their hands. He took a moment to have each person find three people they didn't know and introduce themselves. It was an upbeat and friendly break of about five minutes, with people milling around, talking, and hugging.

Then we moved into a large circle, and Pastor Davis asked the Rev. Jeffrey Streator to describe the symbolism. While Rev. Davis and Rev. Wood-Powe stepped around the circle with silver communion trays, handing each person a clear plastic communion cup filled with water, Rev. Streator described the symbolism of the water. Because of the water's transparency and purity, one is encouraged to let go of grudges that prohibit interpersonal transparency. And if one bears a grudge against someone, before going to the altar for communion the next day during the Sunday morning service, he or she should go to that person and make amends. He stated that "the purity of the water symbolized that 'transparency of love' that should mark the community." Then each person was given a piece of white bread, about a third of a slice lengthwise. I thought we would then eat it. Actually, however, no one ate the bread. Each person got a piece of everyone else's bread. This, according to Rev. Streator, was "intended to build fellowship, to be a symbol of oneness."

Starting with Rev. Davis, the process began: he gave a piece of bread to the person to his left. That person took a piece of his bread, and they hugged and exchanged God's blessing by saying, "God loves you and so do I." Each subsequent person peeled off and followed Davis, forming a second inner circle that moved around the outer circle until everyone had exchanged bread and greetings in a similar way with every other person in the room. I noticed that in the process people stuffed the tidbits of bread they received from others into their little communion cups; at the end all the cups of bread were returned to the altar table, and we sang a stirring rendition of "Amazing Grace." Before closing, Rev. Davis introduced Mother Theodora, who stood hunched over her cane near the altar. He reported that she was one of the oldest members and, he said, "has adopted Love Feast and comes every time, even today when she doesn't feel well." People applauded and Rev. Davis commented that this might have been the most successful Love Feast yet.

During the process of waiting for the bread to come around, I chatted with Ms. Green, a member since 1948 and a stewardess, the ministry group that hosts the Love Feast. She noted that this ritual was new for Big Bethel, even though it had deep roots in Methodism generally. In a later interview she credited this to Rev. Davis's being "a deeply spiritual man, and a visionary." Indeed, the Love Feast and Rev. Davis's enthusiasm for it went to the root of this old church and accounted in large part for its current revival. Such a circle ritual had deep roots in the slave "ring shouts" related to me by another old member, Mrs. King.[1] And out of the solace of such song, prayer, and common spirit, gatherings in this fellowship hall have given birth to schools, financial institutions, local civil rights actions, and many programs of social uplift for members and beyond.

[1] See Art Rosenbaum and Margo Newmark Rosenbaum, *Shout Because You're Free: The African American Ring Shout Tradition in Coastal Georgia* (Athens: University of Georgia Press, 1998).

Yet the storied history of the first black church in the city could not alone keep the church vibrant and engaged today. A downtown church whose members left the neighborhood decades ago faces a peculiar problem of attracting membership and building community. The Love Feast symbolically represented a central thread Rev. Davis used to stitch the community together; as he noted at the ministers' meeting held directly after the Love Feast, "We need to work on fellowship, for commitments to do don't *start* with doing—they start with family. We need to put all our commitments down, take time to become brothers and sisters, and then together go and do." The Love Feast, however, was also about doing. Fellowship served the agenda of "kingdom building." As Rev. Davis often said in his charge to the neophyte Christians who answered the "Invitation to Discipleship" after the sermon on Sunday morning, "Salvation is not a feeling, it's faith; now believe and live like a saved person ought." The church that proclaims "Jesus Saves," through programs that reach all over the city and beyond, finds its taproot in becoming a fellowship of disciples, gathered to feast on love.

HISTORY OF BIG BETHEL
AFRICAN METHODIST EPSICOPAL, 1847–2000
The history of Big Bethel is in large part the history of "the black side," to quote the title of the Rev. E. R. Carter's 1894 volume on the history and present shape of the city. As the railroads expanded in the 1840s, the early residents of Terminus worshiped together in one church, called Union Church. According to Rev. Carter, the whites used the building in the morning, while blacks could use it in the afternoons, but only under the supervision of a white pastor and with the requirement to use "portions of scriptures that refer to passages like, servants obey your masters, etc."[2] As an old former slave named Andrew Montgomery, a resident of Terminus from its earliest days, put it, "The negroes had to consider themselves the shoe soles and the whites the upper leather."[3] Although the exact details are not known, it is not surprising, given the tension of such a situation, that before long an itinerant minister

[2] Edward R. Carter, *The Black Side: A Partial History of the Business, Religions, and Educational Side of the Negro in Atlanta, Ga.* (Atlanta, 1894) 14.
[3] Carter, *The Black Side,* 14.

A view of Big Bethel A.M.E.
from across Auburn Avenue

passed through who preached "the Word as found in Christ Jesus,
regardless of one's feelings." This sermonizing "enraged the
whites," who thereafter "refused the negroes privilege to hold
services in their church house again."

Mr. Montgomery and a number of others brought their plight
before Lemuel P. Grant, a Maine native recently transplanted to the
city as chief engineer of the railroad.[4] A Presbyterian and one of the

---

[4] Carter, *The Black Side*, 15; Charles Rutheiser, *Imagineering Atlanta: The
Politics of Place in the City of Dreams* (New York: Verso, 1996) 140.

leading businessmen in the city, Grant had amassed large swaths of real estate and gave the church a small plot of land on Jenkins Street (now International Boulevard) and Courtland Street. On this plot of land they built Bethel Tabernacle, with the assistance of the Methodist Episcopal Church, South, and were served by a white minister, Isaac Craven, though the church was never listed officially as one of his charges.[5] By 1860 there were 9,554 residents of the city, with 20.3 percent black: 1,914 slaves and only 25 free. While many blacks had to attend the churches of their masters, sitting in the segregated balconies, increasingly they came down from the balconies to attend Bethel Tabernacle.[6]

The Civil War radically changed Atlanta's "black side" as well as its white side. However, instead of viewing the falling shells of the advancing northern troops as the "Great Unpleasantness," they believed that "the shells of General Sherman were the strokes of the hammer of liberty, unfastening the fetters of the accursed and inhuman institution of slavery."[7] While the A.M.E. Church previously met great challenges to its missionary efforts in the South, it prepared diligently for the new challenge of responding to this vast new mission field of freed slaves.[8] As Wesley J. Gaines, the second pastor of Bethel Tabernacle and later an A.M.E. bishop, put it, "The joyful news of emancipation had scarcely been heard be-

---

[5] Interview with Mrs. Mary Ruth Talmadge King; Perlie Craft Dove, "Big Bethel African Methodist Episcopal Church: A Century of Progress and Christian Service," in *Big Bethel African Methodist Episcopal Church: A Century of Progress and Christian Service* (Atlanta, 1968) 11.

[6] Dana F. White, "The Black Sides of Atlanta: A Geography of Expansion and Containment, 1870–1970," *Journal of the Atlanta Historical Society* (Summer/Fall 1982) 208; "Historical Synopsis of Big Bethel African Methodist Episcopal Church," brochure, n.d.

[7] Carter, *The Black Side,* 17.

[8] On the difficult efforts of the A.M.E. evangelization in the South, one could cite the example of Charleston, where Morris Brown led his congregation into the A.M.E. connection in 1820, only to be banned as a result of one of its members, Denmark Vesey, leading a slave revolt. It was another forty years before the A.M.E. church could return to Charleston. See James T. Campbell, *Songs of Zion: The African Methodist Episcopal Church in the United States and South Africa* (Chapel Hill: University of North Carolina Press, 1998) 35; Clarence E. Walker, *A Rock in a Weary Land: The African Methodist Episcopal Church During the Civil War and Reconstruction* (Baton Rouge: Louisiana State University Press, 1982) 20.

fore the African Methodist Episcopal Church of America made its preparations to send missionaries to the South." Led by Bishop Daniel Payne, the A.M.E. Church held its first Southern Conference session in Charleston in 1865. Bishop Payne sent the Rev. James Lynch, from Baltimore, through the upper part of Georgia. While passing through Atlanta, he met a lay preacher from Bethel Tabernacle, Joseph A. Wood, who, after hearing Lynch describe the A.M.E. doctrine and policies, led Bethel into the A.M.E. connection. A year later, at the Annual Conference session in Savannah, Wood and fellow preacher Wesley J. Gains were ordained deacons, and Wood began his service as the first black minister of Bethel Tabernacle.[9] First Rev. Wood, and after two years, Rev. Gaines, labored to build the church in the midst of the city that grew more than fivefold in the thirty years after the Civil War. Much of the growth came through the former slaves who streamed into the city looking for work and opportunity.[10]

Before the war blacks lived throughout the city, a residential pattern know as "marble-caking" or the "back-yard residence pattern."[11] However, the population of the city exploded in the years after the war, especially its population of newly freed African Americans. The city was made the headquarters for the Freedmen's Bureau for the region.[12] Because the majority of the prime real estate downtown and north along Peachtree was owned by wealthy whites, a unique pattern of segregated housing took place, in effect creating "urban clusters" along the "periphery of the city, where land was inexpensive and available in large tracts."[13] New neighborhoods sprung up, including Shermantown, east of the old downtown. When Bethel Tabernacle's membership outgrew its building on Jenkins Street, Rev. Gaines led the church to sell its property and purchase a new site in the center of this new neighborhood on

[9] Wesley J. Gaines, *African Methodism in the South or Twenty Five Years of Freedom* (Chicago: Afro-Am Press, 1969 [1890]) 4; Dove, "Big Bethel African Methodist Episcopal Church," 11–12.

[10] Rutheiser, *Imagineering Atlanta,* 20–21.

[11] White, "The Black Sides of Atlanta," 208–209.

[12] Rutheiser, *Imagineering Atlanta,* 20. This federal agency was set up in 1865 to mediate the transition between slavery and freedom for the South's newly emancipated African American population.

[13] White, "The Black Sides of Atlanta," 208.

Wheat Street (now known as Auburn Avenue) near the corner of Butler Street.

In retrospect, this choice could not have been better—the church was now squarely in the middle of what by the mid-twentieth century was called "the richest Negro street in the world," in large part because of the presence of black-owned insurance and banking companies as well as various churches, small businesses, and the nation's only daily newspaper owned by blacks, the *Atlanta World*.[14] Under Rev. Gaines, the church built a large brick structure, simply called Bethel A.M.E. Church, completed in 1868. During the next twenty years, the city and the church both grew, and Bethel was instrumental in leading the efforts in education. In 1879 the Gate City Colored School was founded in the basement of Bethel, and two years later Morris Brown College was founded in the same way.[15] C. L. Harper, who headed Big Bethel's Sunday School during the 1930s, also served as the first principal of Booker T. Washington High School, the first African American high school in the city. Such examples show the prominence of Bethel and its members, making it commonly known as "Sweet Auburn's City Hall."[16]

Yet, perhaps because of its prominence and size as well as the fine pastors who gave it leadership, Bethel had outgrown its brick church by the 1890s, and the lot next door was purchased for construction of a new church, to be called "Big Bethel." Not long afterward the gray stones were being hauled from the quarry at Stone Mountain, where some of the members worked as stonecutters.[17]

[14] Emmet John Hughes, "The Negro's New Economic Life," *Fortune* 54 (September 1956) 248.

[15] The first board of trustees for Morris Brown College was made up of four former pastors of Big Bethel as well as one prominent lay member, and the first classes were also held in the basement. See Dove, "Big Bethel African Methodist Episcopal Church," 13.

[16] Ibid. While no direct evidence exists for it, one can imagine Bethel at the center of meetings to plan the black community's (1919) voting boycott of two referenda in support of tax increases earmarked for education expansion; finally, a third referendum was offered that included plans for two new black grammar schools and the first black high school, Booker T. Washington. See White, "The Black Side of Atlanta," 215–216.

[17] In my interview with Mrs. King, she noted that the infamous KKK leader and owner of Stone Mountain, Mr. Venable, gave the church a "deal" on granite—any broken pieces, twenty dollars a wagonload.

Although condemned twice for poor construction, in 1891 and 1898, Bishop Henry McNeal Turner declared on the occasion that Big Bethel, the mammoth structure remodeled and reopened for public worship September 23, 1899, was a great structure with a capacity unequaled in the city of Atlanta." While this facility served the community in the aftermath of a terrible fire in the neighborhood in 1917, the newly remodeled church suffered its own devastating fire in 1920.[18] Members were stunned, furthermore, to discover that the insurance on the building, one of the largest black-owned churches in the country, had expired the day before. Rebuilding cost the church dearly; at $135,000, the repairs were nearly half the original price of $300,000.

The church rebuilt in two years time. Yet, despite many donations from well-wishers, the church had to incur a great debt to numerous financial institutions. Crowning the newly rebuilt church, the steeple bore a lighted cross bearing the message "Jesus Saves," which shines over the city today. Still, the struggle to pay off the debt strongly marked the church's focus through the next quarter century. Rev. Singleton, pastor at the time of the fire, hatched numerous ideas to aid fund-raising, including the formation of two concert choirs that alternated at Bethel's services and sang concerts throughout the region.

A decade later the most significant fund-raising idea emerged. Ms. Lula Byrd Jones shared her idea for a morality play called "Heaven Bound," suggesting that if the choir put it on, they would help put the church out of debt.[19] The choir director, Ms. Nellie Davis, a talented musician and an English teacher, took up the idea and developed a full script. The play centered on various pilgrims, portraying diverse life situations, on their way toward the pearly gates. A hit from its first performance in 1930, the play became a staple of the church's life throughout Depression-era Atlanta. The

[18] I follow the dating of Dove, "Big Bethel African Methodist Episcopal Church," 15, who dates the fire in 1920, restored by 1922, and Rev. Singleton's death in 1923; but note the discrepancy with Gregory Coleman in his book *Heaven Bound: Portrait of a Black Sacred Drama* (Athens: University of Georgia Press, 1992) 23, who dates the fire in 1923.

[19] The story of the play, as well as the congregation's history, is well told by church member, former cast member, and now the drama director, Gregory Coleman, in his wonderful book *Heaven Bound*.

play was performed in various municipal theaters and at locations all over the South and has been performed every year since, now in the first weeks of November. In no small part because of this success, the Rev. D. T. Babcock was able to lead the mortgage burning ceremony in 1945.

Ironically, this watershed moment marked a turning point for the church. During the post–World War II years, a process of residential dislocation because of urban renewal and the building of an interstate through the east side of downtown effectively ended the era of Big Bethel as a "neighborhood church." Throughout the 1950s and 1960s, residents who could moved out of the downtown area, primarily to the new middle-class black neighborhoods in southwest Atlanta, where a majority of the longer-time members live today.[20]

The 1960s brought a crisis between the generations sparked by the civil rights and black power movements. These movements affected the church internally, creating tensions between an older generation accustomed to its ways and the younger generation, with new ideas and opportunities, critical of whatever in their view accommodated too much to the dominant white culture.[21] These structural and cultural forces pressed hard on Bethel, so that by the early seventies, a church that at one time was filled for Sunday services with two thousand worshipers now had dwindled to less than two hundred. As Gregory Coleman notes, if members who had moved to the west side of Atlanta had not continued to journey back across town on Sunday morning, "the church might have ceased to exist."[22] The commitment of extended family units like Coleman's kept the church going through lean and difficult years.

[20] During the twenty-year period ending in 1990, real median household income of Atlanta African Americans declined by 26 percent, while the metro area income for blacks rose by almost 43 percent, a change that reflected exactly this migration of middle-income blacks out of the city. See Mary Beth Walker, *A Population Profile of the City of Atlanta: Trends, Causes, and Options* (Atlanta: Research Atlanta, Policy Research Centers, Georgia State University, 1997).

[21] Coleman, *Heaven Bound*, 135ff. See also the seminal work by A.M.E. theologian James H. Cone, *Black Theology and Black Power* (New York: Seabury, 1969), and a lucid discussion of the period in C. Eric Lincoln, *The Black Church Since Frazier* (New York: Schocken Books, 1974).

[22] Coleman, *Heaven Bound*, 138.

In 1980 a fiery young pastor named McKinley Young, himself brought up at Bethel, was appointed pastor. Decades of urban decline left the Auburn Avenue corridor in shambles; brothels, prostitutes, and small-time drug pushers now greeted members arriving for worship on Sunday morning. Rev. Young took the church and the community head-on, radically redirecting the church. As Gregory Coleman describes it, a fundamental shift took the church away from its past, with its "concentrated attention to debts, renovations, and other internal affairs," including the significant work of educational advancement for a generation of former slaves and their descendants.[23] In a new day, with an increasingly more affluent, more educated congregation and with more diverse professions represented, the church shifted its outreach efforts to include "community members who were hungry, without adequate clothing, or in prison." Various programs were set up to respond to the destitute, including the Welcome Table, providing meals, and the Dorothy Young Help Center, providing emergency assistance.

The changes in membership not only affected the program focus of the church; Rev. Young's tenure also brought significant changes in worship and music too. As a harbinger of generational change, some older boards and choirs disbanded, while others, like the contemporary gospel choir, Voices of Inspiration, gained new prominence. Along with a growing trend toward "neo-Pentecostalism" in the A.M.E. Church nationally, the younger Big Bethelites seemed to move away from the more staid anthems and spirituals of their parents' generation toward the more upbeat gospel sound.[24]

While many older members thought the music "too rowdy and too much like the blues to be considered sacred," for the younger Big Bethelites "its emotional appeal reflected the strong African tradition of the ring shouts, hand clapping, and call-and-response handed down from the 'invisible' slave church."[25] Rev. Young's strong leadership in preaching, worship, and music, and the constant

[23] Ibid., 147.

[24] For a discussion of the growing neo-Pentecostal movement in the A.M.E. Church, see Eric C. Lincoln and Lawrence H. Mamiya, *The Black Church in the African American Experience* (Durham, N.C.: Duke University Press, 1990) 385–388.

[25] Coleman, *Heaven Bound,* 153.

drumbeat for community and justice issues turned Big Bethel toward a new day.

When Rev. Young was elected a bishop in the A.M.E. Church in 1992, Rev. James L. Davis, a fifth-generation A.M.E. pastor, quickly moved to uphold Rev. Young's gains while tending to the decades of wear and tear on the building. One of his first actions required fixing the "Jesus Saves" sign that had gone for some time with the "Jes" burned out. He quipped, "We have to find 'us' in 'Jesus.'" With hindsight, though, it is obvious that he had in mind remodeling more than the facility. In fact, his ministry focused on multiple renewals, including a multimillion dollar renovation of the historic church building, but also focusing on renewal of the membership through spirited preaching and worship, Bible study, men's ministries, family and youth programs, and, most boldly, renewal of the whole Sweet Auburn neighborhood through the Nehemiah project. Such changes are the primary focus of the remainder of the chapter, and I turn now to them.

COMMUNAL IDENTITY

By far the most imposing building along this stretch of Auburn Avenue, Big Bethel's grey granite spire rises high above the modest, two-story brick buildings housing businesses and church offices on the rest of the block. As telling for the church's membership, however, one block to the east cars zoom by on the Downtown Connector, a merger of I-75 and I-85 through downtown Atlanta. The freeway both hastened the out-migration from the neighborhood thirty-five years ago and now provides the ease of access for members driving to the church from such suburban Atlanta communities as Smyrna and Marietta, fifteen miles to the northeast, Riverdale, twenty miles south, and Stone Mountain, a similar distance straight east. Walking up to the church on Sunday morning, signs of suburban success are present, such as Mercedes and Lexus automobiles pulling up to park alongside the many more moderate sedans and sport utility vehicles.

As I noted after my first visit, the congregation on a Sunday morning was predominantly African American and of all ages. While the congregation was weighted slightly toward middle-aged to elderly, there was a significant group of younger adults in their thirties and forties and many children. As a rule, dress was very formal, with men in suits and women in dresses. A few women wore large, pastel-colored hats. While the church had long been home to a fair share of educated professional members, its older members still remember days of working as domestics and in other low-end service jobs. Each younger generation, however, grew in the diversity of its work affiliation; the largely public-sector and self-employed work of the civil-rights generation (baby boomers) has given way to much more private-sector employment in the post-civil rights generation (Generation X, or the "busters"). Rev. Davis has especially tried to draw this youngest group into leadership, "planting the seeds now for Big Bethel's future." One evening he told his Steward Board that "when we have young professionals working at major corporations and when IBM trusts them, when CNN trusts them, then the church has to trust them."

The impressionistic description of the church thus far helps bring to the fore why, when asked for one word to describe the church, members often said "diverse." In the face of changing demographics in its membership, one of the biggest challenges Big Bethel faced was being more than a historic elite church on Auburn Avenue. On the one hand, its historical status gave it a unique visibility in the city. Often referred to as "the old landmark," its cachet of historical importance for the African American church in Atlanta was rivaled only by Ebenezer Baptist Church, the home church of Rev. Martin Luther King, Jr., located just a few blocks to the east. As the first black church in Atlanta and the mother church of African Methodism in the region, Big Bethel certainly deserved its designation as a "historical landmark." Its distinction and the hard-earned distinction of its accomplished members made its historical importance central. During the fall of 1995, while worshiping across town so that Bethel could undergo a $1.6 million interior renovation, Rev. Davis said, "This is a tried and proven facility. We're committed to restoring it because it has a place in history."[26] Featured prominently on its Web site, its mission statement, the church's 150th anniversary brochure, and on the sidebar of the thank-you letter sent out to visitors, Bethel's historical consciousness

[26] Patti Puckett, "Rebuilding God's Houses: Bucking U.S. trend, intown churches spend $30 million to spruce up sites," *Atlanta Journal-Constitution*, (Oct. 21,1995) F/06.

embodied the spirit of the A.M.E. Church as an institution that knew the "stony road" it had trod.

On the other hand, however, the fact that the membership lived nearly everywhere in the city but in the surrounding neighborhood meant that the church had to foster an identity that drew its metropolitan membership downtown.[27] As one member, a middle-aged banker who lived in southwest Atlanta, put it:

"We're an urban church and it's difficult to get people to drive all the way in here from the suburbs. They have to drive by nice big churches with easy, flat parking lots, where people can just stroll out to their cars talking on Sunday morning. It's a challenge to keep professional people coming all the way down here—there has to be a draw, there has to be excitement."

While members gave many responses to the question about what they liked at Big Bethel, the "red thread" stitched through all the responses boiled down to spirituality. Mr. Clark, a middle-aged man and trustee at the church, remarked that at his previous church he was "drying up." At Bethel, however, he had found a spiritual leader who would inspire and nurture him. "That's what I get here, and it goes back to Rev. Davis." Another noted that "before Rev. Davis, this was not a tithing church, and not the Word-based church it *should* be. Before Rev. Davis, Bible study was only on Wednesday night, and wasn't well attended." Typical of many members, the renewed spiritual depth in the life of the congregation was credited to Rev. Davis's dedication, energy, and vision.

A key element of Rev. Davis's efforts at spiritual renewal focused on "rebuilding the family of God from the inside," and for him this began with reclaiming an active place for men in the life of the church and the family: "Men are our greatest concern and the greatest way to get back on the right track."[28] Mr. Petty, a member for more than twenty years and a member of the Steward Board and Male Chorus, discussed this in my interview with him:

[27] It is noteworthy that on Big Bethel's Web site, the directions posted only refer potential worshipers to the church via the four major freeways crosscutting the city.

[28] Gayle White, "Big Bethel pastor sees positive sign: 'Rebuilding the family of God from the inside' is church's goal," *Atlanta Journal-Constitution* (May 20,1993) D/26.

"I like to bring my lunch in to Rev. Davis's office, sit down with him, and ask him about what's going on or about some specific issue I need some help understanding. We are in the process now of forming the Council of Men's Ministry bringing together the Male Usher Board, the Male Chorus, the Sons of Allen, and the Fishers of Men Bible Study. This has been an important focus for Rev. Davis because some men will hide in church, and others will just get turned off because other men are not involved."

After a career in computer networking, first for a local university and then for the regional transportation authority, he wanted to bring his professional management experience to the task of organizing the men's ministry. He continued:

"I want to have them all get together on a Saturday to brainstorm, to put their ideas on paper. I learned the team-building approach in the secular world, but even biblically, Moses's father-in-law taught him to organize and delegate. The aim would be to have the men come together, to fellowship and have fun in the church without it having to be a card game or a ball game. I'd like it to be something with spiritual benefit, something that serves the Lord."

Organizing "something that serves the Lord" fit the overall characteristic of Bethel's center of gravity historically and in a focused way under Rev. Davis's leadership. There were many effects of this emphasis on spiritual renewal at Big Bethel, including the men's ministries, but extending far beyond them as well. I will return to examine some of these ministries and their renewal in more detail in the sections on public worship and public work below. I pause here to ask about Big Bethel's fit within the organizational styles and models I discussed above in chapter 2.

STYLES AND MODELS OF CONGREGATIONAL IDENTITY
Simply by nature of its historic and present prominence in the city, Big Bethel fit more on the public/outward-focused organizational orientations and models. In Roozen, McKinney, and Carroll's terms, Big Bethel fit very closely with the churches representing a "civic" style of public engagement.[29] For example, Carmel Baptist, the oldest black church in Hartford, had a proud history of fine

[29] Roozen, David, Jackson Carroll, and William McKinney, *Varieties of Religious Presence: Mission in Public Life* (New York: Pilgrim, 1982) 128ff.

minsters, worship, and music, as well as leadership in civil rights and education. Located in a formerly thriving downtown neighborhood, its fortunes fell as its members moved to the suburbs. Key to the civic orientation was corporate support for the status quo combined with concern for public life and issues. But when it came down to action, members expected the church to educate them on issues but not become a corporate social actor; rather, individual members acted on the basis of considered positions.

Such a description does not exactly fit Big Bethel, for as I will discuss below, its very history and identity, not to mention specific outreach programs, such as the Nehemiah Ministry, blurred such distinctions as public/private and individual/corporate. Further, while Carmel was puzzled about how to respond to the local community surrounding the church and was resigned to stay a "quiet, dignified congregation" separate from the "more emotional, vocal" worship desired by neighborhood residents, Big Bethel worked to reground its ministries in the needs of the community while reorienting its worship in ways that included a wider diversity of tastes and styles of music and worship participation.

But Big Bethel was not an in-your-face, activist church either. Roozen's other public-oriented mission style, the activist church, is critical toward the status quo and doesn't mind ruffling civic feathers to bring issues of justice to the fore. While Becker's models focus more on the form of organizational culture as opposed to Roozen's focus on the content, her evocation of "leader" model churches nonetheless draws in the sort of congregation like Big Bethel, which understands itself as responsible to the public. In Penny Becker's analysis of the "leader" model churches, as I discussed in the chapter on the Shrine above, a premium is placed on "community service, compassionate outreach to the poor, civic involvement, and political activism in the service of religious values."[30] But both "activist" and "leader" congregations depend on the liberal notion of society split into public (male, political, impersonal) and private (female, familial and religious, intimate) realms.[31] Thus

[30] Penny Edgell Becker, *Congregations in Conflict: Cultural Models of Local Religious Life* (New York: Cambridge University Press, 1999) 146–147.

[31] See Jean Bethke Elshtain's *Public Man, Private Woman: Women in Social and Political Thought* (Princeton: Princeton University Press, 1993) among many other relevant works.

more activist congregations are, according to these models, more concerned with public issues than interpersonal intimacy.

Yet, from the perspective of Big Bethel, a key question was: Which definition of public counts? The historic black churches like the A.M.E. have particular characteristics that make them confound such organizational models, and for particular reasons. First, the African American community exists as a counter-public sphere, exemplified in Atlanta by the title of Rev. Carter's book, *The Black Side*.[32] Therefore, when asking about the church's "public" influence, one needs to specify; Rev. Davis's focus on men's Bible study and participation in church may seem private from the dominant liberal paradigm, but such an evaluation would grossly misunderstand both the intention and broad impact such a ministry entails.

Second, the black church, as *the* institution at the center of the black community, necessarily has a complex identity. Such a view was summed up in Lincoln and Mamiya's influential proposal of a "dialectical model" of the black church that holds in one image the tensions between a priestly and prophetic voice, between otherworld and this-worldly concern, between ideals of universalism and particularism, between the communal and the privatistic, between charismatic and bureaucratic organizational forms, and between resistance and accommodation.[33] Big Bethel, as a result of its historic place in the city, its size, and relative affluence, considered itself "one of the vital urban churches in Atlanta" and certainly a "leader" and "civic-activist" congregation. Yet the tensions that ran through the church pushed such a straightforward application of a model toward the sort of complexity Lincoln and Mamiya describe. Whatever the polarities, Lincoln and Mamiya argue that it is most important to stress "the dialectical tension and constant interactions."[34] Roozen and coauthors bow toward such a dialectical view in their conclusion when they note that for their two "activist"

[32] See the notion of the black church as a counter-public sphere in Evelyn Brooks Higginbotham, *Righteous Discontent: The Women's Movement in the Black Baptist Church, 1880–1920* (Cambridge: Harvard University Press, 1993) esp. 10–11; the concept of a counter-public sphere is further theorized by Nancy Fraser, *Justice Interruptus: Critical Reflections on the "Postsocialist" Condition* (New York: Routledge, 1997) 75.

[33] Lincoln and Mamiya, *The Black Church*, 10–16.

[34] Ibid., 15.

case studies, "activist emphasis is complemented by careful attention to pastoral care and nurture of the members."[35]

Another key dialectical tension, mentioned by Roozen et al. in their chapter on Carmel Baptist but not elaborated further, figures prominently in the black church generally, and Big Bethel is no exception. This tension between a highly personal and evangelical theology and a strongly activist and political theology is implicitly bound up in the neon beacon proclaiming "Jesus Saves" atop Bethel's steeple. The complexity is made explicit in Bethel's mission statement:

"Our mission is to proclaim the gospel of Jesus Christ and to communicate to the world through preaching, teaching, evangelizing, worshiping, and stewardship that 'Jesus Saves.' Our goals are to administer to the physical, spiritual, intellectual, and emotional needs of our members and the community through Christian ministries and outreach, and to serve and preserve our surrounding urban community for present and future generations through economic development and empowerment."[36]

Such a wide-ranging mission confounds typical white-church paradigms of liberal and conservative, activist and sanctuary. Juxtaposing an emphasis on Jesus' power to save with the church's duty to extend such salvific power to the worldly needs of an impoverished neighborhood helps make clear in general terms the manner in which Big Bethel is a recognized "leader" congregation in its city, denomination, and nation. It falls to the next two sections to specify this dialectical organizational logic through specific examples drawn from its worship and social-ethical action.

PUBLIC WORSHIP

The most striking thing in my interviews at Big Bethel was that when I asked people where they meet God, rather than saying some aspect of Sunday morning worship, they told me about experiences of prayer and praise in daily life. This one is typical.

"Where do you experience God the most?"

[35] Roozen, McKinney, and Carroll, *Varieties of Religious Presence*, 249.

[36] This mission statement is ubiquitous, printed on the inside cover of every worship bulletin and used by Rev. Davis in his public descriptions of the congregation, as, for example, in his letter on the Big Bethel Web site.

"Personal prayer. He reveals himself most sometimes when I'm not expecting it, like when I'm shaving. For example, a while back, my mother had a stroke and she was in the hospital, and we were not making much progress in her recovery with the medical approaches. So I decided to look into some herbal remedies, and we tried some things and she really responded and was doing much better in a couple of weeks. And one morning I was shaving, looking in the mirror, thinking about my mom and feeling pretty good about myself for the way the herbal remedy helped, and God just spoke to me as clear as day, 'Bill, it wasn't you, it was me.' I was so humbled because, of course, it was the truth. Those types of situations are most powerful. My most intimate time is when I'm meditating— even when I'm driving."

Such a perspective is remarkable for the image of God as personal, intimate, and conversational. And one minister connected this back to both an African sense of the ubiquity of the divine in everyday life and the way that prayer and Bible study prepare one to connect with the Holy Spirit in the midst of Sunday worship.[37] Thus, for Big Bethel, rather than the worship service as the center of worship life for the congregation, it is in an important respect the communal expression of daily praise given up by members as they go about their daily lives.

The dynamic of Big Bethel's communal expression of worship consists of a three-way interaction between the congregation, the clergy, especially the preacher, and the musicians, especially the choir. After giving a brief description of the worship space, I will discuss the interrelation of the three. The shape of the sanctuary beautifully facilitates such a dynamic interaction. The field notes from one of my first Sundays at Big Bethel offer a good sense of the building's layout.

"I walked up the two flights of stone stairs with the flow of finely attired people streaming into the sanctuary. One of the ushers, attired in a white dress and white gloves, held the door and offered me a program, warmly welcoming me to the church. I went

[37] Relevant here are Lincoln and Mamiya's discussion of the black sacred cosmos in *The Black Church and the African American Experience*, 2-7; and John S. Mbiti, *African Religions and Philosophy*, 2nd ed. (Oxford: Heinemann, 1989) esp. 1–5.

through the door and sat down in the second pew from the back. The pews arc in a half circle reaching from one wall all the way around the pulpit and choir area to the far wall, eight sections of pews, each the shape of a slice of pie. A red sweep of carpet curved around the back aisle and flowed down the aisles between the sections of pews leading up to a white, two-foot-high altar rail that also curved in a half circle from wall to wall. The rectangular room has a balcony on three sides, and the white ceiling is some forty or so feet up. The outer walls are adorned by elegant, opaque, pastel-stained glass. The front area holds a small altar on floor level behind the altar rail, with a stone pedestal font next to it. Just above and behind this, the pulpit area is elevated about three feet and holds a row of dark wood carved and padded minister's chairs, thirteen in all, with a silver pitcher and silver goblets set just next to the center seat. In front of this section of chairs, in the exact middle of the pulpit area, a large wooden pulpit stands, holding a very large, black, leatherbound Bible. Just behind this area for ministers, the choir rows rise up from a traditional pipe organ console to meet the golden organ pipes that fill a cavernous space in the back wall. The choir director plays an electronic piano just to the right of the choir, and in tight rhythm with the choir and keyboards, a drum, bass, and Hammond organ keep the beat from down in the far right section of the front aisle."

The congregational arc surrounding the pulpit, lectern, and choir/music space allowed for dynamic interaction between "pulpit and pew" but also across the pews, since such a configuration wrapped the congregation around the pulpit, unlike the traditional "cigar box" church with straight rows of pews receding from the pulpit area. This spatial arrangement, while certainly not determinative, aided the sort of spirit-filled spontaneity that emerged during the services.

While it might seem backwards to take up congregational participation first in my discussion, before considering the "leadership" of the service by clergy and musicians, in this case it is justified because of the dynamic interaction such participation produces with "the Word performed" both in sermon and song.[38] Par-

[38] This wonderful phrase is used in Lincoln and Mamiya, *The Black Church*.

ticipation slides between two poles in Big Bethel's worship: order and the Spirit. Both components are powerfully present each Sunday morning; both have important roots in the denomination's history and current patterns of worship.

Order in worship is a hallmark of the A.M.E. Church, and Big Bethel is no different. Upon entering the sanctuary, a finely dressed, white-gloved usher hands out a thirty-two page program that includes the order of worship on pages eight through thirteen (see figure 4.1). The order of worship itself lends an orderly dignity to the rhythm of participation for the congregation. As the associate pastor, Rev. Wood-Powe noted, "Worship doesn't change that much but follows a pretty basic pattern from week to week." This pattern was standardized in the American Methodist Episcopals Church Hymnal and derives from typical early Methodist patterns of worship.[39] It includes such traditional elements as "The Doxology," sung to a full pipe-organ rendition of the classic tune "Old 100th," and the recitation of "The Decalogue," including Jesus' summary of it, interspersed with sung responses and followed by a verse of the hymn "Nearer, my God, to Thee," concluding with another full pipe-organ "Gloria Patri."[40] This liturgical order provides the backbone of the service and distinguishes Big Bethel, in the words of one young member raised in the A.M.E. Church, "from those new-fangled Christian centers where all the young people go." He stated that when he moved to Atlanta to go to college, "I went to a traditional church, I went to where I was accustomed to, traditional in the sense that a lot of the rituals are still observed."

A culture of dignified care for the order and decorum of worship in the A.M.E. Church has deep roots. In addition, it produces an alternative society in which a dignity not always conferred in the larger society is upheld and made sacred. The organization of the church as a whole, according to A.M.E. historian Lawrence H. Mamiya, "provided an alternative status system for people who

[39] Vinton R. Anderson, "'Under Our Own Vine and Fig Tree': Sunday Morning Worship in the African Methodist Episcopal Church," 157–172, in Karen B. Westerfield-Tucker, ed., *The Sunday Service of the Methodists: Twentieth Century Worship in Worldwide Methodism* (Nashville: Kingswood Books, 1991).

[40] See the *African Methodist Episcopal Church Hymnal* (Nashville: The African Methodist Episcopal Church, 1998) esp. xivff.

FIGURE 4.1—

A STANDARD ORDER OF SERVICE FOR BIG BETHEL A.M.E.

Elapsed Time	*Order of Service (with symbols for worship decorum [41])*
0:00	The Organ Prelude*
0:04	The Moments of Reverence (singing praise songs)**
0:10	The Processional**
0:15	The Doxology **
0:17	My Hope for This Service**
0:18	The Call to Worship **
0:20	The Hymn of Praise ***
0:26	The Morning Prayer ****
0:30	The Prayer Response ****
0:31	The Organ Voluntary *
0:36	The Anthem**
0:37	The Holy Scripture** [one reading]
0:38	The Affirmation of Faith **
0:39	The Preface to the Decalogue **
0:40	The Decalogue **
0:44	The Gloria Patri **
0:45	The Organ Voluntary *
0:45	Worship Through Music *
0:52	The Acknowledgment and Recognition of Visitors *
1:00	The Pastor's Word *
1:02	The Paying of Tithes and Giving of All Offerings and Special Gifts*
1:10	The Offertory **
1:11	The Anointing Service ****
1:21	The Sermonic Hymn **
1:30	The Sermon ****
2:00	The Invitation to Christian Discipleship **
2:10	The Celebration of Holy Communion **** [only on first Sundays]
2:35	The Recessional **
2:40	The Benediction **
2:41	The Organ Postlude *

[41] The following is printed in the Sunday program: "The following symbols found throughout the printed order of worship govern our worship decorum at Big Bethel AME. Please cooperate with our ushers by allowing them to seat

were marginalized in the larger society."[42] It also, according to early A.M.E. bishop Daniel Payne, served to "civilize" and "uplift" a population of ex-slaves he saw as in great need of education, order, and discipline.[43] To do this, Bishop Payne labored to stamp out the worship forms he called "ridiculous and heathenish," the common practices of dancing, shouting, and other elements of black folk-culture inherited from their African roots. While he was largely successful in his efforts at worship reform, in a new day his position would increasingly come under attack.

Even during his life, many resisted Bishop Payne's vision for worship and church life, saying, as one congregation's chief steward did to Payne upon dismissing him from their pulpit: "You have too fine a carpet on your parlor floor, and you won't let them sing the cornfield ditties."[44] Likewise, when I asked one middle-aged member, a steward who was active in the choirs, about his first impressions of Big Bethel upon joining in the late 1970s, he said, "Big Bethel had a reputation. People said to me, 'That's the sophisticated church.' They don't say, 'Amen.'" This dramatically changed in the 1980s with the pastorate of Rev. McKinley Young, who introduced many changes, including more spirited worship and a contemporary gospel choir, the Voices of Inspiration. One man, an original Voices choir member, told me that early on the traditional choirs did not allow them in the choir loft but instead made them sing from around the piano. Such resistance gave way over time as the changes led the church to grow dramatically, and its newer membership increasingly supported the revival of what one can only called "spirited worship."

---

and direct you during the service. *Worshipers may enter quietly and reverently; **Stand/No entering or leaving; ***Stand/Enter, remain standing; ****No entering or leaving."

[42] Lawrence H. Mamiya, "A Social History of the Bethel African Methodist Episcopal Church in Baltimore: The House of God and the Struggle of Freedom," in James P. Wind and James W. Lewis, eds., *American Congregations*, vol. 1, *Portraits of Twelve Religious Communities* (Chicago: University of Chicago Press, 1994) 227.

[43] Mamiya argues that Payne's influence on the worship and culture of the A.M.E. Church was so profound that its history must deal with pre- and post-Payne eras. See "A Social History of the Bethel African Methodist Episcopal Church in Baltimore," 236; also, Walker, *A Rock in a Weary Land*, 21ff.

[44] Ibid., 238.

The distinctiveness of the spirited style of worship lay in how it interwove with the order of worship in a series of building crescendos; the emotional building dynamic of order and spirit marked the congregation's participation, as well as the clergy and musician leadership. I can better examine this by offering an illustration of the dynamic from my field notes describing the first portion of the Sunday morning service during August 1999 when I began fieldwork.

"I came into the sanctuary, and the choir and ministers were crowded across the back arch of the aisle. About fifty people were scattered throughout the pews, mostly standing and singing along with the music and leadership of the minister of music, Jacques Green. He is an energetic man of medium build, close-cropped hair, and an intense and focused, but very radiant face. He plays the electric piano and leads singing during the first Moment of Reverence period of the service, directly after the more traditional (Bach) organ prelude. The words of the songs were printed in the program and while some sang without looking at the words, others looked at the words, and still others came in, sat down, and paged through the program without singing at all. The songs were 'Give glory to God, saints,' 'Welcome into this place,' and 'Thank you, Lord.' This time was filled with the various individual worship responses, a phenomenon that continued throughout the service. One middle-aged woman in front of me swayed to the songs, both arms stretched upwards, at turns clapping her hands and exclaiming, 'Thank you, Jesus.' Others, swaying and singing, held their hands outstretched in front of themselves, elbows close to their sides, eyes lifted upwards or closed. Others simply stood and sang. Some looked around or seemed to be in deep thought, looking at one spot for quite some time. The overall atmosphere was clearly building, and the music increased in intensity until the processional hymn, 'There is a Name I Love to Hear—O, How I Love Jesus,' began and the ministers and choir all processed down the main aisle, separating into two columns at the altar rail, each filing around and up to their seats. While the choir sways and claps and the director encourages the congregation to stand and sing louder and more energetically, the ministers all paradoxically come to their chairs and kneel on the floor for the remainder of the hymn, assuming positions of prayer, hands on the seat cushions of their chairs. As the song ends the organist moves smoothly into the Doxology with no break in music or level of energy. The ministers turn and stand, joining in the singing, some uplifting hands as are some in the pews. The Doxology, a formal song offering praise to the triune God, ends quickly, and a few moments of settling take place during which most sit down and a few remain in sort of spirit-filled ecstasy, hands outstretched or held over head, shouting 'Thank you, Lord. Thank you. Thank you, Jesus.' The woman in front of me stomped her foot for emphasis on THANK you, Lord."

The Bach organ prelude, usually played ten minutes before the service officially begins, usually passes with a minimal number of parishioners in the building. But as the music shifts to contemporary praise songs and members flow in to find their places in the pews, the service seems to suddenly rise above an invisible threshold of energy, and numerous people rise from their pews, beginning to praise God in their own style. During this time the ministers, acolytes, choir, and numerous ushers fill the back aisle, lifting the volume and energy in a dynamic way when the processional hymn begins. With the encouragement of the choir and musicians, aided by the ministers arising from prayer at the foot of their chairs, the Doxology takes this first cycle of praise just another step higher, leading to various ecstatic outbursts throughout the congregation.

While of course it matters how each service goes on a particular Sunday, I found four such cycles of building during the service, each seemingly settling down to a beginning level of energy more elevated than the last. Not accidentally, the second and third cycles climaxed with the choir selections and the last with the sermon. The first choir piece, titled "The Anthem," tended to be a more traditional piece, either a choral anthem ("Almighty Fortress") or as was the case on this particular Sunday, a spiritual ("Done Made My Vow to the Lord"). While these hymns usually elicited enthusiastic applause, they did not usually move as many people to stand, raise their hands, or shout.

The second choir piece, titled "Worship Through Music," was nearly always a contemporary gospel song, on this Sunday a tune with piano, drums, and a head-bobbing beat. The song concluded with a repeating chorus of "He never failed me, He never failed me

. . . yet," first with accompaniment, and then simply voice and drums, over and over, "He never failed me; he never failed me." With dozens of people standing and clapping, the choir ended to shouts of "Amen" and "Thank you, Lord." For the next few seconds, the musicians played a quiet reprise of the tune on the piano as choir members and people in their pews remained standing, caught up in the Holy Spirit.

According to Jacques Green, the minister of music, a movement of the Holy Sprit had been blowing a revival through black church music since the mid-seventies. He tied it to Methodist tradition, saying, "As with John Wesley, with his 'heart warmed' experience, so also now hearts are being warmed." When I asked how he knew this was happening on a given Sunday, he said, "I listen for the Holy Spirit. One Sunday the song the choir sang was pretty, but didn't have its downbeats, it wasn't sharp, and it didn't move people. The work, the intention of my work, is all about whatever is done has to bring people into Christian living. It has to move people." He works "to pick up on the spirit of the congregation on the vibe of the service, and then through musical leadership put some coals on the fire, you know what I mean? Help the Holy Spirit."

The view of the essential role of music in the worship service was reinforced as I spoke with people in the church. One middle-aged woman who had been a lifelong Lutheran before moving to Atlanta and joining Big Bethel succinctly compared her two experiences: "The Lutheran service, well [and she turned her shoulders slightly to the side, lifting the one near me, scrunched up her face, and stuck out her tongue], but I really like the music here. It's up-beat, it lifts you up." Indeed, the music minister in an equally bold statement said that what he does on Sunday morning works to support and enhance Rev. Davis's preaching. Such support is key, he argued, "because on Sunday, if the music is off, it will kill the service. People will go somewhere else." One of the choir members I spoke with underscored this view:

"God may speak through the song and to realize that God might do this, somebody's life might be touched through this song, somebody might decide to choose Jesus as Lord and Savior *because* they heard something in this song, so now just as weighty, as heavy, as much weight as we put on the Word, really in African American worship a lot of weight is put on the music. Cause when we pray, musicians are supposed to play softly, when we sing, even when the preacher's preaching, sometimes there might be a little background music."

While the sermon and the invitation to discipleship were the mountaintop destination in the service, the music was the vehicle that got the congregation there and prepared them for what they would behold.

However, the music ministry did not deal with an emotionally simple congregation; the diverse congregation meant that the music ministry worked actively to make space for a full range of musical expression in the service while attempting to avoid what one person named "losing focus" and another called "coldness." A young choir member noted that "some days Bethel is kinda cold, cause folk done come in [he exhaled loudly and sat stiffly upright in his chair], you know, and some days are wide open, I mean you can sneeze and people start praising the Lord." The music minister noted that "music works as a catalyst for worship. Anytime it's getting out of focus, I have to pick it up." Music also, he argued, worked to make the congregation more mature, and therefore more open to the movement of the Spirit. It did this, he argued, by avoiding a focus on one type of music:

"Some churches are taking praise choruses and making them central and losing what else the music ministry has to offer. That's not good, though. For example, if I went to Southern [University] and only took music classes, no science, no math, I'd be underdeveloped. The church is an institute of higher learning, and appreciation grows with variety. Education leads to more mature Christian people, able to be in various places. Without the openness, the Holy Spirit gets closed out, you know, the Holy Spirit's movement in their lives."

He noted that he varied musical expressions and used five forms explicitly: hymns, anthems, spirituals, traditional, and contemporary gospel. Each, he argued, is marked by "a different style, harmony and form of instrumentation, pauses, diction, dynamics, and feel, and therefore how they touch people."[45]

[45] He even suggested that the tonal resonance of the chords in different styles of music had different effects on the listeners and together contributed

Patrick Clayborn, a young adult member and director of the contemporary gospel choir, noted a practical reason for this diversity of music, something Rev. Davis hinted at in my first meeting with him:

"There is a struggle between those who would hold on to traditions too tightly and maybe those who would let go too freely. I mean, so you have this mix, and so it's like in the music, there is this call for 'we still want anthems to be sung,' and 'we want spirituals,' and 'we want gospel,' and I have a problem with no one. Any form of music gonna praise God, I'm for it, but I guess my thing is to make sure that the music is going to give God praise and bring the people into praise."

Each style of music played to its constituency, yet each aimed at a singular goal of drawing people into praise of God. However, in order to accomplish this aim, Patrick was cautious of the various pitfalls associated with the styles of music.

"With the Anthem, the pitfall is if the choir is [he pretends to hold a music folder in his hands, looking down at the pages of music] and they never look up to make connections, sometimes it just falls down through the cracks in the floor, and it never gets off, but we can do the same anthem, and I said put the paper down and let's internalize, and we did and there was a moment of worship where you could tell the spiritual needs were being met. Same with spirituals, where you're doing it because we used to do it or it can be a point of transcendence where we can ascend, where we can make those connections with each other and with God. The pitfall with gospel music is you get caught up in the entertainment and so the loud music, you're popping your fingers, swinging on your feet, thinking you're at the club on Saturday night and not trying to worship."

The tensions inherent in musical styles ranging across the spectrum from order and tradition to freedom and the spirit were evident in the leadership of the clergy as well, and the divide goes to the heart of the senior pastor, Rev. Davis. A self-declared traditionalist in worship taste, he loved hymns and the worship order. Yet he was highly aware of the diversity among his ministers and his

---

to a more mature development. He compared specifically the gospel cord—C G E C—to the choral chord—E C G C.

congregation. On my first meeting with him, he noted that worship taste ranged widely in the congregation. He mentioned an Emory University neurologist who was one of the leading enthusiasts for more spirit-filled worship, while a particular Atlanta University professor worshiped in a very cerebral way, content to sit quietly during worship. In a minister's staff meeting, however, Davis put his view on the line; he told his ministers that "we don't do high liturgical worship here; we don't do it. I know what liturgical worship is, we should know it, we should know what is proper; we just don't do it." It is a model of worship new to the church since Rev. Davis's arrival, according to one member; it is "openness to new things in worship, to worship that has an order but is Spirit-led."

Yet, despite Rev. Davis's efforts to encourage such spiritedness, his commitment to church order and keeping the morning on schedule pushed against just such an openness to the Spirit. The conflict between these two aspects of the service really came alive to me in my second month of fieldwork at Big Bethel. I knew that the early service was going to be tight in terms of time given the addition of communion to the order of service and Sunday school looming with its fixed start time at 10:00 a.m. The Sermonic Hymn was, "Alas! And Did My Savior Bleed," a hymn that has four verses plus a beloved chorus between each and sung repeatedly after the verses were done ("At the cross, at the cross, where I first saw the light"). And Rev. Joyce Young, who "lined" the hymn, enthusiastically lined the entire hymn, all four verses and the chorus.[46] By the time the congregation was finished with the chorus for the final time, the choir as well as many members were really singing.

Rev. Davis stood up and walked to the pulpit, effectively ending the song with that go-around of the chorus. While Rev. Streator, sitting just to the left of the podium, bent over in his chair, repeatedly shouting at the top of his voice, "Thank you, Lord" and others

---

[46] An old Methodist tradition of reading a hymn before it is sung, likely with roots in a time when few if any worshipers could read and hymnals, such as existed, were scarce. See Portia K. Maultsby, "The Use and Performance of Hymnody, Spirituals, and Gospels in the Black Church," in Melva Wilson Costen and Darious Leander Swann, *The Black Christian Worship Experience* (Atlanta: The ITC Press, 1992) 141–159.

shouted "Hallelujah," most people quickly sat and Pastor Davis softly prayed that his word be God's word and that "as you bless other pulpits across town right now, bless this one that as the word goes forth, it might fall on fertile ground." He ended the prayer— as if to acknowledge that he stopped the song too early—by singing in his gravely baritone, "At the cross, at the cross," and that was just enough for the piano, bass, drums, and choir to pick up the tune and beat just where they left off, and the congregation joined in one last go-around on the chorus. But just one more. As they sang that verse, Rev. Davis was behind the pulpit, opening his Bible, and looking out, ready to read.

The particular sermon Rev. Davis preached that day, entitled "The Problem of the Borrowed Ax," served as further evidence for the tension of order and spirit. First of all, the typical sermon—and this one was no exception—contained in miniature the cycles of building and release present in the service as a whole. The sermon began slowly with an astute analysis of the impact of technological change in modern society and its impact on the African American community, building to its first climax about fifteen minutes into the sermon. Then, as he began to deal with the text, taken from 2 Kings 6, he built up rhetoric and emotion each time as he reached a key point in his message, beginning with the biblical text and building through example and application to contemporary living.

Rev. Davis preached mightily, but then at a peak point he stated, "Now next Sunday I'll tell you the problem with the borrowed ax." Laughter erupted in the sanctuary, and he continued, "I'm gonna let them have Sunday school on time, huh?" He stopped his ser-mon midway because of time constraints—and finished it the next Sunday.[47] Rev. Davis had explicitly developed a more traditional style of African American preaching, a style that depended on building emotional as well as intellectual participation, and by the movement of the spirit, evoked calls and shouts of participation from the congregation.[48] Yet, as with my discussion of the spirited-

[47] I deal more with the content of this sermon in the next section on public work.

[48] See Maria Mallory, "Soul-stirring sermons: Traditional black preaching draws forth two-way communication between pew and pulpit," *Atlanta Journal-Constitution* (May 8, 1999) B1; also the classic by Henry H. Mitchell, *Black Preaching: The Recovery of a Powerful Art* (Nashville: Abingdon Press, 1990).

ness of other aspects of the service, spirit-led preaching coexisted somewhat uncomfortably with a formal order of service and time schedule for Sunday morning activities.

Two pairs of events, each held more occasionally than the weekly round of meetings, rehearsals, and Sunday morning worship, need to be discussed as I close out this section. First, the Love Feast and holy communion were held monthly on the weekend of the first Sunday of the month, as I noted above. While the Love Feast described above avoided such time constraints by its Saturday morning time slot, the celebration of holy communion that the Love Feast anticipated suffered under the practical effects of time constraints as well. While the altar, set just below the pulpit, was diligently and respectfully cared for by the stewardesses, the fact of its architectural sublimation under the pulpit represented a real sublimation in the worship practice of the church.

According to Rev. Davis, the communion table is "the ultimate table," for which he, the clergy, and the stewards and stewardesses have "a high responsibility to keep holy." Yet it is held once a month, and at the very end of the service, taking up less than one fifth of the total time. Additionally, the emotional structure of the service builds and peaks in the sermon and invitation to Christian discipleship, leaving the communion service in an ambiguous place. It is not surprising, then, that no one I interviewed mentioned communion when I asked what was important to them in worship.

In the second occasional worship event each year, the choirs put on two major events: a sacred drama titled *Heaven Bound* in early November and a Homecoming Christmas Concert in early December. *Heaven Bound,* as I noted above, was developed in the 1930s as a means to pay down the debt incurred to rebuild the church after the fire of 1920. The play, now presented more than eight hundred times, has just one living member of its original cast. Yet new members have been inducted into the performance, and the power of the simple story intertwined with hymns and spirituals continues to attract large audiences. This is in part because of the talented vocalists who were part of Bethel's old concert choirs, upon whose shoulders the pageant fell.

During the early 1980s, due to tensions between younger members of the new gospel choir and the older members of the concert choirs and *Heaven Bound* cast, the younger members concentrated on building their own annual attraction, a Christmas concert.[49] The past twenty years calmed the tensions, and many of the same choir members sang in both events. The concert, a combination of Handel's *Messiah*, contemporary gospel numbers, and traditional seasonal hymns, embodied some of the issues reflected in the worship life of Big Bethel generally. The *Messiah*, sung in A.M.E. churches since a famous performance in New York in 1839, reflected the deep-rooted tendency for an elevated, cultured style of worship that could "vindicate the race."[50] And indeed, Big Bethel's choirs included some excellent voices, carrying the *Messiah* along with great vocal skill and passion.

The whole first section of the program leading up to intermission consisted of selections from the *Messiah* except the last song, "Total Praise," a contemporary gospel song based on Psalm 121. This juxtaposition marked the order/spirit tensions that ran through the congregation's worship in the most stark way. When I got home that night, I wrote:

"The people who like the traditional music such as the *Messiah* sit quietly in their pews, some singing along with the words to favorite parts. Yet those who love the contemporary gospel music move their bodies; they stand up, raise their hands, shout out loud, and the choir does the same. So, when they began the song 'Total Praise,' the feel and look of the sanctuary changed. For instance, a woman to the right of me immediately stood up and raised both hands upwards; a homeless man behind me to the left began shouting , 'All right, Big Bethel, let's have some *church* now'; and the choir stood up, swaying, and lifting their hands as they sang powerfully and loudly."

Exactly because the tensions inherent in A.M.E. worship were so deep, reaching back to the church's infancy, they did not have any

[49] The existence of these two late-fall events, *Heaven Bound* and the Christmas Concert, gave silent witness to the history of tensions between the generations— those tending toward more traditional worship and music and those who favored the more contemporary. These changes and tensions are recounted in Coleman, *We're Heaven Bound,* 147 ff.

[50] Indeed, Daniel Payne heralded this performance in 1839, a landmark in the development of African American sacred music. See Campbell, *Songs of Zion,* 42.

easy resolution. And it may be that insofar as they coexisted within the worship of one congregation, the diversity of the congregation— across class and income as well as education and job status—may continue to coexist.[51]

PUBLIC WORK

During the fall I spent at Big Bethel, the Christmas Concert not only served as a pinnacle event in the church's worship life but was also the capstone event in a major, month-long focus on out-reach ministry. The "Come on Home for Christmas" program was begun by Rev. Davis early in his tenure at Big Bethel and was billed as "the largest outreach event of the year." At the Quarterly Conference in December, Rev. Davis remarked to Presiding Elder Wicker that he and his wife were invited to attend the various events, especially the Christmas Concert, for in Big Bethel's work through these events, they "would really see the church being the church." The program stretched over the first weeks of December and consisted of four distinct aspects. First, the program simply encouraged members to attend during December, and through various means, the pastoral staff extended that invitation. Second, the program invited and coordinated transportation for sick and shut-in members to attend a Restoration Service of worship with holy communion on a Saturday morning. Afterward each one was given a modest financial gift as a sign of love and support. Third, the congregation traditionally sponsored a Giving Tree Project in order to be a blessing through the giving of gifts to needy children. When I was there, however, the church adopted a "Christ Family" whose mother had died a few months earlier, leaving fourteen children from age seventeen down to twenty months. Rather than split the family up, the deceased mother's two sisters, both of whom lived in Atlanta, adopted the children and planned to keep them together as one large extended family. The congregation made

[51] While generally in the A.M.E. and at Big Bethel, the neo-Pentecostal influence is led and supported by highly educated clergy and lay members, the spirited nature of the worship encourages a wider class spectrum, including especially the working poor, than the traditional "order and decorum" worship fitted more tightly to a middle-income and middle-class constituency. See Lincoln and Mamiya, *The Black Church*, 386–387.

them honored guests at the Christmas Concert and presented them with a shower of gifts and financial support.[52]

The Christmas Concert, the last of the four aspects of the program, not only honored the "Christ Family" as guests but also invited any "brothers or sisters who are homeless" to be "our special guests." The plan included members bringing "a gift of warmth— gloves, socks, etc.— to share with a homeless person." In addition, they intended to share dinner with the homeless after the concert. However, as my field notes describe, this idealized vision did not work out in every detail:

"The first half of the concert lasted nearly an hour and a half. Although it seemed like a change in plans, Rev. Davis took the podium below the pulpit area and welcomed their guests from 'the homeless community,' thanked them for coming, and said that he understood that because of time constraints, they would have to go now downstairs to eat 'in order that they be able to get to the next place where they are required to be.' (He never said the word 'Shelters.') He asked the congregation to applaud their presence as an offer of support for them and had all the people who brought gifts of warm clothing for them stand in order to show a tangible sign of support for them. Then he asked that they be excused and go downstairs where the men's ministry was waiting to serve them dinner. I went downstairs a few minutes later, and the scene looked like this: they had three long tables set up running north-south across the fellowship hall and one serving table running east-west at the south end of the hall. The line of men (with a few women; almost 100% African American) wound along the table and along the east wall of the hall."

A quick estimate: 30 men serving and between 150 and 200 men and women eating. I was most struck by the dignity shown to the homeless, speaking with them and to them in respectful tones, inviting them for a "cultural" event, for a gift of practical assistance, and for a meal intended to be, if not actually, shared. As I returned upstairs to my seat, the program continued with Rev. Davis and the chairwoman of the event handing out nine institutional gifts of between $500 and $2,000 dollars. In giving to such pro-

[52] See S. A. Reid, "Orphaned children are church's 'Christ family,'" *Atlanta Journal-Constitution* (December 23, 1999) J1.

144

grams as the Butler Street YMCA and St. Joseph's Mercy Care, they suggested that they were following Jesus in helping the needy and "assisting institutions which are doing the same."[53]

In total, the "Come On Home for Christmas" program shared over $16,000 and much more in material gifts and food from a whole host of people, while at the same time providing spiritual nurture for the congregation through worship, music, and service. Yet it would be deceptive if this whole event were reported in terms that fit more closely with an approach to outreach based on a "client-type" social service model. This program and its various events found its grounding in two sources, both deeply rooted in the church.

One source was the example and inspiration of Jesus. Rev. Davis put it this way: "[The Come On Home for Christmas program] is the way we show the Christ in us." Another member, a middle-aged woman who was active in various leadership positions and church ministries, put it this way: "The way we believe here is, Jesus saves lives, *and* Jesus saves communities. We're just being a part of that work." Jesus pervaded the members' talk about prayer life, and it pervaded the public prayer, worship, and song in Sunday services.

Second, and hardly less influential, was the strong tradition of self-help within the A.M.E. Church generally and Big Bethel, as well.[54] The struggles of the A.M.E. Church over authority and autonomy with whites combined with the strict discipline of Methodist theology to produce a self-reliant and independent church. The church depended on such an ideology of self-help in gaining ownership of its own property, in encouraging financial success of its members through entrepreneurship, and in viewing its missionary efforts to the freed slaves as attempts at vindication

[53] The organizations were Christ Homes, Inc., a group home for abused children; Southwest Hospital, which provided medical services in an underserved African American community; the National Mental Health Association of Georgia; Crossroads Community Ministries, which provided services to homeless people; Harriett G. Darnell Senior Multi-Purpose Facility; Austin T. Walden Middle School, a neighborhood school with whom they had an ongoing relationship; and the Christian Council of Metropolitan Atlanta, which specialized in immigration and refugee resettlement activities.

[54] See Robert B. Hill, "The Role of the Black Church in Community and Economic Development Activities: The Legacy of Self-Help," *National Journal of Sociology* 8 (Summer/Winter 1994) 149–159.

of blacks' capacity for self-governance, education, and economic success.[55] Rev. Davis explicitly associated the church with this tradition, noting in a brochure developed for the 150th anniversary of the church that Big Bethel "represents the philosophy of our Founding Fathers of self help. Big Bethel is more than just a structure. It exemplifies a theology which highlights the intervention of God into the African American experience."

Big Bethel's outreach ministries were grounded in this A.M.E. tradition of self-help and empowerment, a perspective that was articulated and reinforced most markedly through worship and especially preaching. Rev. Davis's sermon "The Problem of the Borrowed Ax," which I discussed briefly above, provides a remarkable example. The sermon was based on a text from 2 Kings, where a group of young "sons of the prophets" approached Elijah, the prophet, and convinced him that their quarters were too small, that they needed to move and build a bigger dwelling. Suggesting a site near the Jordan, they set off and began to cut wood to build the new dwelling. Suddenly the head of the ax of one young man flew off and landed in the river, and he cried, "Alas, master, for it was borrowed," and it was this last section that Rev. Davis focused on in his sermon. After reading the text, he challenged the congregation that if "you stay awake with me the first fifteen minutes, I'll keep you awake the next twenty minutes," a comment that received shouts of "Amen" and "Watch out." A short extract of his beginning offers a taste of his rhetoric and focus during those first fifteen minutes:

"In a world that is swiftly becoming a smaller and more competitive place, we are constantly being challenged to develop new skills and to upgrade the skills we have in order to keep up with the rapid pace of this changing world, and the changing trends and the changing times. Like no other time in the long, exasperating, marathon of human existence, change is occurring so quickly and in so many ways and so in every aspect of our lives that we literally stand at the doorstep of what Huxley calls the brave new world. Change, inevitable change, and on a drastic scale, are the hallmarks of our time."

[55] This is discussed extensively in Walker, *A Rock in a Weary Land;* Campbell, *Songs of Zion;* and in Lincoln and Mamiya, *The Black Church.*

Rev. Davis highlighted the fact that while some welcome the change, others ignore and deny it, wishing to return to the "ways of yesteryears." He chided the church for being slow to change, and warned that the new world coming would simply leave them behind. He argued that the church *ought* to be the most changing, responsive institution in the community, and while it was that in the past, it seemed to have lost its way from the front burner of social and economic development to the back burner of bagging up lunches. He quickly hedged his critique by stating:

"realizing that there is nothing wrong with that but there's a changing world out there. There ought be someone in this congregation this morning that ought to hear this word and declare I know about computers and I'm gonna volunteer four or five of my hours to teach somebody else computer skills in the computer lab. There ought to be some folk in this congregation right now who work on a job where they give software away and they ought to go and petition their— somebody ought to hear what I'm saying— ought to petition their boss when they get back to the job tomorrow morning, Mister, I need two pieces of software to go on my church's computer because the world is changing, and the church has to be in the front of that changing order, somebody ought to say amen."

With this flourish, he finally got to the sermon, to the text, and the three main points he drew out of it are all implicit or explicit in the excerpt above.

First, the young prophets told Elijah that they had outgrown their current place; they knew what the problem was. Rev. Davis chided the congregation for taking this first step and thinking they'd done something. "It doesn't take a genius to tell me what's wrong with something. My car broke *[laughter]*. My air conditioner won't work." The young prophets, Rev. Davis noted, had thought long enough about the problem to have a solution to offer. The plan was to go down to Jordan and cut some wood and build a new dwelling. Davis ran out of time without getting to the problem of the borrowed ax, and so declared that he'd finish the next Sunday, saying, "You were supposed to be here anyway," a recognition that this was the second Sunday in "Perfect Attendance Month" at Big Bethel.

The next Sunday, after a spirited rehearsal of the previous week's "Part A" of the sermon, he turned to the second half of his sermon, focusing on the changing world he discussed in the beginning of his sermon. In such a changing world, Rev. Davis declared, "if we're going to be in this race for the new world, we got to, we got to know we got a techno-trinitarian pneumatological religion and a God who goes with it, somebody say, Amen [*shouts of* Amen! *Laughter*]." And with such a situation, we can't get by with borrowed axes that represent not luxuries but the necessities of life: "not waiting on the lottery to hit, but education, somebody say amen, axes here was not the Mercedes, axes was the Chevrolet that'll get you to work."

He continued, now really hitting his stride and his central point, with three fundamental problems with borrowing an ax. First, "when you borrow axes, you leave your destiny in the hands of somebody else."

"When you start borrowing your necessities [alright. Preach, preach] you're leaving your destiny in the hands of other folks. You didn't even get it. [go ahead] When you borrow your ax, I'm not talking about the lawnmower, I'm talking about your ax, when you borrow your ax, you leave your destiny in the hands of other folks, and that's always dangerous. That's always problematic. When you borrow your ax, you're leaving in hands of other folk your destiny, somebody else determines your ability to succeed in life or fail in life, when you borrow your ax, somebody else has the responsibility of calling the shots. If we could borrow the ax, we have to ask somebody else, if we have to ask someone to borrow their ax, then we're giving them the power over our lives that we ought not ever give anybody. When we bor—we better start learning how to get our own ax, because if we don't, somebody will always be able to predetermine how far we will go, what our altitude in life will be, what our attitudes will ultimately turn out to be, there is a problem when you borrow other folk's axes because they determine what you do and how much you do. Just when they get ready to pull their ax back is just when you need the ax most. You better start getting your own ax, buying your own ax, sharpening your own ax, getting your stuff that you need, that's the reason we ought to be banking with each other, that's the reason we ought to be shopping with each other, that's the reason we ought to be spending with each other, that's the reason we ought to be elevating each other, because when we don't do that, we are borrowing somebody else's ax. [preach, preach.]"

Second, Rev. Davis argued, when you borrow an ax, you never know what condition the ax is in. People tend to give you something they are not using, rather than risk parting with the tools they depend on day to day. One compelling example:

"Try to borrow from somebody who is really using their computer as an ax, and see what they tell you, you want to learn how to use the computer and you don't want to buy one yet but you just want to borrow somebody else's computer ax and see what they do for you. They give you one of those old antiquated things they got down there in the basement and they try to make you feel like they done something for you. Now it does not run this program and it does not run this one either, but you can learn the fundamentals on it. Because when you're trying to borrow somebody else's ax, they ain't giving you their good stuff, they're giving you what's left over. Somebody ought to say amen, [amen]."

The third problem with a borrowed ax is that you might lose it. And here Rev. Davis used his final moments to remind people that despite the necessity of their own efforts, they don't really have something unless it is given from God, and it is to God that they ought to go first when they set about getting new tools for the new world. When the young prophet was swinging his ax, the head flew off and into the deep water of the Jordan River. It happens like that, too, Rev. Davis concluded:

"The truth of the matter is isn't that where most of us lose the stuff, when we try to go through the deep waters without help from somebody else, I lost it in the deep waters, I don't know where you lost it, but I'm sure somebody in this place this morning has lost it at one time or another. You lost it when you got so filled with yourself that you forgot God's doing a work through you, and you ain't doing it yourself. You lost it when you start finding more time to do your stuff outside than inside. You lost it when you start thinking more about your job than the giver of your job, you lost it when you got to the point of believing you were all of that and a bag of chips too. You lost it when you forgot that God gave you everything and everything belongs to God. You lost it when you start thinking everything that you are all of that and everything you made belong to you."

This remarkable sermon did many things, but its extended rehearsal here pointed to the powerful rhetoric of self-help that pervaded Rev. Davis's sermons and the church's ethos generally. The discipline, hard work, and individual effort might sound like a straight Protestant ethic overlaid in the African American experience. Yet, note the importance of total dependance on God combined with a strategic interdependence with the African American community as a whole that marks a distinctive point in the black version of the American dream. And the sermon did not simply speak in generalities, but as the discussion of corporate donations of software suggested, offered practical advice on how to implement the theory in practice.

I now turn to the multitude of ways this theology of self-help works itself out through the multitude of social ministries, especially focusing on the area of economic development, a major focus during the time of my fieldwork. In a video highlighting the church's various community ministries, such programs were named the Health Ministry breast cancer screening; Habitat for Humanity; the Piece of the Rock Ministry, helping people through the arduous process toward home ownership; the Andrew Ministry, sharing the gospel with those in the immediate neighborhood; the Computer Ministry, teaching computer skills to members and others; Juvenile and Prison ministries; and the various ministries under the Richard Allen Outreach Center: the Dorothy Young Help Center, offering emergency food and clothing; Project Reach, working after school to counsel and tutor low-income neighborhood kids; the Welcome Table, providing bag lunches for homeless people; My Sister's Place, providing transitional shelter for homeless and battered women with children; and the Homeless Intervention and Prevention Project, providing housing along with remedial and skill enhancement programs for residents.

Such a laundry list is both overwhelming and uninforming. Were they all supported equally? Did they fit equally into the mission of the church? In answer to these questions, I offer a more focused look at two key programs focused on self-help and economic development in the rest of this chapter. The short answer, however, is that while in general outreach ministry was highly valued, programs that embodied the emphasis on economic empowerment and self-help received stronger attention and fit more snugly into the mission of the church.

The video mentioned above was meant to highlight Big Bethel's role in the community, but its aim was especially to cast a vision of "God's people returning God's land to serve God's purposes" on the occasion of a mortgage burning. Before Rev. Davis's tenure, the church had not purchased a piece of property for more than a century. But by the eighth year of his tenure, through a program dubbed the Nehemiah Ministry, they had not only completely renovated the church interior and exterior but had also purchased fourteen dilapidated lots on their block or nearby, and renovated, occupied, and paid the mortgages on two of them. This was part of an overall project called "Vision 2000: Making a Difference Where We Are Serving, Witnessing, Growing in Christ," which envisioned a "Big Bethel Village" on their section of Auburn. The church was taking time out this particular Sunday to formally burn the mortgages on two lots and recommit itself to its surrounding community. Named after the sixteenth book of the Old Testament, the project drew a three-pronged strategy from the example of the biblical Nehemiah. The project aims were "reclaiming the land, rebuilding the people, and replenishing the health of our economy."

After the showing of the video, Rev. Davis took the pulpit and led applause, thanking the committee in charge, and said to the congregation, "Weren't you just proud?" "How can we not commit to be a part of what we're doing, of what God's doing through us, in this place?" The placement of this celebration in the middle of their stewardship focus on commitment of time allowed the mortgage-burning and video-celebrating community ministries to highlight Rev. Davis's consistent effort to increase involvement by the members. He said, "Turn to your neighbor in the pew and say, 'You ought to be ashamed of yourself if you haven't found your space in God's place.'" He said everybody ought to be a part of something, and the Nehemiah Ministry was a great opportunity to make a difference. He invited the head of the board of trustees, Mr. Baxter, to come up and call for Nehemiah commitments. He reiterated the importance of the whole church participating and said that this regular giving was how the mortgage burning could take place so soon after buying the property, and then asked that each family give $30 per month. Little green cards were provided to facilitate recommitment, and families were asked to fill one out, whether they already participated or if they wanted to begin. Everyone willing to make the commitment was then asked to walk forward and place the green commitment cards into two crystal bowls, each on a pedestal near the altar railing.[56]

Rev. Davis then introduced councilman C. T. Martin, reminding the congregation of the important fact that "we don't work alone, but in partnership with others, including the city." Councilman Martin commended the congregation on the contribution of the Nehemiah project to the systematic rehabilitation of the Auburn Avenue corridor, noting that "if you *own* the land, you *control* the land." At this, Rev. Davis burst out in applause, beaming his smile, and the congregation followed suit.

Yet, in an ironic twist, it was the city's ineffective efforts to control drugs and crime on Auburn that helped spark the project soon after Rev. Davis's arrival in 1992. He stated at the time that "if we're going to stay on Auburn Avenue, we find it necessary to save the community if we're going to save the church." The first step was the commitment to stay, and though they never seriously considered moving out of the city, their decision to stay couldn't have been a bigger statement. The church, owner of its property and building since the mid 1940s, secured loans to carry out a nearly $2 million interior renovation followed by a $1 million exterior renovation. And during this whole period, the church was buying boarded-up and abandoned lots nearby, with visions of a federally insured credit union and a multi-purpose community center to host everything from daycare to job training. Rev. Davis summed up his sense of divine obligation: "If everybody is going to run from the valley, we're saying the valley is damned. If there's anything we're saying, it's that it's in the valley where ministry should be developed. That's where you get the best results." The

---

[56] Given above the regular giving (tithes and offerings), Nehemiah giving averages nearly six thousand dollars a month.

Nehemiah Ministry and its visions of community uplift and empowerment were Big Bethel's flagship on this front.

The Big Bethel Federal Credit Union was one Nehemiah Ministry outgrowth already bearing fruit. Chartered in June 1995, the credit union was a ministry in and for the membership of the church, housed in one of the first properties purchased through the Nehemiah Ministry. When it opened, it was one of only three minority-owned credit unions in Georgia. "The whole idea," Rev. Davis said, "was to teach our people something that is not learned unless taught. And that is the process of saving. We practice tithing for God, but we need to learn saving for ourselves, too, because a people without money is a poor people." Another member, whose career in finance both in the private and public sectors led him to heavy involvement with the Nehemiah and credit union ministries, noted the need for the credit union in my interview with him:

"There is a continuous and strong benevolent pull in the life of the church. Many people have emergencies and special needs, and they often turn to the church. They, the members who have these sorts of needs, they don't want a handout, but they need a helping hand, a loan to get them past a trouble spot, and can repay the loan in time, but because of debt load or credit difficulty might have difficulty getting a loan at an established institution. So the credit union is intended to lessen the benevolent burden on the church."

He also noted that the credit union could cash checks, eliminating the fee charged by check-cashing stores; members could apply for auto or home equity loans; and the youth could establish savings accounts in order to learn the virtues of thrift. One of the board members of the credit union, an officer at Coca-Cola, headed up the youth focus and sponsored a booth at the back-to-school celebration (the Sock-em Jubilee) and a Christmas savings program.

The many social-ethical ministries of Big Bethel, and especially the economic-oriented ones, drew on the experience and expertise of the lay leadership. One middle-aged man, a longtime computer systems manager and steward of the church, put it this way: "I get so busy, but the Lord just helps in putting things in the right sequence. It has been a challenge training in science but living a spiritual life, because spiritual life is not logical; in a spiritual life I have to let the Spirit lead." In part, he says, this happens when he "can take knowledge I learned in the secular world and put it to work in the church." Numerous members spoke of leading such ventures as exhausting yet fulfilling. Most leaders of the congregation were busy professionals and lived some miles from the church. Often they told me that Rev. Davis's energy and commitment inspired their own. Further, as one trustee shared regarding his leadership in the purchase of several properties, the connection between spiritual nurture and service is central:

"You have to be fed, you have to be nurtured and then you can open up *[he leaned his six-foot frame back in the chair, both arms high above his head in a V shape]*, then you want to serve, then it's gratifying to put my shoulder to the plough. With Rev. Davis, we have a called man here, a true man of God. I'm grateful for the opportunity to follow a committed person, and to share my talents."

I was especially struck by this articulate young man, a choir member, as he tried to articulate the ways the Spirit leads into service. I had asked him about the congregation and their response to the spirit in worship. He said this:

"If I have a cup and I fill the cup up with water up to the brim and I say is it filled, you might say, oh yea, and I put another drop in there, and another drop, but is doesn't overflow, so can I really say it is filled if it does not overflow? So once something is filled it is actually being filled with the very thing that is within it. So worship, if we're looking for a connection that's going to overwhelm and fill until we're baptized with the very thing that fills us, then the life that we lead ought to be one for service that begins to permeate and baptize the sanctuary in which we worship and flow down the steps and goes down the street and how that happens, in so many different ways, right? The church may decide to acquire all the properties so that the drug users and drug pushers get pushed out. Or we're constantly trying to put up help stations, clothes closets, I mean how, how that baptism takes place could happen in so many ways, we do bag lunches and send them over to St. Luke's, we do Habitat for Humanity, or when we do the Grady Homes Andrew Ministries. I mean, how does, how does the Holy Spirit overflow?"

Chapter Five

"The Church at Work": Central Presbyterian Church

OPENING SCENES

January 30 was the second Sunday in a row on the heels of a bad ice storm. It was a very cold and foggy morning. The previous Sunday, with power outages and treacherous conditions through-out the Metro Atlanta region, I did not go to church—I stayed home and kept warm. But later, on the Internet, I read the Rev. Ted Wardlaw's letter in Central Presbyterian's newsletter, *The Weekly*, titled "The Grace of Bad Weather."[1] It celebrated the "intrepid Centralites" who came in to church anyway and noted how in the midst of responding to the storm, and to life without the conven-iences run on electricity, our common human need of community became clear. So I went to church that morning anyhow, in spite of bad weather, determined to see how these intrepid Christians gath-ered during inclement weather. I planned my arrival so that I could attend the last session of the adult and youth winter studies program, entitled "Blessed are the Peacemakers: How do we respond to violence in our community, nation, and world?" The program concluded discussions throughout the congregation ever since Rev.

---

[1] For parity with the other chapters and for ease of identification, I have referred to Rev. Wardlaw throughout this chapter, even though all members call him Ted, and he himself does not like the pretense of formal titles. I hope the benefit of this choice outweighs its obvious shortcomings.

155

Wardlaw preached a particularly powerful and challenging sermon on August 29 titled "A Christian Response to Violence."

He preached this powerful sermon after a white supremacist, Buford Furrow, Jr., fired an assault rifle into a Jewish daycare center in Los Angeles and later that day killed a mail carrier, Joseph Ileto, simply because of his skin color. In the sermon Rev. Wardlaw laid out statistics making the case that American culture has a fascination with violence and that the center of this fascination–the gun–has become our "golden calf." While he noted that such direct talk about guns and a culture of violence from the pulpit would make some uncomfortable, he challenged them to channel their responses into an examination of the issue.

Arguing that depersonalization was the first step of violent acts, Rev. Wardlaw challenged the youth to "pledge that this year in school you will not participate in those acts of mental violence that tear down somebody else. I challenge you instead, in the name of Jesus Christ, the Prince of Peace, to treat your fellow students with respect." Further, he challenged adults to be involved with children, especially in the crucial transition to adolescence; adults need to "stop neglecting our children. We need to pledge, right here and now, to reinvest in their lives and in the lives of our families." And while he noted that many things can be done to stem the tide of violence, he paused to focus on a basic issue to face: easily accessible handguns and assault weapons. In response, the members as citizens can advocate for "meaningful and significant gun control laws." And, as Christians, members can "repent—we can change our whole way of thinking—when it comes to the topic of violence." We can do this, he concluded, "because God desires it of us," and therefore "all of us have a role in redeeming our world, in disarming its violence." All eight adult education classes and the high school class joined together on four January Sunday mornings to consider personal and public responses.

That particular Sunday morning I made my way down to the atrium of the Health Center in the Oglesby Building, just to the southwest of the sanctuary. I had read that for this Sunday's presentation of the "Blessed are the Peacemakers" study, representatives from the DeKalb County Schools would talk about youth and violence. I walked into the room, found a cup of tea at the back, and took a seat among the rows of cushioned chairs. People greeted me and asked me if I was a visitor and where was I from. I introduced myself and told them about my study.

A balding man in his late sixties began the event by acknowledging that we should not worry too much about starting on time and keeping on schedule, given the weather—people would come as they were able. At this point there were only six people present, including one of the two speakers and the facilitator. The latter said that previous surveys about these sort of events found that people wanted more singing and opportunity for community, which he felt had happened nicely that morning. He passed out song sheets and said he thought that the Spirit would make up for what our numbers lacked but to "give it our all." One man played the electric piano, and we sang the old spiritual "Were You There" and then "Beneath the Cross of Jesus." The volume was good and the harmonies striking, given our small number.

By the end of the songs, both guests were present. DeKalb County school board member Elizabeth Andrews and DeKalb County Schools student services director Gary McGiboney spoke about their nationally recognized success on issues of school safety and youth violence in the DeKalb County school system. Their object was to describe the reality of guns and violence they faced over the last ten years in the DeKalb schools and to emphasize the key programs that have effected change. Their statistics were overwhelming, yet they focused on issues that the members could respond to with concrete measures. They noted that the best predictor of school violence was violence in the home and that the height of problems centered around age thirteen, exactly the age when parents begin to loosen the controls on their children (letting them have a TV in their rooms or go to the mall unsupervised, for instance). The best response, the speakers emphasized, was positive attention to kids by loving adults, whether parents or mentors. Their take-home message was that the schools can't do it alone; the problems come to school from troubled homes and a troubled society. By ten o'clock the room was full, with about thirty people, including a mix of ages ranging from teens to middle-aged couples to the elderly. The presentation concluded with a few minutes of vigorous discussion about conflict resolution and the need for character education in the homes, not just in the schools.

Afterward the speakers shared flyers, including "Talking with Children About Violence" and "A Parents Guide to Television Violence," a "You *CAN* have an IMPACT" flyer from the Coalition to Stop Gun Violence, and packets of information encouraging advocacy for Georgia House Bill 308, the "Adult Firearm Parental Responsibility and Children's Protection Act 2000." One class member told me that two weeks before, the program hosted state senator David Scott, who spoke to more than one hundred people about legislation he was trying to pass to make parents legally responsible for the weapons they kept in their homes. I picked up some pamphlets and headed upstairs toward the sanctuary for worship.

On the way I chatted with Professor Beth Johnson, who taught New Testament at the nearby Columbia Theological Seminary and was a relatively new member. She asked if I'd read *The Church That Stayed*, a congregational history published in 1979 and given to every new member upon joining the church.[2] I responded that it was a glowing portrait that I'd enjoyed very much. She promptly retorted that many in the church felt they needed a new history written and that Rev. Wardlaw had an author in mind to undertake such a task. She thought that my term "glowing" for *The Church That Stayed* was apt, but "the trouble is that it is *too* glowing and doesn't tell enough of the story, like why was the church so progressive on labor issues and so slow on civil rights?" Anyway, she said, she'd look forward to seeing what I found through my research. Leaving me a bit taken aback, she headed upstairs to gather her children from their Sunday school classrooms.

In retrospect, I should not have been surprised by her sharp comment; if anything at all, Central Church embodies a Reformed theology-influenced impatience with its status quo, knowing that it is called beyond its present achievement to join God's great work in the world. In his annual report to the congregation, passed out after the worship service this same Sunday, Rev. Wardlaw challenged the membership to recommit itself to the church's work, saying "after all, God's already out there, waiting for us." Such a

[2] John Robert Smith, *The Church That Stayed: The Life and Times of Central Presbyterian Church in the Heart of Atlanta, 1858–1978* (Atlanta: The Atlanta Historical Society, 1979).

commitment was evident simply in the presence of people who braved cold and ice to attend the winter study session that morning. Further, their commitment to taking on tough issues, such as violence in society, extended from the minister in the pulpit to the members in Sunday school to their engagement as citizens advocating for new laws and as families involved in schools and home life. Undergirding it all was their Christian responsibility for disarming the world's violence "because God desires it." Such commitment gained energy through regular surveys and self-studies, most recently a "staff design study" and a "space study," both aiming to make internal church operations serve the mission more effectively.

Such studies occurred at regular intervals throughout the past century, recommending everything from starting a transitional shelter for homeless women and children to encouraging "more singing" during educational events. It may be that the congregation's "moral reflexes" were exemplified as much by this relentless self-assessment in the service of strengthening their long-standing identity as "the church at work in the heart of the city" as by their well-recognized community ministry programs themselves– the Health Center, the Outreach Center, and the Night Shelter. Such striving for a stronger witness, in the case of the congregation's consideration of peace and violence, as in its life in general, exemplified the "center" of Central Church—a people gathered to study and sing and pray and preach to God's glory, and then together do God's work in the world.

THE HISTORY OF CENTRAL PRESBYTERIAN CHURCH, 1848–2000

Central Presbyterian Church was born from a conflict within the membership of Atlanta Presbyterian Church just a decade after its founding and only seven years after the dedication of the congregation's modest brick building on Marietta Street. The conflict was described as a quarrel about whether or not to demand the resignation of Pastor John E. DuBose. In its report on taking official action, the Flint River Presbytery mysteriously declared that

"in view of the prevailing differences of opinion in the Atlanta Church on matters not involving any vital principle of doctrine or

A view of Central
Presbyterian Church from
the State Capitol steps

church polity, and yet threatening to disturb, if not destroy, the
peace and prosperity of the church, it be and hereby is directed
that the said congregation divide and constitute two distinct
congregations."[3]

Although speculation is dangerous, recent historical research
suggests that a plausible reason for the dispute revolved around
the question of unionism, centered on the issue of slavery. These
disputes, dominant in Presbyterian debates throughout the first
half of the nineteenth century, were overlaid by the theological divide among Presbyterians between the Northern-dominated, liberal, and abolitionist "New School" and the Southern-dominated,
traditional, and slavery-justifying "Old School."[4] Most Southern

---

[3] Ibid., 4. The group that eventually formed Central supported Rev. DuBose,
numbered about forty, likely somewhat less than half of the congregation.

[4] These developments and positions are discussed in great detail by Ernest
Trice Thompson, *Presbyterians in the South,* vol. 1, *1607–1861* (Richmond, Va.:

Presbyterian churches would have been expected to tow the "Old School" line, allied as they were with the agricultural interests dependent on slavery. However, Atlanta's population, although predominantly Southern, also attracted numerous northerners because of its growing importance as a commercial and transportation center.[5] These families included some of the leading civic and business leaders of the city in the decade of Central's birth.

It was exactly some of these Northern-born leading citizens of the city who championed Unionist positions up to and even during the Civil War. Historian Thomas Dyer, in a recent work entitled *Secret Yankees: The Union Circle in Confederate Atlanta*, details the remarkable story of Amherst and Cyrena Stone, who moved to the city in 1853 and were among the founding members of Central Presbyterian. They were leaders in a circle of Union supporters throughout the war, despite intense pressure from Confederates to show loyalty through financial, material, and personal pledges of support to the Southern war effort. Cyrena worked with others to carry food and money to Federal troops held as prisoners of war in Atlanta at the same time that she nursed Confederate soldiers in her home as an outward sign of proper loyalty to the Confederacy. A close family friend, fellow church member, and mayor of Atlanta during the 1850s, William Markham, felt strongly enough about his support for the Union that he attempted to sell his steel plant. This attempt was forcibly denied by the Secretary of the Navy, whose shipbuilding plans depended on the steel. In response, Markham ordered workers to maintain minimum production levels for the remainder of the war. Such examples as Stone and Markham made a case for significant Union sympathy among early Centralites.

It is certainly not clear if the question of Unionism was at the heart of Atlanta Presbyterian's split in 1858, even if such events were clearly present in the congregation's life at the time. Even if

---

John Knox Press, 1963) esp. 323ff. and 530ff. As early as 1836, these issues split the General Assembly, the Presbyterians' yearly national governing body. Thompson notes that "Southern commissioners expressed the conviction that abolitionism was a natural child of New School heresy, and New School representatives retorted that bigotry and slavery were inseparable" (386).

[5] Harvey K. Newman, "Some Reflections on Religion in Nineteenth-Century Atlanta: A Research Note," *The Atlanta Historical Journal* 27 (Fall 1983) 50.

such was the case, it is not clear whether sympathies were rooted in theological controversy, pride of nation, or abolitionist conviction. In fact, these three were often intertwined. Although the Stones owned slaves by way of an estate settlement handled by Amherst, in which an elderly woman begged him to tend after her "servants," they found the institution of slavery morally reprehensible and worked to give these slaves freedom, work, and ownership of property in the city. Furthermore, a member of another founding family of Central, Col. Lemuel P. Grant, gave a plot of land in downtown for the building of the first black church, Bethel Tabernacle. While not known to be active in Unionist circles, it is likely that he had abolitionist sympathies, having recently moved to Atlanta from his native Maine.[6]

Rev. Wardlaw and other members of the church suggested to me that Central's roots may have been in a split within Atlanta Presbyterian Church over slavery. I have found evidence making this conclusion quite likely. Certainly it seems safe to move beyond Smith's portrayal of Central as solidly in the camp of the Confederacy in *The Church That Stayed.* While all church records up to 1869 were destroyed when then ruling elder Moses Cole's home burned, Smith takes bits of evidence showing support for the Southern cause as a clear indication of the church's pro-secessionist position. It is reasonable to assume, as Smith does, significant support for the Southern position, given that public sentiments forced even the most ardent Unionists to engage in at least token signs of allegiance to the cause of the Confederacy. Yet the new historical details I have pointed out support the version of the history members recounted to me. Departing from Smith's account, members read their current progressive identity back to their founding in a moral claim against slavery and war.

Once on its own, Central quickly made plans to build its own sanctuary and purchased property in the fashionable southeast

---

[6] Bethel's church was destroyed by the Federal troops and the land taken from the black owners, but after the war Grant ordered return of the property and signed the deed over to them. The sale of this property facilitated the purchase of Bethel's present site on Auburn Avenue. Edward R. Carter, *The Black Side: A Partial History of the Business, Religions, and Educational Side of the Negro in Atlanta, Ga.* (Atlanta: 1894) 15.

section of downtown, across the street from the newly completed City Hall. After worshiping in City Hall's basement while its church was being built, the congregation moved into its high-steepled brick building just two years later. Many of the elite membership lived in nearby mansions, with trimmed lawns and white picket fences Indeed, as of 1876, the church had not one male member working as an unskilled laborer, and only 17 percent who worked in well-paid, skilled-labor jobs. This was representative of the white Protestant churches (Baptist, Methodist, Episcopal, and Presbyterian), whose members were of similar socioeconomic status and together made up only 7 percent of the roughly two thousand residents of the city.[7]

Given the strong investments these families had in Atlanta, and especially in its real estate, it is not surprising that whatever doubts they may have had about the Southern cause in the Civil War, their life afterward depended on first saving and then rebuilding their devastated church and city. The church building survived the war, thanks to Father O'Reilly, priest at the Immaculate Conception Church next door. O'Reilly convinced General Sherman not to burn a number of downtown churches and other structures in order to protect the Catholic parish. Still, although it remained standing, after Sherman's departure Central's building was not in good shape. Its basement had been used as a slaughterhouse and kitchen during the Union army's four-month occupation. With a pastor returning from a Union prisoner of war camp, the church membership scattered by the Union army's imposed evacuation of the city, and a blood-stained and reeking facility, Central Church faced as remarkable a challenge of rebirth as did the entire city of Atlanta.

Between 1865 and 1890 the population of Atlanta more than doubled and by 1910 had increased fourfold again. During this time of upheaval and rapid growth, the city's churches and their elite members upheld strong moral standards for themselves and the city generally. At Central, during the pastorate of Rev. Leftwich, such moralism turned in on itself, relentlessly bringing charges against its members for all manner of wrongdoings and nearly destroying itself in the process. Such high-minded moral consciousness

[7] Newman, "Some Reflections on Religion in Nineteenth Century Atlanta," 50.

163

was rooted in the Presbyterian ethos that recognized a divine command ethic calling for human holiness in response to God's law.[8] This ideal, undergirded by practical modes of discipline to encourage adherence, was common practice in nineteenth-century Southern Presbyterianism.[9] Yet the very difficult, decade-long tenure of Pastor Leftwich during the 1870s was marked by a battering of the congregation with constant rumors, accusations, and the imposition of formal discipline of members for "habitually absenting themselves from public worship," drinking, dancing, gambling, dueling, and all manner of individual moral lapses. An effort by some members to force Leftwich's departure split the congregation, already deeply frayed from the years of internal accusations.

By 1883, when the Rev. J. B. Strickler succeeded Leftwich, the membership had declined to thirty-nine, its size when first founded twenty-five years earlier. However, this seemingly bleak period proved to be an axial moment for the church, moving it onto its course toward an established reputation as a spiritually deep, intellectual, and socially progressive "church at work in the heart of the city." The two events most clearly responsible for this monumental shift in the church's fortunes were Strickler's founding of the Young Men's Prayer Association and the arrival of a new member named John J. Eagan, only thirteen years old at the time.

Strickler's tenure as pastor, from 1883 to 1896, bordered on the miraculous. He almost resigned soon after coming to Central when

[8] Reformed historical theologian John H. Leith notes the Reformed tendency to highlight *sanctification,* the movement of believers to conform their lives to the will of God motivated by fear of eternal damnation, at the expense of *justification,* the offer of God's unmerited forgiveness and grace. See *Introduction to the Reformed Tradition: A Way of Being Christian in Community* (Atlanta: John Knox Press, 1981) 79–80.

[9] William Davidson Blanks' Th.D. thesis from Union Theological Seminary in Virginia studied both the expressed moral ideals and their enforcement in nineteenth-century Presbyterianism. While he found that catechetical training with the Westminster, Longer, and Shorter Catechisms was a significant source of enforcement, they contributed to the almost singular motivation: fear, either of disciplinary censure or damnation or both. *Idea and Practice: A Study of the Conception of the Christian Life Prevailing in the Presbyterian Churches of the South During the Nineteenth Century* (Richmond, Va.: Union Theological Seminary, 1960) esp. 270ff.

Union Seminary in Richmond, Virginia, offered him a professorship. Yet, after several leading men of the congregation appealed that decision, the presbytery ruled that Strickler should continue to serve as pastor. The ruling was providential for Central. Strickler's deep spirituality, focus on prayer, and mission outreach through the Sunday School, increased the church membership to 473 within one year. Two and a half years later Central built a new church, heralded in the local news report as "the most beautiful church ever occupied by an Atlanta congregation." Strickler's pastoral spirit healed old wounds, and his passion for prayer infused the congregation. The Young Men's Prayer Association (YMPA) meeting, held on Thursday evenings, became an active force for mission in the neighborhoods surrounding the downtown. By 1890 Central's own busy Sunday School superintendent was also head of the Sunday Schools for five other mission congregations throughout the city.[10] According to John Robert Smith, the YMPA led the church in the work of "purchasing sites, erecting buildings, supplying leadership, employing ministers, and furnishing members."[11]

The second key event shifting Central away from its former troubles and setting the mold for its future character had its origins just before Dr. Strickler's arrival when the thirteen-year-old John J. Eagan walked forward to join the church. Although it is not common to invest one man's role with such pivotal importance in the more than 150-year history of a church, in the case of Central, Eagan was to have a defining effect on the congregation. When within the one-year period between 1899 and 1900 he inherited his uncle's fortune, became superintendent of Central's Sunday School, and devoted himself to the principles of the "social gospel," these events set in motion a profound influence not only on Central but also on Atlanta and the nation.

Eagan's pious mother faithfully brought him to church, and he later remarked that Dr. Strickler was the great spiritual force of his life, training him to give himself fully in leadership of the church.

[10] See the discussion of the Sunday School movement as a part of the Protestant response to urbanization during the nineteenth century in Paul K. Conkin, *The Uneasy Center: Reformed Christianity in Antebellum America* (Chapel Hill: University of North Carolina Press, 1995) 143–146.

[11] *The Church That Stayed*, 40.

Because his father died when he was only five months old, his mother and he had moved to the Atlanta home of her brother, William Russell. Eagan went to work in a grocery store while still a young teenager and soon left high school to pursue full-time employment. He believed even as a young man that hard work, disciplined savings, and prudent investment would make him a rich man. Soon his uncle offered him a job in his tobacco store. Russell was an exacting boss, once deducting the cost of a new lock for the front door from Eagan's salary after the boy had lost the key, but his nephew's diligence impressed him. Much to everyone's surprise, when Russell died in 1899, he left his entire business and much of his significant real estate holdings to Eagan, making him one of the wealthiest men in the city overnight.

Even as his business dedication and success were being acknowledged, his contribution to his church also received affirmation. While he had been a leader in the Young Men's Prayer Association, working diligently in the Sunday School mission projects, his election in 1900 as Sunday School superintendent marked a new threshold of accomplishment and responsibility. He threw himself into the work, focusing, according to a report at the time, on three areas: "building a new building for the school, lifting the training and dedication of the teachers, and producing a growing commitment to Christ on the part of his young scholars." He shared his pastor's evangelical zeal. In an article in the November 5, 1905, issue of *The Weekly*, he described his primary goal for the Sunday School ministry:

". . . signs indicate God's presence in our school in unusual power. Last Sabbath without any fanfare about fifty of your fellow students expressed their desire to lead Christian lives and accept Christ as Savior. Our hope and prayer is that you too will accept Christ as your Savior, now and always."[12]

The Sunday School had an enrollment of 250 when Eagan began his superintendency. Driven by his zeal for souls, he soon built the largest Sunday School in the denomination, with more than a thousand in attendance each week.

[12] Smith, *The Church That Stayed*, 45–46.

Given Eagan's success in business and church undertakings, the stage was set for a remarkable encounter when he and his mother hosted the prominent social gospel preacher Dr. Josiah Strong, who was delivering a series of lectures in Atlanta.[13] Dr. Strong took a keen interest in the young businessman and spent long evenings talking with him. For years afterward he continued the relationship, sending Eagan letters of encouragement and new books to provoke his thinking. A friend and colleague from the Inter-Racial Commission, Dr. W. W. Alexander, recalled asking Eagan late in life about the root of his radical social ideas, and Eagan told him the story of his encounter with Dr. Josiah Strong. Alexander recalled Eagan telling him that Dr. Strong "interpreted Christianity in terms that I had never before heard, emphasizing the social implications as the central thing in Christian ethics." As a result, Dr. Alexander recollected, the "most interesting thing about Mr. Eagan was his consistent and thoroughgoing application of the principles of Christianity to every phase of life. He never failed to see the Christian implications in any social, economic, or political situation."[14]

The practical implications of Josiah Strong's influence upon Eagan's life are stunning. Even a partial listing of his accomplishments helps drive home how profoundly Eagan's leadership helped to shape Central's developing congregational character, even up to today.

- 1907—Eagan, fellow Central elder Marion Jackson, and others led an effort to meet the needs of destitute men on the streets of downtown. They leased a building and began providing bed, board, and baths, as well as Bible study and worship. Though they soon realized the job was beyond the capacity of their congregation alone, the idea they implemented lives on today in the offshoot of their work, Atlanta's Union Mission ministry to the hungry and homeless.

[13] Strong's exposé of the nation's social problems, *Our Country: Its Possible Future and Its Present Crisis,* was first published in 1891 and, according to Martin E. Marty, did for the Social Gospel movement what *Uncle Tom's Cabin* did for the Abolitionist movement a generation earlier. See Martin E. Marty, *Modern American Religion,* vol. 1, *The Irony of It All 1893–1919* (Chicago: University of Chicago Press, 1986) 23ff.

[14] Robert E. Speer, *John J. Eagan: A Memoir of an Adventurer for the Kingdom of God on Earth* (Birmingham, Ala.: American Cast Iron Company, 1939) 101.

- 1911—Eagan was chosen chairman of the executive committee of the Men and Religion Forward Movement in Atlanta, the root of today's Christian Council of Metropolitan Atlanta. At the movement's national congress in New York that spring, a stirring address by Jane Addams inspired a prolonged attack on Atlanta's "red light" district and the city officials' collusion with its operation. Eagan and his friend Marion Jackson, a lawyer, took out a series of large and very popular advertisements in the local paper, publicizing the facts in the situation and tying these to well-chosen portions of Scripture.
- 1914—Eagan and Jackson led the effort to open Central to striking Fulton Bag and Cotton Mill workers and spoke out in support of better working conditions for them.
- 1919—Eagan helped to found the Atlanta Commission on Interracial Cooperation and expanded its work to the entire South, easing the transition of 200,000 black soldiers from military to civilian life. The commission eventually set up committees in every Southern state capital and in 800 counties, using a method of resolving crises by bringing together leading white and black citizens to frankly discuss all points of friction.
- 1920—Eagan traveled to New York with Dr. W. W. Alexander, director of the Interracial Commission, to hear Seebohm Rowntree of England, a Quaker, speak of his progressive views on business. Eagan was very troubled about his ownership of a large business (The American Cast Iron Pipe Co.), feeling he should give it up for more Christian pursuits. However, he was much impressed with Rowntree's view: "I feel that I should make every job in my plant such a job as I would be willing to see one of my own children work at."[15] At this comment Eagan gripped Alexander's knee and whispered, "That's it, that's it." This experience pushed him toward a commitment to use his business as a laboratory for experiments in the application of the Christian principles in industry.
- 1922—Eagan's great concern for the impact of industrialization on poor mothers and children led him to suggest the creation of a Baby Clinic at Central after discussing the idea with the Mothers' Sunday School class and enlisting its help and a

[15] Quoted in Speer, *John J. Eagan*, 181.

corps of volunteer medical professionals to staff the clinic; this ministry continues today as the Central Health Center.[16]

These examples together speak to the force of social conscience brought to bear on Eagan and his singular impact in galvanizing the congregation's growing consciousness of being responsible for the city. Such an emphasis began with Dr. Strickler's mission Sunday School outreach to poor neighborhoods in the city and carries up to the present.

Yet, during the period of Eagan's life, the city was growing rapidly, and the old elite constituency of Central were moving from downtown to new suburban neighborhoods accessible first by trolley and then by automobile.[17] By the early 1930s only 18 percent of the congregation lived in the old downtown, the majority having moved north and east to the new "garden suburbs." As members moved, some transferred membership to congregations closer to their homes. In addition, a number of prominent downtown churches, including First Presbyterian, sold their properties and relocated to the north with their membership.

Such demographic trends, common in many cities, must have given the young Rev. Stuart Oglesby pause when he assumed Central's pastorate in 1930. The church and its new pastor must have been reflecting on its changing circumstances. A 1931 issue of *The Weekly* included a map that depicted the distribution of members' residences and their distance from the church in all directions. The stock market crash of '29, which launched a decade of economic stagnation, put further pressure on Central, forcing it to scale back programs. Yet, as he instituted his pattern of regular pastoral visits to members, Oglesby must have slowly realized that the majority felt a moral commitment to their ministries in the downtown area, especially the Baby Clinic.[18] On his third anniversary, Oglesby gave voice

[16] Examples are culled from Speer, *John J. Eagan,* and from Smith, *The Church That Stayed.*

[17] See Dana F. White and Timothy J. Crimmins, "How Atlanta Grew: Cool Heads, Hot Air, and Hard Work," in Andrew M. Hamer, ed., *Urban Atlanta: Redefining the Role of the City* (Atlanta: Atlanta Historical Society, 1980); and Howard I. Preston, *Automobile Age Atlanta: The Making of a Southern Metropolis, 1900–1935* (Athens, Ga.: University of Georgia Press, 1979).

[18] Smith writes that "one of Dr. Oglesby's earliest formed convictions after arriving on the scene was that the Baby Clinic, after only nine years of service

to what would slowly become an institutionalized self-understanding of the church as facing the temptation to move but staying downtown. His message in *The Weekly* in early 1933 stated that

"there are three classes of members in Central today. One class believes that the days of our Church (in the downtown area) are numbered, and the end of our usefulness—if not our existence— is almost in sight. Another class loves 'dear old Central' and 'wouldn't have it die for anything in the world,' but yields to the urge of convenience in sending their children to nearer Sunday Schools as well as attending themselves most often in other churches. The third class believes there is need of a great downtown Presbyterian church in Atlanta, that our problems, though great, are not insoluble, that our field of usefulness and service was never wider or more urgent than today, and that insofar as we give ourselves in unselfish and devoted service to our work, the Lord will cause the Church to prosper. The pastor is grateful that the third class is in the majority among our members and trusts that their tribe may increase. He takes his stand unequivocally with them."

Oglesby pursued this decision through pastoral nurture, believing that such work would foster commitment to the congregation;[19] through prophetic preaching, attempting to inspire and instill a vision of a downtown church in service to the city;[20] and through strengthening that service.[21]

---

to needy families, had already made itself far too indispensable to abandon by relocating Central somewhere else." *The Church That Stayed*, 84. Rev. Taylor, pastor in the late 1960s, commented in a newspaper article that "this clinic had the effect of tying us to the downtown community—almost like a mission outpost." Rick Nichols, "A Church Involved in the Heart of the City," *Atlanta Journal and Constitution Magazine* (Sept. 14, 1969) 9.

[19] During his twenty-eight year tenure, Dr. Oglesby logged (literally—he had a pastoral logbook with notes on every member) almost forty thousand pastoral visits, a remarkable average of twenty seven per week, and this basic fact is viewed by many as the glue that held the far-flung congregation together in its focus on common membership and mission.

[20] In his more than three thousand sermons and nearly as many weekly messages in *The Weekly*, Dr. Oglesby constantly rehearsed the distinctive mission of a downtown church at work in service of the city and its most needy, thereby furthering the work of the Kingdom. This simple sentence, taken from

By the time of Dr. Oglesby's retirement after twenty-eight years of service and Central Church's one-hundredth anniversary, the church was highly regarded both in the city and in the denomination. Thanks to Dr. Oglesby's pastoral work and to Church Night suppers, which became a weekly institution early in his tenure, the sense of community and commitment to the church were high. Yet the advent of a new pastor, the Rev. Fred Stair, and a self-study of the congregation's needs found the church having to face the difficulty of going forward with three old, increasingly expensive and inadequate buildings. The Second Century Program, remarkably ambitious for a congregation whose membership had been in slow decline for a decade, offered a comprehensive attack on the problems. Through a difficult nine-year period, the church persevered, and in 1967, as the Rev. J. Randolph Taylor arrived at Central, the new Oglesby Building (for office space, the clinic, education, and the choirs) and some renovations to the sanctuary and fellowship hall were completed.

While the building program absorbed enormous energy through those years, its stated rationale all along was to better serve the needs of the inner city. Little did they know how dramatically this new facility would be put to use. Just four months after Taylor arrived at Central, Dr. Martin Luther King, Jr., was shot and killed in Memphis. Riots broke out in cities across the nation, and some 200,000 people streamed into Atlanta for King's funeral. Taylor called an emergency meeting of the session to determine how Central should respond. After considering several options, including sending a letter of condolence to Ebenezer Baptist, it decided instead to pass an act enabling the church to be available for anything it could do. The next morning the Southern Christian Leadership Conference (SCLC) called and asked the church to help provide accommodations for the mass of out-of-town visitors.

---

one sermon, gives an example. "I believe in the downtown church because it offers to its members so many satisfying, Christlike opportunities for service."

[21] The Baby Clinic served four thousand to six thousand patients a year, and in addition to a staff of volunteer doctors and nurses, it drew on legions of volunteers from the church to help run the clinic, sewing clothing for young patients, doing follow-up visits to patients' homes, and leading devotional services before each clinic.

Mayor Ivan Allen remembers vividly the phone call he received at home that day from Rev. Taylor:

"'Mayor,' he said, 'it was unanimous. Our Board of Deacons voted on it and we are housing 300 Negro citizens already tonight. We'll provide meals for several thousand during the march when they pass by the church, and we'll have living quarters for as many as we can take. We're going to need 600 blankets.' 'Reverend Taylor,' I said, 'there's only one job bigger than my finding six hundred blankets, and that's your opening up your church to Negroes. You've got'em.'"[22]

With Central setting the standard for response, many other white churches in the city followed suit by offering food and housing to the mourners.

This galvanizing event reinvigorated Central's commitments to the city and a renewed focus on new ways to "open its doors." The congregation hosted a vigil and rally for the SCLC one year after King's death; it began active support of a literacy program, a boys and girls club, and a new child development center, aimed at underprivileged families residing in nearby housing projects. Taylor preached social justice from the pulpit and challenged his people to be "an action church." These activities were the greatest challenges to the scope of Central's social vision since it hosted a rally for the striking workers from the Fulton Bag and Cotton Mill fifty-five years earlier.

For some members, though, the challenges were too great. From 1967 to 1968 the church lost 20 percent of its members and 40 percent of its offerings.[23] While some left because they were unable to support what they viewed as "new social activism," most members found this development to be a maturing and development of what Central had always stood for. Further, new members were attracted, although of a decidedly different cast than those who had left. By the time the Rev. P.C. Enniss came in 1976, the membership was younger and less conservative—but also less wealthy. As if

[22] Ivan Allen, Jr., with Paul Hemphill, *Mayor: Notes on the Sixties* (New York: Simon and Schuster, 1971) 212.

[23] Appendix C, "Membership and Financial Statistics 1953–1978," in "Report of Task Force on Priorities and Directions, Central Presbyterian Church, January 1980."

foreshadowing the growth and success of the church over the next twenty-five years, these newcomers were attracted by the combination of challenging preaching, fine music, and Central's engagement in community ministries. For some, Central Church served as a "last hope" for continuing in the organized church.[24]

Interestingly, the combination of a period of strong focus on public life and significant changes in membership left the church feeling strong in vision and mission but weak in its internal bonds. A self-study done to prepare a vision for the 1980s found that members of all sorts felt the need for more pastoral support and nurture. Not surprisingly, the top five priorities resulting from the study all focused on internal process, participation, and renewal (for example improving the process of assimilation and involvement for new members or creating a series of neighborhood parishes for social and service connection, both of which are now part of the church's program). Building community anew became a focus as a new generation of members at Central Church worked to make it their own.

The self-study also warned against resting on the laurels of a historic and well-known church and community ministry. The study pushed for more emphasis on working *with* rather than *for* the people involved in social programs and raised the question of effort spent on service versus social action and change. These remained key issues for Central's expanding range of social programs, including the Night Shelter. Opened in 1980 after a homeless man froze to death near the church, Central responded to a growing homelessness crisis with shelter, food, and in 1983, the Central Outreach Center, to provide general emergency assistance to those living on the street. While a $2 million renovation to the 1927 Campbell-Eagan Building in the late 1980s recommitted Central to its social service programs, including the Night Shelter, members continued to seek a balance between social service and social action for change.

At the end of the decade, while searching for a replacement for Rev. Enniss, the church again undertook an extensive self-study in preparation for ministry in the 1990s. The study noted that the church had a history of delaying repairs on its facilities, and soon

[24] Smith, *The Church That Stayed*, 102–108.

after the arrival of the Rev. Ted Wardlaw in 1991, undertook a multimillion-dollar capital campaign aimed at full restoration of the sanctuary, Tull Fellowship Hall below, and the Oglesby Building, as well as adding significantly to the permanent plant maintenance endowment. Under Rev. Wardlaw, the church has continued on the path set by his predecessor, seeking to find the correct balance between the inner life of the parish and its active outreach to the city. Focusing on this balance both draws together emphases from various moments in the congregation's past and simultaneously moves it into a new era. The heart of this "new era" vision is captured in the fourfold exhortation Rev. Wardlaw gives to those joining the church:

First, be in worship regularly, for nothing is more important.

Second, find a place in the life of the church to serve; in other words, find a place to inhale, but also to exhale God's love.

Third, get involved in Christian education, and not just on Sunday morning, so you can exercise your mind to the glory of God.

Fourth, be generous financially, by giving time, talent, and resources out of the abundance that God has given us.

By the end of the 1990s, the church was a growing, dynamic congregation, pressing into God's future for it, in Wardlaw's felicitous phrase "at the corner of power and powerlessness." I turn now to these most recent events and years to examine the present contours of Central's worship and work.

COMMUNAL IDENTITY

Central has stood for a century and a half in the old downtown, the symbolic heart of Atlanta. Surrounded by the modern edifices of politics, law, and the economy, its solid, gray, granite spire signals a solid presence, as if the building itself, just by being there, preaches a word to the city. But while the church is directly across Washington Street from the Georgia State Capitol, and across Martin Luther King, Jr. Drive from the World of Coca-Cola, it sees itself as also neighbor to Capitol Homes, a nearby public housing complex, and to the multitude of men, women, and children living on the city's streets. As one member put it,

"there is something very powerful in the symbolism, the church being surrounded by all these representative edifices of power, and there we are, and also right across from this temple of American advertising, and then to have the heart of the homeless population and we're there, how blessed we are to be there."

As this quote implies, location leads to mission: in Rev. Wardlaw's words, an ongoing discussion of ways to be "faithful right here where we've been put."

It is the people, though, and not the edifice, that animate the church, and they give the church its commitment and character, carrying forward the mission of a place that has drawn them into the force of its ongoing story. On any given Sunday nearly four hundred members converge on Central from all quadrants of the city.[25] Although parking is a perennial issue, it has been resolved for the moment through an underground parking deck that it shares with the State Capitol and the Catholic Shrine of the Immaculate Conception, located just behind Central. Sunday dress code is generally formal, with suits or sport coats and ties the norm for men and dresses or suits typical for women. However, it tends to relax in proportion to the age of the member (younger equals less formal, as a general rule). While predominantly white, the church has a noticeable number of black members (about 5 percent) as well. During its early days the church counted some of the city's business elite among its membership, but it has not been that way for more than a generation. The congregation has always had a fair number of self-employed professionals, and that pattern continues today, with a solidly upper-middle-class core of lawyers, doctors, and ministers leading the professional categories.[26]

Such analysis, however, cannot tell the story of how these people come to worship in the same stone church, miles from their homes, and there share a ministry to a neighborhood strikingly different from the ones in which they reside. What emerged from my research is a remarkable combination of community nurture and civic commitment particular to an activist downtown church. If

[25] Central's Web site includes directions from all sides via Atlanta's major freeways as well as a Mapquest link for those who need specific directions and a map of the way. See http://www.central-presbyterian.org/about_us/directions.html.

[26] The congregation has always had a large number of lawyers, with around eighty currently, or about 10 percent of the confirmed members.

civic commitment represents the roots of the church's identity, its sense of family and of elective community nourishes those roots. Asked what has kept the church a strong downtown church over the years, Margaret, a retired school teacher and longtime member, replied:

"Its mission, it has a definite mission in the city, to care for the homeless, the outreach office, its mission has kept it here more than anything else, and always has, back before my time when they thought about moving, and decided to stay, and mainly it was the Baby Clinic, that sort of thing, because without that there's not much reason to come downtown."

Indeed, as Martin, another longtime member told me, the church's mission to the city was set a hundred years ago during what may have been its most pivotal period:

"My contention is that the pivotal moment, the foundational event, was the presence of John Eagan, during that whole period of the social gospel. Basically it turned him around, and that guy went into high gear, and it really set the standard for what Central was all about."

These views are confirmed by the church's self-presentation over the years in brochures and anniversary pamphlets describing the church as focused on "bringing to pass the reign of the Kingdom in this present world," "a church at work in the heart of the city," and "a force for love and justice in the city." Central Church has, in one sense, never struggled with the departure of its membership from the immediate neighborhood. Since its founding it has felt itself a ministry in and to the city, a vital force for good in the midst of Atlanta's civic center.

Yet, ever since the late nineteenth century, the church was defined as centered on "spirituality and mission." While the motif of mission to the city dominates its public brochures, comments about the community spirit present in worship are rarely excluded. Banks, a lawyer in his early forties, noted this complementarity when he told me, "I wouldn't have gone here in the first place if it were not for the outreach. I keep coming because of the worship services, but I came to Central because of outreach." While he noted that he was drawn to the worship service, especially the sermon, he also noted the importance of an atmosphere of welcome and community that draws people in:

"When you're a visitor at our church, you are not overwhelmed but everyone goes out of their way to speak to you, you know, an elder is designated to speak to you, it's just very welcoming. There are people there in coat and tie, there are people in blue jeans, it's a very welcoming environment that you don't run into at bigger churches that have three services a day, and not everybody knows each other. I mean I don't know if I'd go to Central if it had three services a day."

Such a warm and hospitable environment, combined with excellent preaching and a commitment to social outreach, together often lead new members to describe their experience of Central as finding a "home." Yet it is a particular sort of homecoming, fitting for an old, downtown, mission-oriented church like Central. According to a parent whose kids grew up at Central, "I think our lack of facilities strengthens us. We don't have a big family center or whatever the hell they're called now, you know, you don't come to Central to play basketball, you know, the youth group went to Costa Rica." While it is important to members that social and youth programs are strong, they believe that these programs should be marked by Central's character, and therefore *not* be their image of a run-of-the-mill suburban church. As another parent commented, reflecting on raising her children at Central, "We had young children, and I wanted them to know that there was more to Atlanta than out there in the suburbs."

While Central's core identity, being a spiritual community ministering to the needs of the city, has been in place for most of a century, it nonetheless is undergoing an evolution under the guidance of its current minister, Ted Wardlaw. Paradoxically, he has attempted to build the church by breaking down any self-satisfied sense of itself it might entertain. First, he has developed a theological critique of the church's core identity, for years rooted in the claim that while other churches moved from downtown, Central was "the church that stayed." The critique, according to Wardlaw, began a sort of conversion within his own thinking. Over the course of the last years, and in part influenced by reading the Canadian theologian Douglas John Hall, Wardlaw has increasingly seen the mission of the church, not as transforming the culture, but as being faithful in it.[27] He eloquently yet subtly developed this position in a sermon the last week in Lent (2000) entitled "We Wish to See Jesus." Recalling the first time he heard one of his favorite hymns, he noted how he always loved the majesty of it:

". . . the stirring sense I got singing this hymn in a packed house while the choirs and clergy came marching in. 'Ride on! Ride on in majesty! Hark! All the tribes hosanna cry; O Savior meek, pursue Thy road with palms and scattered garments strewed.' And the image that came to mind was of a Jesus at the top of his game, a master of the universe, all decked out in kingly fashion to receive his adoring subjects. And though I'm embarrassed to admit this, it's taken me almost twenty years to get beyond the majesty of the hymn itself in order to notice the utter irony that dwells within its words. It was only a few years ago that I noticed the last verse of that hymn, and it came to me like a slap in the face: 'Ride on! Ride on in majesty! In lowly pomp ride on to die; Bow Thy meek head to mortal pain, *then* take, O God, thy power and reign.' Do you wish to see Jesus? Then don't start with categories of power. Look instead amid the landscape of pain and suffering, and you will see One who understands pain and suffering."

This shift, evoked in a Lenten sermon and a hundred other ways in his daily ministry, boils down to a shift of vision, a shift from defining glory as the tempting applause of the world to defining glory as faithfulness to the way of the cross, a life of servanthood revealed to us in Jesus.

Persuaded by his argument, many members I spoke with are increasingly uncomfortable with a vision of Central that pats itself on the back for being the "church that stayed." Noted one member, "First of all, it's a bit of hubris—the Shrine is still there, Trinity is

---

[27] This marks a change from the late nineteenth-century Presbyterian and social gospel view of John J. Eagan, who literally wanted to apply the principles of Christianity to all realms of society. At that time the new century was optimistically thought of as the "Christian century." Now, in the late twentieth- and early twenty-first-century experience of a post-Christian society marked by powerful secular influences and increasing cultural and religious diversity, the question of the church's survival and integrity come to the fore.

still there."[28] Reflecting on a Sunday School discussion, another described what he believes Wardlaw to be aiming at with his critique:

"Ted points out that 'the church that stayed' is, hey, *we're* the church that stayed. It's a bit of snobbery in itself, and the debate is: Are we cocky or are we just proud? Do you say I go to Central and you're cocky about it? And the lesson that Ted and the leaders of the class tried to teach us is we're lucky, we *get* a chance; it's not that we're great because we do all these things for these people downtown, and this is the message, this is what Ted's sermons teach you—it's not, we're not good people because we help the homeless people down here. We're lucky enough to be given an opportunity to help'm, and that's the way we have to remember it—it's okay to be proud of your church, but don't ever think you're getting pats on the back because you go to Central."

Opportunity language fills the talk of members and ministers alike—opportunity not for haughtiness but for humble service.

Ted Wardlaw employs such theological critiques of Central's ego as a means to strengthen its identity and mission. He picked up the vision in place upon his arrival, attempting to put the ministries in balance after an overemphasis on social action during the heyday of the late 1960s and early 1970s. And he has taken this effort at balance to a new level in rhetoric and action. His oft-repeated analogy to breathing—find a place in this church to inhale but also to exhale God's love—finds grounding in his efforts to build community. One couple listed the things that worked in this way: the worship, with lunch served afterward; the choir; the Sunday School for the kids; the Block Party, when the street is closed for a church-wide party; the all-church retreat at Montreat, North Carolina, over Labor Day weekend. They struggled to put words to the whole, saying:

"Ted, I would describe it, Ted has developed, Central used to be a place where people just went to church and we all ate together on Sunday, and now Ted has turned it into this thing that's going on . . . it's an around-the-clock community, and I think that's where

---

[28] The Catholic Shrine of the Immaculate Conception and Trinity United Methodist Church both share the Capitol Hill area with Central and both date back to the early decades of the city.

Ted had made the real difference, and that's why young adults or mid-life crisis adults like us [*laughter*] want to come back down."

They noted that their favorable assessment extended to those who have been hired since Wardlaw's arrival at Cental, especially Paul Osborne, the church's first full-time director of Christian Education. A strong builder for the youth program, Osborne has also been an advocate of building a family feeling at church: "We have an opportunity here, in spite of all the obstacles, to become a powerful intentional community. The more time we spend together in and away from this place the better. We are the family of God, and family time is important."

The new vision, a chastened and more introspective interpretation of Central's claim to be the "church that stayed," was developed in the late 1990s under the title "Being Centered . . . Becoming Central." They stake a fundamental claim on being centered in the midst of shifting tides in a society no longer predominantly Christian. In facing up to this, they discern that the church has moved into a new era in its history. This new era is marked by the need to "intensify our nurture of each other" in the face of contemporary challenges: new growth in membership, largely young adults and young families not predominantly from a Presbyterian background, requires enhanced education; increasing poverty and homelessness, especially among women and children, require renewal of outreach; the increasing diversity of society calls for deeper reflection on the means of hospitality; and shrinking governmental services heighten the need to recommit to a facility that can serve the long-term needs of the city and its most vulnerable residents. The next sections on public worship and public work take up these challenges and the ways Central has responded. In concluding this section, I briefly turn to an examination of how such a multifaceted vision fits into the organizational styles and models developed in chapter 2 and subsequently applied in each of the case chapters.

Styles and Models of Communal Identity
Central clearly orients itself toward this-worldly efforts, articulating a vision that makes the reign of God more manifest rather than using the world as a springboard into a heavenly reward. This fits

squarely within the civic/activist mission orientations described by Roozen et al. Further, because Central goes beyond concern for and education about various social issues to take communal action, it fits well as having an "activist" orientation. Central typically does not protest in the streets, although it has hosted protests within its walls; rather, the members more often use their social capital, resources, and commitment to foster institutionalized responses to social problems. While Central grew up in a prestigious neighborhood, by 1940 its membership had shifted to distant suburbs as nearby neighborhoods gave way to commercial expansion, new freeways, and urban renewal. And now Central is beginning to feel the positive consequence of gentrification as young professionals rediscover some of the remaining old neighborhoods near the church.

A dominant "social gospel" ethos focused the congregation on social issues, an emphasis only heightened at Central by a reformed vision of the city as its proper field of ministry. Such theological emphases made the church and its various programs places of hospitality for street people, neighborhood folk, downtown office workers, and legislators and others needing meeting space. Yet, remarkably, a period of intense social outreach led to a conscious effort to balance more intentionally social outreach with congregational worship and nurture. Such a combination of an activist and a sanctuary orientation, by renewing the energies of its committed members, often appears dynamic and attractive to newcomers. While according to Roozen this does not assure survival in the downtown, this "balance" formula has led to steady growth for Central in the past decade.

However, the success of social programs presents various threats. On the one hand, there is the question of whether institutionalized social programs with paid staff can motivate active and continued involvement by members; on the other hand, do such short-term social programs put the church's conscience at ease or goad them on toward long-term solutions helping to fundamentally change the problems they attempt to respond to through their outreach? Further, the church members' relatively high level of education and employment status make it most difficult to actually welcome those it serves into its common worship and fellowship. Roozen et al. respond to this last difficulty by differentiating between more civic-oriented, establishment activist churches and those more on the edge, more prone to radical critiques of the establishment. In an interview, Banks, a Central member, had his finger on this exact issue:

"The thing I always find so challenging is that if you go speak to Ed Loring, who runs the Open Door Community,[29] you know, he is the guy who picked up the phone and called Buddy Enniss and said did you know that someone just froze to death where they can see the steeple, and that's what was the genesis for getting the night shelter. You don't even want to start writing a case study about Central before talking to Ed Loring, who will blast Central, I mean he is out there, he's on the edge, but there are people like him on the edge, and people like Ted Wardlaw and the rest of them, who are doing so much, they need someone out on the edge to keep them pushing, to see what more can they do."

So remarkably, though Central "fits" most neatly with the activist orientation, it embodies significant, if not essential, elements of civic orientation, supporting as a rule change within the current systems of society.

Such is similarly the case when Central's life is overlaid with Penny Becker's four categories for organizational form or process; while Central best "fits" a leader model, it depends strongly on the logic of the community, family, and house of worship model. Central fits the leader model because of its embrace of a view that religion is and should be "public." In light of this, it feels itself a player both in denominational politics and in the mix of issues concerning the center city, especially on issues of homelessness and the welfare of the poor. Not only that, but these programs and politics are central at Central; they have a feeling that what they do defines them in the eyes of others. Central does these things, as Becker suggests, driven by a strong doctrinal and missional vision, led by the pastor and strongly endorsed by the membership as a whole.

Yet the leader model deemphasizes the language of family, commits few resources to worship development and community building, and rejects the view that church is about meeting individual

[29] The Open Door Community, an intentional Christian community shared among homeless and non-homeless people in a large house on Ponce de Leon in Atlanta. Peter M. Gathje, *A History of the Open Door Community*, MTS thesis (Atlanta: Emory University, 1988).

emotional and psychological needs. Instead, this model supports an ethic of service and civic commitment. Central, like Downtown Baptist in Roozen's study, has come to realize that such an ethic of service and civic commitment, what Becker calls "public religion," can benefit from a foundation in an ethos of elective family relationships. This family is a community built through commitment not only to public concerns but also to commonly expressed religious convictions and to the emotional and quite personal needs of persons one cares about. As Lelah, a single young adult member at Central told me, "People at Central quite literally got me through the darkest days of my life."

In support of its public presence downtown, and doubtless because of it, I noted how much of Central's life revolves around meals—from the weekly meal after church to meals before meetings, from the meal shared with homeless guests at the Night Shelter to the Maundy Thursday meals hosted in homes of elders and clergy, from the regular parish get-togethers to the pledge dinners held during stewardship season. In ways that quite consciously defy neat categories of activist and leader (as well as their pitfalls), Central Church weaves itself together into a strong-fibered community through all manner of social, educational, and civic activities. A new series of brochures, developed to aid in evangelism and public relations, includes a brochure titled "Central Community," sent with a cover letter to everyone who visits. In contains twenty pictures, twelve of activities inside the church and eight of activities outside; more telling, it opens to a page with pictures of the State Capitol and Central's sanctuary, with the church's mission statement in between. It reads:

"Central Presbyterian Church is a community of disciples of Jesus Christ who come together in central Atlanta to worship, serve, and be nurtured by God. We come as to a wellspring, bringing our thirst and emptiness, only to discover that our cup is filled by the living Word, Who sends us to be with those in need and to call forth God's justice in a chaotic world. We live the on-going story of 'The Church That Stayed,' joining generations of Central members and others who share this vision to proclaim the Gospel."

The mission statement of an activist church, yes. Yet oddly concerned with matters spiritual, and slightly too poetic, lingering too much on "our thirst" for a single-issue social-justice organization.

183

Central Church knows itself to be needy before the God of heaven and earth and, paradoxically, before the poorest of the poor, despite its relative wealth, status, education, and facilities. As one woman, a frequent volunteer at the Shelter's foot clinic for homeless men, commented, "My understanding of Jesus' discipleship is clearest when I volunteer at Central's foot clinic—a time when we who have so much wealth and power are servants, washing the tired feet of our brothers in Christ." They've learned the hard lesson that if a community desires to commit to the long term, it must tend to its own sources of mission *and* spiritual depth. The next sections will focus more closely on these issues: their wellspring in public worship and their calling forth of God's justice through commitments to public work.

PUBLIC WORSHIP

When I spoke with Central members about worship, they almost always started with the preaching. In fact, the worship and pastoral leadership in worship are so dominated by the sermon that the process of finding a new pastor is generally referred to as "filling the pulpit." Yet this knee-jerk reaction to my question always gave way, sooner or later, to conversation about music, about Rev. Wardlaw's liturgical innovations, and, to my great surprise, members' strong emotional experiences during everyday, week-in and week-out Sunday worship services. The signature effect of Wardlaw's reforms has been to draw sermon, music, and the whole progression of the service together in a way that makes sense to many (but not all), even moving some members to tears as they find their own lives suddenly folded into God's own life and presence in their midst. After a description of the physical space for worship, I will address these issues in turn.

Central's sanctuary is strikingly beautiful, having been substantially renovated in the mid-1990s. While the congregation worshiped next door at the Shrine, workers brought the sanctuary back to its late nineteenth-century splendor. My field notes from early in my research offer some sense of what a visitor sees:

"I took MARTA downtown on this cold, grey, overcast winter day. I walked up to the church on Martin Luther King, Jr. Drive under the shadow of the Capitol building, following an older, grey-haired

184

couple walking arm in arm. They crossed the street and turned along in front of Central's grey granite front. As they turned to ascend the stairs, two elderly men, equally well dressed in dark suits and ties, opened the glass doors inward, greeting us with a smile, and welcoming us to the church. The doors open into a dark-stained wood entryway laid out across the front of the building. Straight ahead, white-robed choir members were processing up the stairs from the hall below, turning in front of us, and heading up the side stairs to the second-floor sanctuary. I followed them up the dark wood stairs, carpeted so that the footsteps only gave muffled testimony to the ascending crowd. Parallel stairs arose from the other side of the entry room and met with our stairs in a hallway opening through two sets of doors into the sanctuary. Here greeters welcomed people and passed out the worship program. Other people continued on up additional stairs leading to the balcony wrapped around three sides of the sanctuary walls. The worship space is a big square room painted a warm white, with quite high ceilings and dark wood beams supporting across the width and length of it. The three main pew sections are arranged in semicircle fashion. The baptismal font, a thick wooden column in the shape of cloverleaf with a bowl inset in the top, rests just to the right of the raised pulpit area. Rising up a few steps, a marble platform holds the dark, ornately carved altar, pulpit, clergy chairs. Beyond a short barrier wall, a large brass cross on a pole directs one's eyes upwards, past the choir rows and the organ console to the organ pipes encased in a huge archway rising up from either side of the pulpit area to a peak near the ceiling."

Looking forward to the front, one sees a remarkable density of symbols: altar, pulpit, and cross in direct alignment, lifting, as if with the music itself, up through the choir into the heavens. But just near the altar and pulpit, a baptismal font sits stodgily, reminding all whose eyes rest upon it of their own watery passage way into the community of faith.

Yet if these symbolic focal points converge at the front of the worship space, only one physically and symbolically dominates: the pulpit, and the Word of the Lord proclaimed from it. The whole progression of the order of service revolves around the Word: first gathering, then proclaiming, then responding to and sealing of the

Word, and finally bearing and following the Word into the world (see Figure 5.1). Furthermore, it is easily the portion of the service to which the most time is devoted.[30] The sermon is most prominent in responses of those whom I interviewed and talked with informally over meals and in the hallways. One member who joined the church in the early 1970s and was not a Presbyterian at the time joined because of the preaching. When I asked him what it was about Rev. Taylor's preaching, he recalled:

"the topicality of it all, I mean he was talking about the war in Vietnam, he was talking about civil rights, he was chair of Atlanta's interreligious community, Randy just wanted to be out there . . . he spoke out on a lot of social issues, and a couple people left the church because of his stands on social issues, but I got there when the church had gone through this, the whole Martin Luther King funeral, you know, it was one of the most important things in the history, I wasn't there but I've talked to people who were there, and it had a significant impact on their lives."

Weaving together elements of the pastor's personality and politics and the church's identity and history, this quote exemplifies how the "Central pulpit" is expected to address the key issues of the day, in the church, and outside its walls.

Rev. Wardlaw, while not backing off taking political stands, has also expanded the emotional range of sermons, in the best sense of classical rhetoric, entertaining the congregation and moving them by story and Scripture and personal anecdote. This has particularly been important in drawing a growing number of young adults, singles, and families. The following report, given by a young couple I interviewed together, offers a glimpse at the effect of his style:

[H] "I clearly think a lot of Ted, his sermons are awesome, I mean he really is a strong preacher, and I think that everyone can relate to them in a different way, from their own perspective, but even that young adult class that we were in last year, people would quote Ted's sermons from last year, 'remember that sermon where Ted said . . .' they're very, well . . .

[30] While an examination of the elapsed time on Figure 5.1 shows that communion does take about as long as the sermon, a sermon is preached every Sunday, while communion historically fell only once a quarter and now does so monthly.

FIGURE 5.1: A STANDARD ORDER OF SERVICE FOR CENTRAL PRESBYTERIAN CHURCH

Elapsed Time	Order of Service
	Gathering Around the Word
0:00	Opening Organ Voluntary
0:02	The Common Concerns of the Church
0:05	The Ritual of Friendship
0:06	The Call to Worship
0:07	Hymn
0:12	The Call to Confession
0:13	The Confession of Sin
0:14	The Kyrie Eleison
0:15	The Declaration of Pardon
0:16	The Response
	Proclaiming the Word
0:16	The Prayer for Illumination
0:17	The First Lesson
0:20	The Psalter
0:26	The Second Lesson
0:30	The Sermon
	Responding to the Word
0:50	The Affirmation of Faith
0:52	The Peace
0:54	The Offertory Sentence
0:55	Anthem at the Offertory
1:04	The Doxology
	Sealing the Word (Communion on first Sundays)
1:05	The Invitation to the Lord's Table
1:06	The Communion Hymn
1:11	The Great Prayer of Thanksgiving and Our Lord's Prayer
1:16	The Communion of the People
	Music During Communion
1:24	The Post-Communion Prayer
	Bearing and Following the Word into the World
1:25	Hymn
1:30	The Charge and Benediction
1:31	The Closing Voluntary

[B] "They make a very strong impression, they provide a great deal of guidance, it's a pure reformed Presbyterian, he's got the greatest lessons . . .

[H] "You learn a lot and yet you laugh, he tells funny stories.

[B] "And he's not afraid to challenge the congregation, to be better as individuals."

Asked to give an example, they both immediately said, "That's an easy one, he did one on gun control not long after Columbine," the same sermon that sparked the winter program "Blessed are the Peacemakers," discussed in the opening of this chapter.

As many members as said the sermon was very important to them also quickly noted their love of the music at Central. Dorothy, a secretary to the four pastors before Rev. Wardlaw, noted that the music program ranks "as one of the church's greatest programs." Currently headed by a music director and staff organist, Central has five choirs, including three age-graded youth choirs. Blessed by two long tenures by heads of the music ministry since the early 1950s, the music program prides itself on producing top-quality music from an all-member, all-volunteer choir.

But the key is not simply that they do well in their musical undertakings. In part, the positive reaction is simply love of singing and an opportunity to participate. The congregation sings between six and ten different pieces of music each service, not including additional choir anthems or special music. One older woman commented to me that while sermons are "the key thing . . . we do sing a lot, it's very meaningful, it gives the congregation a chance to participate, not just sit back and have somebody else up there, intoning all these things." A young woman noted that often the words will "just hit me, in a personal way, connecting God to what's going on in my life." And another noted that "the service is pretty energetic and contemporary, you walk out with a smile on your face, you learn something, it just makes you feel good." Such positive connection between the music and the members is intentional, even a subtle form of preaching again. The minister of music told me that through careful text selection, she tries to offer "deeply articulated statements of the faith that can deepen the theological language of many young members who join because of Central's outreach and have no theological depth at all." While this may be an exaggeration to make a point, nonetheless many members noted that since the arrival of Rev. Wardlaw worship has changed, and young families and singles keep joining at the rate of about forty per year.

Such care in planning is one of the key innovations Rev. Wardlaw has offered the church. Each Monday morning the pastors and music staff come together, a template of the worship program for the next week in hand, and work out the details. As on the particular Monday morning I attended, however, they spend time on a critique of the Sunday just past, noting what worked and where they had trouble. That morning they brainstormed with the associate pastor, Rev. Kelly, about her sermon and looked at more than ten options before finding a sermon hymn. The organist, Michael Morgan, notes the date each hymn is sung in his hymnal, on the top of each hymn's page; that way they can follow the rule of thumb that says wait at least six months before singing a hymn again.

Such careful planning is noted by members, and it matters to their experience of worship. A younger member who had served on a committee for an intern from nearby Columbia Theological Seminary said, "I never knew how much energy the staff puts in during the week planning the worship. I was just in awe that they really put so much thought into it, you know." An elder who has seen a number of pastors come and go simply said Rev. Wardlaw's work in worship "has transformed it." "How?" I asked member after member. "How is worship different now?" One elder summed up the feelings of many I talked to; she simply said, "More ritual." And another elder said, "Ted liturgicized the service so much more. I think of just the opening, 'The Lord be with you.' I mean that was unheard of. We don't bother with that sort of stuff, you know. Let's just sing!"

When pressed for details, members noted three main changes. First, as someone told me, "Things hold together," explaining that the service is thought through, with hymns and music and prayers done in ways that work with the lessons and sermon. Second, an opening section of the service, including a formal call and response, greeting, and rite of confession and absolution. A young woman told me that "I do like after the confession of sins, when we get a moment of silence, a moment of prayer. A couple of

189

weeks ago it got skipped, and I was, like, where's my silent prayer!" Third and most contentious is a heightened sacramentalism. An elder recounted to me that when Rev. Wardlaw came, the sacramental rituals "had gotten real sloppy," and when Rev. Wardlaw arrived, he said "just very dogmatically, 'we're going to do this by the book,' we're going to do baptism with all the words and all the actions, you know what I mean, and make that an important ceremony again."

I attempted to observe responses to such liturgical innovations in Sunday worship. Having spent the previous four months at Big Bethel, where movement and vocal response are quite animated, I had to refine my analysis of movement and response in worship. Before long I had recalibrated my observation, and I began to attend to the relative body angle and posture in the pew. After one Sunday I commented in my field notes that

"I noted more today than before that the congregation almost never responds to what is said or proclaimed from the front except with formal sung responses, such as the sung response to the declaration of pardon. And when people pray, they literally don't do much more than (at the most) fold or overlay their hands and slightly bow their heads. Many keep looking about, keeping the exact posture they had before, say like the man in front of me who had his right leg over his left, torso turned slightly to the left, shoulders tilted that way, and was picking his fingernails, which he continued to do through the prayer."

In short, I wasn't finding much outward expression to help me assess people's experience of worship's ongoing reform.

In talking informally and through formal interviews, however, I indeed found fascinating and quite remarkable evidence. Rev. Wardlaw's reforms meet some resistance, especially from those elderly members most deeply formed by a spare Reformed aesthetic in matters of worship. While they are willing to accept some change, their disquiet comes with a guarded, worried tone. One elderly member told me that since Rev. Wardlaw came, "there's more ritual than there was. He likes that. I don't mind it. I don't want it to go much further [*nervous laughter*]. It's more like the Episcopal Church, not totally, but I see little elements in there." A special sore spot with some older members is communion by intinction, which Rev. Wardlaw has instituted every other month, a process that requires members to rise, process forward to the altar, and receive the bread and cup from the ministers rather than the traditional way with a corps of elders delivering the bread and trays of individual cups to be passed through the pews. Such a practice evokes worries, even for some who are generally supportive. One member who sees grounds for theological concern likes intinction; he told me, "I know it's not the real thing and I'm not Catholic, but it means more to me doing [intinction]."

Despite the reservations of some members, these liturgical interpolations, generally, and in the case of the sacraments in particular, have also helped foment a quite un-Presbyterian flowering of emotional experience in worship, especially among the growing numbers of new members, many of whom, in the words of Margaret, an elder and lifelong Presbyterian, "don't seem to be dyed-in-the-wool Presbyterians at all, they're everything in the world!" One woman, a member for two years and raised marginally Episcopalian, told me about her first experiences in worship:

"I don't even want to sound like I'm born again, because I don't mean to be that. I don't like that phrase, but the first month of church, I would say, I cried at every service, like the first month or two, mostly joy, something Ted had said, or the children's choir sang and they were so cute and so sweet, or I don't know, but I, Mr. what's his name played his fiddle. There was something neat or happy that just touched me for like the first two months, the first eight weeks, and still every now and then, but it was just really a happy feeling."

Another, an elder and member for many years, reflected comparatively to when he first joined in the early 1970s: "Well, I would come away from the services where Randy had preached a powerful sermon, very cerebrally . . . touched, you know. I would walk away, and I thought about it a lot." His analysis of worship today strikes a different tone:

"You know, during and after worship, but at points *during* worship, I mean I'm moved, I'm emotionally moved, and I was telling someone about this one time. There were people sitting around, and I said, you know, I mean I'm a bit of a marshmallow anyway, but I said I was literally moved to tears, and they said, 'Oh, God, yea,' and I started to realize that as I looked around the congregation, that's when I realized that you got a bunch of people blubbering. How un-Presbyterian can you get? You know, we're not going to get into any more ecstatic modes of worship, I'll tell you that, but for a Presbyterian to shed a tear in worship, holy cow! John Buss, one of our new members, wonderful guy, former Catholic, I mean John and I can't keep from crying in the service."

Though not prone to the sort of visible spiritual ecstasy prominent in Pentecostal-style worship, I observed a sort of passionate and intense worship, whether it was singing, listening, or responding to various call-and-response portions of the service. My interviews helped me to look for the sort of clues–eye contact, bodily posture, facial expressions–that signaled members' subtle but powerful modes of engagement.[31]

In the face of renewed sacramental practice, I also heard various positive experiences. Some are simply attracted by Rev. Wardlaw's principles on the matter. As I showed above, he came in with a bold agenda regarding the church's sacramental ministry. And this impressed a number of my interviewees, including this one: "[Rev. Wardlaw] is very big on the table, you know. A lot of churches, they move all that stuff away for a wedding. Ted won't let that move. He makes the table stay out there, the church is still the church."

This same member commented that he "really liked" the change in communion to intinction, and I asked "Why?" He said, "The symbolism of me and that person holding the cup, they speak directly to me, instead of somebody handing me the traditional tray, and like, don't drop it. Those two people who really mean it are holding the cup and the bread and it's more symbolic." He continued, "The procession to come up there . . . I just enjoy watching the people come up." Another member, who is strongly in favor of the change, thought the congregation "did communion that way because it's been done that way for so long, until now we try the method of intinction, and well, just the discipline of coming for-

---

[31] See David Yamane's work on religious experience, in which he argues that one can't really ever get at another's religious experience directly. We have to rely on narrative reports of such experience. See his "Narrative and Religious Experience," *Sociology of Religion* 61:171–189.

ward, getting out of your pew, not just sitting there waiting for your shot glass to be delivered."

The long-term success of these innovations seems assured, in part because even the detractors seem to be pleased with the overall growth and health of the congregation, and despite reservations about Wardlaw's enthusiasm for ritual, they are pleased with his leadership generally. But more than that, the new worship style is supported by the many who are experiencing a new emotional and spiritual depth in worship.

While many find the exact reasons for this new experience in worship mysterious ("he's made communion more meaningful, don't make me say how, because I can't think [laughter]"), it is having a profound effect on Central's life. One leader articulated this in a way that makes an appropriate segue toward the final topic I will consider—Central's public work:

"I haven't taken time to analyze it, but whatever is happening, the impact is measurable. I don't know, I don't think I leave that service wanting to go out and feed hungry people. That's not the issue. I already wanted to do that, but first of all I'm *personally* energized by the worship experience, and then I go out and do whatever else, however I choose to express that. Which way is more the question, and it's very different, *very* different than hearing a sermon on something. That's important, too, but it's not just a message to the head."

PUBLIC WORK

Although Central is increasingly critical of its legacy as "the Church That Stayed," its renewal of worship, emotionally and spiritually engaging its members, assures that its most public work—its presence in downtown Atlanta—will continue with strength. Central *did* stay, and in staying, has over time committed tremendous time, energy, and millions of dollars to maintain and expand its facility, in service of its members to be sure, but ultimately in service of its mission in the city. While Rev. Wardlaw told a newspaper reporter that their $2.7 million renovation would "simply glorify God," he not only gave an answer right out of the Westminster Catechism[32] but also clearly intended the corollary

[32] "Q. 1: What is the chief end of man? A. Man's chief end is to glorify God, and to enjoy him forever." "The Westminster (Shorter) Catechism," in The

that God is present in the midst of all human activity. Thus the pamphlet developed as part of the capital campaign to raise the money took as its title "Preserving Our Inheritance," not defining "inheritance" in the obvious sense of a facility but in the edgy, reformed sense that the members are called to recommitment to God's ongoing work in the city. The pamphlet concluded with proclaiming that Centralites are "stewards of a great inheritance—a century-old pledge to love and serve the city from a strategically positioned site in the heart of Atlanta."

Central Church's recommitment as stewards of this century-old pledge of love and service to the city plays out most clearly in its well-institutionalized ministries of hospitality and service: the Health Center the Child Development Center, and the Outreach Center and Night Shelter. However, its pledge to serve the city extends in a multitude of ways, from its Music in the City program, which attracts downtown workers for noon concerts, to its participation in tutoring and after-school programs with Capital Area Mosaic, to its latest efforts to establish transitional housing for homeless women and children. After briefly describing the main programs run by the church, I will conclude the chapter by demonstrating the promise and peril of Central's style of social ministry by examining the process of developing the transitional shelter for women and children.

The Baby Clinic, begun, as I noted above, at the suggestion of John J. Eagan in the early 1920s, served for nearly sixty years as a ministry of and by Central Church as a primary-care site for those without insurance or resources. Stewart Oglesby, son of Rev. Oglesby, who served as chair of the clinic board for many years, told me that the clinic was run on a completely volunteer basis, including medical staff and support staff, and that his personal doctor served also as medical director. One woman, Dr. Lelia Denmark, served at the clinic for more than thirty years. In response to increasing homelessness in the 1980s, the clinic broadened its approach to include a variety of primary-care clinics, including testing and free prescription drugs. In 1992 the

Presbyterian Church, USA, *The Constitution of the Presbyterian Church (U.S.A.): Part I Book of Confessions* (Louisville: The Office of the General Assembly, 1999) 175.

church entered into a partnership with St. Joseph's Hospital, then expanding a system of "Mercy Mobile" health centers around the city and looking for a fixed site. Since that time it has been known as the Central Health Clinic. Early on, the clinic expanded to include ob-gyn care and includes both pediatric and women's clinics, free HIV testing and education, mental health counseling, and other relevant services for the destitute and the working poor, who generally qualify for Medicare or can pay a nominal fee but do not have resources to pay for insurance or the full cost of care.

The Child Development Center (CDC), a day-care and preschool program started in the early 1970s, also aims to serve those living in the area who are without resources for high-quality child care. The CDC also sees its mission as providing an outreach to the many workers in downtown corporate, state, and city offices. Begun in partnership with nearby Georgia State University, the CDC has continued as a learning lab for early childhood research. It also continues to focus on class and race diversity among its seventy-five or so families, with scholarships currently supporting 20 percent of the children. While Central has supported the CDC by providing space (including utilities and maintenance), a significant contribution to its budget, endowed scholarships for low-income families, and supplies, personal involvement has traditionally come through church members whose children attend.

The Night Shelter and Outreach Center both began in the early 1980s in response to a growing crisis on the streets of the city. The Night Shelter for men, run from November 1 through March 31, provides hospitality to eighty to a hundred homeless men per night. The second oldest church shelter in the city and the only one still run solely by volunteer effort, Central Shelter is in large part a host for their own program, given the multitude of churches, public and private organizations, and schools that provide the volunteers who greet guests, make and serve a warm dinner, breakfast, and sack lunch, provide beds, towels and showers, and on Wednesdays tend to guests' sore and often neglected feet. Since the late 1980s the shelter has been jointly housed between Central and the Shrine, its next-door neighbor.

The Outreach Center was at first a simple, volunteer-staffed office responding to the flood of requests for emergency food, tokens for public transportation, or counseling. Rev. Kimberly Richter, an associate pastor during the late 1980s and early 1990s, systematically expanded and deepened the vision for the Outreach Center, and with Central's support hired a full-time director to oversee implementation of the vision. Today staff and volunteers work out of a suite in the Oglesby Building and are prepared to welcome a diverse range of people—homeless, immigrants, unemployed residents from nearby public housing, and others—with coffee and a pastry, employment materials, use of a phone, and one-on-one counseling to assess what can be done.

Both the Health Center and the Child Development Center were, during the time of my study, largely perceived to be disconnected from the majority of the members and even the leaders of the church. During my first Session meeting, the interim associate warned the church that they must face "the disconnect between the low numbers of people involved in Central's various outreach ministries and the commitment to outreach ministries we in fact have." Various task forces are in the process of evaluating everything from use of facilities to self-studies of the ministries discussed above in an effort to stitch the vision and practice together again. It will not be easy, however. When I asked an elder about the interim associate pastor's comment, he confided that

"we *have* lost something. I'm on a task force trying to work with the Health Center, and since Mercy Mobile took over, they've tried to become independent and used our space, which is a significant savings for them, and then they come to us with financial problems, saying they want help, and we say, where have you been lately? You know, all of a sudden they want to be friends again. We're trying to get some conversations going about how we, how that relationship is going to work."

Most hopeful may be the work of the Community Ministry Council, which has spent the last year listening, month after month, to the leaders of all its outreach ministries, working to understand the issues they face and the ways Central can become personally reinvested in the ministries.

Such a disconnect has not been as prevalent with the Night Shelter and the Outreach Center. This in part is the result of much higher numbers of active volunteers. During the recognition of shelter volunteers at the end of the 1999–2000 winter season, Kathy, the Community Ministry Council cochair, asked everyone in the congregation to stand if they had helped at the shelter during the year. The pews creaked as nearly three-quarters of the packed church stood to their own enthusiastic applause. Yet the fact that these ministries loom large in the lives of even those who do not volunteer indicates their location near the heart of Central's self-understanding. When I asked what keeps her from being the sort of person she thought a member of Central should be, an active member and mother of two told me:

"I'd have to say that being involved in the homeless shelter, I would like to do that, but we have small kids, but I also, I'm a little fearful of it. I don't know where to go. I don't know what to do. I don't know what to expect. I don't know if I would know how to handle a certain situation. So the kids are probably a good front, but I have my own, because I've never done it before. I have my own fears about doing the night shelter, spending the night there. Do I really want to do that? I don't know, and that's selfish. And the same thing with the foot washing thing, which I think is awesome, between you and me, there's no way I could go and wash feet, and that's terrible. And I could overcome it. Do you think I'm terrible for admitting this? But that would be a very hard thing for me to do."

Even in her fears and reluctance, she acknowledges the importance of these ministries for the congregation—a member *should* do them, even if one actually does not.

I pondered this dilemma of high ideals and splintered commitments out loud as I talked with various members and listened to Session discussion on a range of issues. One member began to get at the problem when I pressed him on why Central members seemed somewhat disconnected from their own ministries, programs they are committed to in general.

"Well, they all began small, but as they grow, they become unmanageable for our size congregation. We don't have the size membership to support them by ourselves, and we support them financially, but a lot of us are not able to volunteer on a regular basis. I definitely can't. I've got such a frenetic schedule I can't be regular about anything."

In this introspective comment a number of key factors surface that contribute to an almost inevitable dissociation over time between the membership and its outreach ministries. These factors are connected to the congregation's social taxonomy: highly educated, white-collar professionals, many with children still at home, and very few who live near the church. First, the membership's strong theological commitment to serving the needy means that when it sees a need, it comes up with the financial resources and organizational know-how to respond. Second, and relatedly, their response tends to be toward institutionalizing a program. They receive satisfaction in using their workplace skills in law, finance, and administration for the purposes of Central's ministry and also feel more confident in the future success of the program, knowing it will have full-time, professional management which they feel is needed but which they cannot provide within their own overcommitted lives. As one lawyer noted when I asked how membership at Central changes his family's life, "As Ted says, 'breathe in, breathe out,' and we're involved, we're overvolunteered because we're trying to breathe out."

The current initiative to start a transitional shelter for homeless women and children exemplifies this paradoxical logic of dissociation between the membership and its core social ministries. In the late 1990s the Outreach Center noted an increasing number of homeless women with children and worried that the city lacked facilities for these people. The congregation quickly acted to set up a task force to examine potential program models throughout Atlanta and beyond. After considering an emergency shelter modeled on the Night Shelter for men, the congregation decided to focus their energy on a transitional housing model that could host a family for several months, aiding them in regaining a home and a more stable living situation. The task force then studied options for developing this idea and settled on a partnership with Decatur Cooperative Ministry (DCM), a local organization with experience in such programs, to help guide the development of the program.

Members of the task force worked simultaneously to raise funds, find a suitable home to buy, clean, and furnish, and organize an official advisory board to run the shelter, drawing on the model of the Child Development Center. The February Session meeting, when a draft constitution and by-laws were discussed, was an incredible display of thoughtfulness and forethought, eliciting a concluding comment from Rev. Wardlaw: "You all are frisky tonight. This is all strengthening this document, so I appreciate your diligence." The process had taken an enormous amount of energy, time, and commitment on the part of literally hundreds of members, drawing on a multitude of skills and professional knowledge at various points. After the first family is chosen via their partner agency, Decatur Cooperative Ministry, Central members will be able to assist the family by providing services needed, including mentoring, tutoring, and coordinating child care while the parent attends workshops at DCM, and similar activities.

Although in the case of the transitional shelter for women and children the outcome is not assured, I detect the same type of process as with other Central outreach ministries. It draws out members' educational and work-related skills in getting the programs up and institutionalized, while over time also marginalizing the program from the church by professionalizing the ministry, thus making it less dependent on volunteer support in the long run. This may be a good thing, for it fits squarely within the grand tradition of voluntary organization in the United States. Churches like Central exercise their moral sensitivity through responding to needs, and very often spinning these off into independent organizations in responding to the needs they see. While this may be a strength of such a process, Central's distinctive communal identity somehow depends on a more vital and gut-jolting connection to the plight of the needy. As an elder put it as we concluded our interview,

"The real challenge is going to be how to keep outreach ministries, real hands-on ministries, viable and directly related to everything we are. And, you know, there's talk, for example, that, 'shouldn't we move them somewhere?' But my fear is, out of sight, out of mind. For better or worse, it's best when you sometimes climb over somebody on the way to a meeting, ah, to see that reminder, you know?"

Part Three

Conclusion

Chapter Six

The World in the Church in the World

The larger question of this study, namely, does Christian worship form and sustain a people committed to a greater public good, has been explored through the framework of a character ethics claim that worship forms distinctive Christian public witness. My main argument, as developed in part one, was that such a "linear model" of formation draws on an idealized notion of church and a simplistic notion of formation, thus masking how the particular communal identity of a congregation marks out the conditions of possibility for its life, worship, and work. While these claims were implicitly substantiated in the case studies, it remains for me to do so in a more analytical and comparative way and to suggest the implications of this claim for the larger question about churches in public life.

To do this, I first reiterate the shortcomings of the "linear model" of worship formation implied in character ethics approaches. Then I introduce the concept of communal identity, its implications for traditional church-world distinctions, and the way various social sources of such identity imply various styles of faithful churches, each with its own "sense of public" to which it is responsible. Lastly, I illustrate the role communal identity plays in relation to public worship and work by proposing an "interactive model." Such a model allows me to indicate the ways in which communal identity structures the possible styles of worship and work within a congregation, the ways that "worldly" influences are constitutive of the congregation's life, and finally how worship is, and is not, powerful in forming Christians and their public witness in the world.

203

THE PROBLEMS WITH A LINEAR MODEL

Many leading authors writing on worship and ethics depend upon a linear model of relating the two, basically suggesting that participation in worship forms individual Christians and the church. Through such formation Christian social-ethical witness is made possible (see Figure 6.1). Individual authors have nuanced positions, including the recognition that the liturgy and most modern Christians who gather to worship are shaped by secular "fields of force" that compete and conflict with the story of Jesus told through word, prayer, and song. Don Saliers singles out the mass media and its ubiquitous message that says "you are what you have" as a counternarrative constitutive of such "fields of force" against which the church attempts its own formation.[1] Even with such an admission, the fundamental model is not changed. External social forces are portrayed as competitive influences, mal-forming Christians, while the church and its worship offer the hope of proper and powerful Christian formation. It is exactly this linear framing of the question—that the church's worship (or the world's social forces) directly form Christians—that my research suggests is misguided. When significant attention is paid to the role of a congregation's communal identity, both the simple linear framing of the formation process and its assumption of a church-world distinction are called into question.

THE NEGLECTED ROLE OF COMMUNAL IDENTITY

Liturgy and its enactment are infused with the particular social and cultural characteristics of membership and location. This is nowhere more profound than in the complex identity of the community gathered to worship in a particular place. Who they are and who they are becoming exist in a dynamic interrelationship with the acts of worship, mercy, and justice which they enact and which influence them in return. I recognize that there is an infinite regress of complicating factors when one looks closely at the sub-

---

[1] Don Saliers raises these questions forcefully in his "Afterword: Liturgy and Ethics Revisited," 216ff., written in response to a book of essays reflecting on his 1979 article on liturgy and ethics. See E. Byron Anderson and Bruce T. Morrill, eds. *Liturgy and the Moral Self: Humanity at Full Stretch Before God. Essays in Honor of Don E. Saliers* (Collegeville, Minn.: The Liturgical Press, 1998).

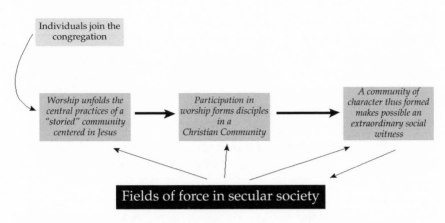

FIGURE 6.1—A LINEAR MODEL OF THE RELATIONSHIP
OF WORSHIP AND ETHICS

groups or, beyond that, the diversity of individuals, who make up one congregation.[2]

Implications of Communal Identity
Given such diversity, I draw on recent research in congregational studies showing the power of a dominant communal identity (a "mission orientation" or "congregational model") within a congregation. A communal identity provides a structuring logic based in ideals and a mode of living that fits with such ideals hand in glove. Such an identity, according to Becker, serves as a "local public" that mediates between the individuals and large-scale institutions and organizations.[3] Though often explicit, the many implications of a congregational identity and its practical logic are usually not conscious. I claim that such a practical logic shapes a "sense of public church" that frames who the congregation sees as its responsibility, as well as the language it uses and the practices it enacts as a response to its particular sense of public responsibility.[4] Such an identity and its practical logic make some things and ways

---

[2] Penny Edgell Becker makes this point exactly. See *Congregations in Conflict: Cultural Models of Local Religious Life* (New York: Cambridge University Press, 1999)158f.

[3] Ibid., 194, 198.

[4] Ibid., 158–159.

of doing things natural and right, while others are awkward or not even thought.[5]

Thus, in any particular congregation, the question of the roots of that common identity comes to the fore. If the church is a "storied community," as Stanley Hauerwas claims, then exactly which stories constitute such an identity? Since the members not only worship God together in particular churches but are also involved in many other spheres of social life, such a claim begs to be set in context in order to make sense. And it will not do to simply roll out church-world distinctions; in so many ways the church is "worldly" *even* insofar as it serves as a counter-society that shows the world that it is the world, as Hauerwas is fond of saying.

While few theologians take the church-world rhetoric to Hauerwas's heights, many do implicitly trade on church-world distinctions in arguing for a stronger Christian witness in the face of vast changes in Western societies and even more so, globally. Even Robin Gill, who explicitly critiques Hauerwas for his rhetorical excess, in the end builds his own case for a distinctive church culture by drawing on Hauerwas's teaching companion at Duke, Harmon Smith.[6] Thus it may be fruitful for me to use the example of Hauerwas's theological point about church and world to show exactly how such language goes wrong, even in relation to his theological point.

When Hauerwas deploys church-world distinctions to portray the church or worship as a social ethic, he is fundamentally working under the influence of the separationist logic of the Anabaptist tradition. The left-wing Reformers described themselves in *The Schleitheim Confession* of 1527 as "we who have been and shall be separated from the world in everything and completely at peace."[7] It is well known

---

[5] I take this to be a main contribution of the notion of *habitus* as a means to speak of such a non-conscious practical logic framing the scope of possibilities. See pp. 60–63 above.

[6] Gill draws extensively from Harmon L. Smith, *Where Two or Three Are Gathered: Liturgy and the Moral Life* (Cleveland: The Pilgrim Press, 1995). For many years Smith has co-taught a course, "Christian Ethics as Worship," with Hauerwas at Duke University and developed the book out of this teaching experience. Hauerwas discusses the course in his *In Good Company: The Church as Polis* (Notre Dame: University of Notre Dame Press, 1995)153–168.

[7] "The Schleitheim Confession of 1527," in John Leith, ed., *Creeds of the Churches*, 3rd ed. (Louisville: John Knox, 1982) 283.

that Hauerwas draws this perspective from the late John Howard Yoder. In his own words (and some of Yoder's), his point is this:

"If the church's first task is to make the world the world, that is its fundamental social and political task. Such a claim is often resisted because it sounds so intolerant, which of course it is, but it is an intolerance based on charity that would have the world saved by knowing that it is the world. If the church does not worship rightly, how can the world know that it is the world exactly to the extent it does not willingly glorify God. As Yoder puts the matter in *Body Politics*, 'stated very formally, the pattern we shall discover is that the will of God for human socialness as a whole is prefigured by the shape to which the Body of Christ is called. Church and world are not two compartments under separate legislation or two institutions with contradictory assignments, but two levels of the pertinence of the same Lordship. The people of God is called to be today what the world is called to be ultimately.'"[8]

In the context of such a theological position, such claims as "liturgy is social action" and the sacraments are "the essential rituals of our politics" make logical sense. The church is not responsible primarily to make society better, more just, or more at peace; rather, the church, by its life together, enacts God's intentions for social life, becoming a righteous society that provides a model for the world to follow also, although it does not.

My argument is that sociologically uninformed dichotomies between the church and the world, because of the simplistic and holistic understanding of culture implied, really harm their own efforts to better lead the church in being the church exactly because their crude cultural lens cannot see the ways in which they are bound up with the world in their very ways of being church.[9] With

---

[8] See Hauerwas, *In Good Company*, 249, n. 12, and Yoder, *Body Politics: Five Practices of the Christian Community Before the Watching World* (Nashville: Discipleship Resources, 1992).

[9] After all, this point is made by Ernst Troeltsch, who argued that the Christian church and its host cultures have mutually influenced each other from the beginning. See his great work *The Social Teachings of the Christian Churches* (Louisville: Westminster/John Knox, 1992 [1912]). See a similar critique leveled at John Milbank in Kathryn Tanner's *Theories of Culture: A New Agenda for Theology* (Minneapolis: Fortress, 1997) 97ff.

a more complex understanding of culture, two intimately related facts emerge. First, one recognizes that multiple kinds of faithful churches exist. Second, the tensions they face in sustaining their style of faithfulness are also multiple. These two, kinds of faithfulness and kinds of tensions, usually share an elective affinity with the social characteristics of a congregation's membership. Therefore, seeing how a church is *both* in *and* of the world helps with the very particular tasks of being a church in *but not of* the world. A return to the example of holy communion, discussed in chapter 2, can serve as an example here as well.

The Shrine, as I discussed earlier, is a congregation that embodies remarkable diversity, and this fact has become central to their eucharistic celebration. In contrast to a segregated and segmented society, they claim a oneness in the Body of Christ effected through participation in the sharing of Jesus' body and blood present in the bread and wine. Undergirded by an expansive global church, they perceive their unity in the "one Lord" to be reality and, through their choice of membership in this community of faith, fold their own lives into this ideal and its practical implications for their lives. Just such a focus on diversity, though, among a predominantly middle-class professional membership, tends to depend on the language of "tolerance" and respect for "private individual choice" rooted in the liberal individual traditions of American life (especially influenced by John Locke). Thus Father Adamski saw a key challenge for his ministry in offering theological language and ritual enactment to ground such notions of unity in diversity, with the Eucharist at the center of such efforts.

Big Bethel's evangelical theology and sense of decorum in worship translate into a formal communion practice focused on the sacrificial death of Jesus on the cross. Sharing in the redeeming blood effects the forgiveness of sins, fortifies believers in their struggle to live right, and holds out the promised heavenly reward to all who persevere in this world of woe. The theology is rooted in the suffering of African Americans in the United States, and its enactment embodies the claim that though the world forsakes them, the Lord of Heaven and Earth died for their sins, bought their freedom for a price, and calls them to a holy life that begins now as they work together for the freedom and uplifting of their brothers and sisters. What becomes of such a theology of communion when increasingly members are well-to-do doctors, lawyers, and corporate managers remains to be seen, but its themes of sin and neediness before God can become unattractive to upwardly mobile members, encouraging a deemphasis of communion, or as in some independent black megachurches, its virtual eclipse by preaching and upbeat praise and worship. Given the rehabilitation of the Love Feast at Big Bethel, such a total deemphasis seems unlikely. Rather, the ritual's action turns toward an emphasis on spirit-filled connection to God and to one another in a community of love. Such a ritual focus fits more nearly the needs of a mobile, transient, and thus less geographically rooted post-civil rights generation.

Central's tradition of holy communion in many ways parallels that of Big Bethel. Presbyterianism, Central included, is known for doing things in good order, and communion is a ritual case in point. Yet its theological emphases draw it away from Big Bethel's evangelical, salvation-oriented understanding. Combining a common Protestant view of the meal as a remembrance rather than the real presence of Christ and a peculiar Calvinist focus on God's divine sovereignty that effectively de-centers the question of an individual's salvation, the meal takes on the ethos of a rededication to God's mission in the world as revealed in Christ.

Central's own particular social gospel twist on this dedication to God's mission has, ironically, drawn many newer members with no particular commitments to Presbyterianism, its theological heritage, and its rich language of calling and commitment to follow Christ into the world. Called "young secular humanists" by the minister of music, these members are attracted to the church because of its social ministries and the charisma of the pastor, not by shared understandings of Christian belief and practice. While the minister's agenda of liturgical reform is in part an effort to draw this diverse younger cohort, offering them a ritual center, a wellspring of faith from which to nourish their social commitments, such changes in the worship and especially communion quite unsettle the longtime members, whose sense of proper order has lost most of its flexibility.

Some Sources of Communal Identity

While these glosses on the interrelation of communion and communal identity in my three case-study churches are quite brief, they underscore my point that traditional church-world distinctions depend on ignoring or minimizing communal identity and its impact on the church's life, worship, and work. In an effort to think through the multiple sources of communal identity in relation to case examples that show its impact, I attend to five salient components.[10] Often such influences are parsed along church-world, secular-sacred lines, but I intend to consider them all as characteristic of the church's identity, shaping its particular mission and the tensions it faces in fulfilling that mission. While there are undoubtedly others, I will focus on these: (1) congregations's social context; (2) members' social worlds; (3) denomination/polity; (4) local culture/history; and (5) dominant ecclesiology. My argument is not that these *determine* the congregation's life; that would imply the erroneous assumption that they could be something else freed from these "constraints." Rather, I am trying to indicate that such components of congregational identity represent the very conditions of possibility for its life in a real sense—the earthen vessel that bears the treasure of the gospel. I'll take each in turn, noting its characteristics and offering examples drawn from my case studies.

Social context is a broad category that potentially includes the structural location of the church building in relation to its surrounding community and also the social structure and geography of that community itself, the broader population demographics of that community, and its particular cultural characteristics. The development and changing fortunes of downtown Atlanta (especially patterns of racially segregated housing tied to economic globalization and large-scale processes of deindustrialization) mean that the social realities of many people living in downtown neighborhoods have been bleak. Further, access to social services, government offices, and shelters concentrates the city's homeless population nearby.

[10] In thinking these through I benefited greatly from previous work in congregational studies and especially the methodological reflection by Jackson W. Carroll, William McKinney, and Wade Clark Roof, "From the Outside In and the Inside Out," in Carl S. Dudley, ed., *Building Effective Ministry: Theory and Practice in the Local Church* (New York: Harper and Row, 1983) 84–111, which effectively described the approach taken in David Roozen, Jackson Carroll, and William McKinney, *Varieties of Religious Presence: Mission in Public Life* (New York: Pilgrim, 1982) discussed in chapter 2 above.

Each of the three congregations has responded to these issues with various programs. St. Francis' Table, the Saturday lunch for the homeless at the Shrine, and the Central Night Shelter, housed at both the Shrine and Central, are established ministries called forth by virtue of the Shrine and Central being located in the old downtown of a sprawling metropolitan area. The slow abandonment of the central city by families, businesses, and even churches created the conditions for high concentrations of people with few options. The churches' physical location, then, offered options for concrete social outreach simply by the fact that homeless and hungry people constantly knocked on their doors and slept on their steps. Yet, while the commitment to stay and to reach out through various ministries to these many needy people helped to establish these churches as committed to action, the fact that most of their middle-class professional members live in nicer neighborhoods scattered all over the metropolitan area adds a "commute tax" to any activities they participate in at church. This fact, while regularly overcome, nonetheless haunts many a planning meeting and gives cause for realism in estimating participation in a particular event.

The *members' social-worlds* category is quite self-evident for the most part; it refers to the sorts of things asked in a typical U.S. Census questionnaire, such as gender, race, age, socioeconomic status, educational level, and so on. Also important, however, are the ways these cold facts imply the influence of a whole set of cultural values, assumptions, and influences. For instance, extensive research has been done on the so-called baby-boom generation, who were born in the aftermath of World War II and came of age in the turbulent 1960s.[11] In the American professional middle-class population generally and especially as the baby boomers reach middle age, sociologists have noted an increasingly common and influential "individual-expressive style" of moral understanding and commitment. This growing trend increasingly impacts the culture of many congregations made up of this demographic slice.[12]

[11] Among the many authors working in this area, Wade Clark Roof has distinguished himself as the most influential. See his *A Generation of Seekers: The Spiritual Journeys of the Baby Boom Generation* (New York: Harper, 1993) and *Spiritual Marketplace* (Princeton: Princeton University Press, 1999).

[12] Penny Becker gives a good overview. See *Congregations in Conflict*, 211ff.

A few examples here can illustrate how such an individualist ethic shows up differently in each congregation. Big Bethel seemed the least susceptible to this sort of experiential-expressive form of commitment, in part no doubt because of the inherent historical solidarity and sense of collective identity forged through centuries of oppression.[13] Recent research suggests that this unity is at least under stress, if not fundamentally broken, by the growing economic and social mobility of the black middle class.[14] Churches like Big Bethel counteract the forces pulling the black middle class away from their historical connection to, and responsibility for, poor African Americans in part through the A.M.E. identity and mission focused on self-help for the downtrodden and in part through their commitment to a downtown neighborhood populated primarily by the poor.

Central and the Shrine seem more susceptible to such an individual-expressive ethic. While the Central effort to respond to gun violence did include more systematic structural analysis, it largely turned to individual actions as a response. Similarly, the Shrine Outreach Committee's work on death penalty issues also focused primarily on individual responses to a complex social problem. This is not surprising, given the context of Atlanta with its booming regional economy driven by technology and service-sector jobs. Ken, a Shrine member, offered a summary of the power of religion that embodies such an emphasis on expressive individualism: "All religion is personal. It's not the institution that does things, it's people."

Especially relevant here, in the case of the Shrine's experience, is an Outreach Committee discussion about what action to take at the end of the series of events on the issue of the death penalty. On the one hand, personalizing the plight of those on death row allows Shrine members to express their values and appeal to others in their efforts to do what they see is right. Such a perspective echoes an appeal to a religious individualism as old as our nation. As Betti

---

[13] On this see the fascinating discussion in Seymour Martin Lipset, *American Exceptionalism: A Double-Edged Sword* (New York: Norton, 1996) 113ff.

[14] See Arthur S. Evans, Jr., "The New American Black Middle Classes: Their Social Structure and Status Ambivalence," *International Journal of Politics, Culture, and Society* 7 (Winter 1993) 209–228.

suggested in an Outreach Committee meeting, asking for corporate action by the Shrine is in a sense misplaced because commitment to this issue is "a matter of the heart." Such a focus on the heart clearly made a way for Ken to rethink his position on the death penalty. Such is the power of an emotional appeal. Social critics worry about the interplay of changing modes of commitment tied to loosening ties to social institutions, especially the question of the durability of commitments based on "my experience." Yet the prevalence of such language for commitments may not be an adequate mirror of the depth of values and commitments, at least for active members of an organization. As I argue below, this may be because strong organizations attract commitment and then work to root that commitment in deeper and more stable connection.[15]

On the other hand, such dependence on the modes of expressive individualism limits the scope of response—almost all suggestions for concluding the death penalty program were individual, interpersonal, and emotion-based: writing "friendly stuff, like a pen pal" to a death- row inmate, adopting a death-row inmate, or most astonishing, constructing an "angel tree" allowing members to select a death-row inmate complete with a name and heartwarming story to post on the refrigerator. Such personalism can flatten moral language and imagination, thus hiding questions about its fairness and legality, not to mention moral judgement. Further, the personalism precluded any discussion of turning this nascent heartfelt connection toward systemic and institutional policy analysis and a more sustained collective response. The one exception to this avoidance of collective response, a powerful suggestion of corporate prayer on behalf of those on death row, focused on individual death-row inmates whose stories they knew.[16]

By *denomination and polity,* I have in mind two central and related matters. First, there is the influence of church structure tied to ideas of governance practically expressed in local organizational

---

[15] Becker, *Congregations in Conflict;* Paul Lichterman, *The Search for Political Community: American Activists Reinventing Commitment* (New York: Cambridge University Press, 1996).

[16] Becker notes that none of her models seemed conducive to systematic critique of racism, economic justice, etc., a fact she ties to the expressive style dominant in the middle class. See *Congregations in Conflict,* 210.

structure but influenced through connections to larger expressions of a church from local expressions such as the Atlanta presbytery, the Catholic archdiocese, or A.M.E.'s Sixth Episcopal District, on up to national denominational offices. But second, there is also the influence of traditions in terms of core beliefs and ritual styles. Both of these aspects are integral to local culture/history and dominant ecclesiology, the two remaining components of communal identity to be discussed below. I give an example of the influence of the more structural side of denomination and polity there. I will focus here on polity and core beliefs.

One Sunday, while in the new members' class at Central Presbyterian, Rev. Wardlaw was teaching about Presbyterian history and doctrine. He had once read that H. Richard Niebuhr believed all Christian churches to be "practical unitarians," despite their creedal profession of a Trinitarian God. Niebuhr thought that reformed churches like Congregationalists and Presbyterians focused on God the Father, sacramental traditions like Catholics and Lutherans on Jesus, and Pentecostal traditions like the Church of God on the Holy Spirit. While Presbyterians in general may fit Niebuhr's typology, I nonetheless found that each of my case congregations were unitarians of the second Person, Jesus, but with different emphases, not just the sacramental one that Niebuhr suggests.

In each case the theological vision derives from their denominational heritage and contributes to framing the particular "public" they see and engage. First of all, Central's strong history of outreach, rooted in a social-gospel understanding of practical imitation of Jesus, draws their congregation down from a singular focus on God the Father. Yet it is just this sense of God as Sovereign Lord over all the world that undergirds their confidence that the whole city is an extension of their congregation. On this basis they believe that they are and are to be a "church at work in the heart of the city." For them, the tension is between a theology of the first and second Persons of the Trinity.

Second, at the Shrine a deep sacramental sense of participation in the body and blood of Christ roots their core theological tendency, expressed in their frequent singing of the hymn "We are the Body of Christ." On this basis they view the atoning work of Christ on the cross as sufficient for all, allowing them also to see the whole city as their purview. Yet this expression is markedly less political and mundane compared with Central's. The Shrine's theology of sacramental participation in Christ invites individuals into an experience of conversion and reunion with another reality, in a sense above the world. Yet, as Father Adamski was fond of saying, "We must bear witness to this new reality with our lives and actions."

Third, the blue neon sign on Big Bethel's steeple has proclaimed its message "Jesus Saves" to the city for almost eighty years. In a real sense, their public is those who are lost; they are the only one of the three churches that includes an altar call in every service so that the lost may come home. Yet, in a way that confounds typologies built on white Evangelical churches, Big Bethel's Jesus has a holistic vision of salvation more typical of the traditional black church. Big Bethel's vision of evangelism includes saving their neighborhood from drugs and decay while offering practical assistance for a new life in the here and now. Jesus saves, Big Bethel believes, starting immediately. Increasingly, the A.M.E. church, including Big Bethel, has embodied a neo-Pentecostal emphasis in their faith and worship, pulling their christocentrism into a direct encounter with the Holy Ghost.

Local culture and history are intimately related to issues of denominational affiliation. Here one should pay attention to pivotal points in the living memory of the congregation. These, while not always remembered accurately or even remembered at all, hold the key to fundamental aspects of the congregation's identity. In my cases, each congregation's roots in the founding of the city contributed to their commitment to stay downtown and their efforts to maintain a vital presence there. Further, local culture includes all the things done—worship, eat, learn, serve— and the artifacts needed to do these things—a building, hymnbooks, a kitchen, as well as the beliefs and values that are expressed as people talk about their life together.

A key example of this, and one central to my larger question in this book, is worship. Each church uses denominational hymnbooks and follows a pattern of worship typical within its respective tradition. Each sings, prays, reads Scripture, preaches, and celebrates sacraments. Yet, in terms of the overall flow, style, and emphases, the worship services are quite divergent. In terms of emphases, a most obvious divergence is that the Shrine celebrates communion every week (daily, actually, since they have Mass seven days a week), while Big Bethel and Central do so only one time per month. Over the course of a month, then, average Sunday worshipers at the Shrine will have spent approximately an hour and a half participating in communion, while worshipers Big Bethel and Central will spend only twenty minutes. Yet, because of the relatively greater emphasis placed on the sermon at Big Bethel, especially, but also at Central, the average worshiper will in that same month have listened to a sermon for an hour and a half to two hours, while at the Shrine a worshiper will have listened to sermons for about only thirty minutes (Figure 6.2).

These somewhat traditional Protestant-Catholic differences in emphasis play out in even more divergent styles and forms of worship, creating a significantly different feel in each. For instance, the flow of a liturgical service is a more balanced orchestration of parts, peaking once at the sermon and again at the communion. A

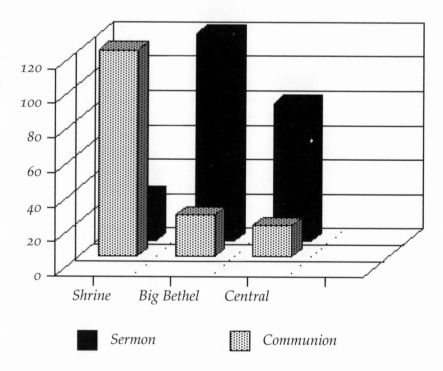

FIGURE 6.2—MINUTES IN ACTIVITY PER MONTH

thematic service, however, builds its rhythms as it goes, moving toward a climax in the sermon and, if they have one, the altar call. While Central's service is moving somewhat from a thematic service to a liturgical service, especially on communion Sundays, the rest of the time it remains more strongly thematic in form.

Music in each fits the movement of the form and serves its needs in terms of emotional mood and movement. Big Bethel's worship moves along supported in its emotional energy and focus by constant music, both in the explicit musicality such as hymns and anthems but also the implicit musicality in preaching. Even during prayer or communion, an organ or solo voice will pick up a musical theme designated for the moment or drawn from earlier in the service and offered as an improvised theme. Central's worship highlights the hymn form that allows full congregational participation, and their use of four-part harmony and alternating leadership on verses (now choir, now women, now men) exemplifies the way they've made this form their musical expertise. The Shrine has its own distinctive form of call and response led by a cantor, not only for the responsorial psalm but also for congregational song. While the cantor sings the melodic verses, the congregation joins in repeatedly for the chorus. Yet the long silences are what is most distinctive at the Shrine. For instance, following the reception of communion, the congregation sits in silence for more than a minute on an average Sunday, a practice that reaches its height in the ten-minute silence following communion on Holy Thursday.

In each case there is a kinetic connection between the structure of the music and basic body movement, breathing, and rhythm. This, in turn, is rooted in the social history of the music related to the social and cultural worlds of the members (e.g., at Big Bethel, in the suffering of the spirituals and the blues; at Central, the emphasis of the Protestant Reformers on the "priesthood of all believers" that highlighted the congregational hymn form; and at the Shrine, medieval monasticism and repetitive chant transfigured by the Second Vatican Council), all of which create the "sense of style" in each church.[17] All this matters for my argument because such

[17] I've drawn generally on my conversations with Don Saliers on this point, as well as J. Nathan Corbitt, *The Sound of the Harvest: Music's Mission in Church and Culture* (Grand Rapids: Baker Books, 1998), and Glenn Hinson, *Fire in My*

forms and a sense of style set parameters within which worship is meaningful for worshipers. They bear in their bodies the memory of music that "feels like church," in part accounting both for the quietly weeping Presbyterians and for the shouting African Methodists. When worship does not work, it is likely because it has strayed too far from the sense of style embodied in the congregation's communal identity to be recognized as "how we do it here."

Lastly, *dominant ecclesiology,* in the sense of congregational models or mission orientations, draws together and frames the expression of influences from the other four components of congregational identity. Each of the congregations I studied had strong dominant ecclesiologies as leading, civic-minded churches (something which I looked for in selecting them and which is highly typical of downtown mainline churches).[18] While there are a number of reasons for this, one key is the simple fact that although everything else has changed, these church buildings are still there, following their ideals, enacting their missions, and people choose to join these congregations because they also hold those ideals and wish to participate in enacting such a mission. Their choice is not simply the kind of choice that "maximizes their self-interest" or "fills out a rational life-plan," as some theories would say.[19] Rather, these are choices that are intended to express moral values and to find communities that serve to sustain the commitment to these values. One of the reasons, undoubtably, why these congregations maintain their strong sense of mission lies in offering people something to commit to, providing them a community of people whose commitments al-

---

Bones: Transcendence and the Holy Spirit in African American Gospel (Philadelphia: University of Pennsylvania, 2000). The latter is a stunning ethnography of a single gospel program performed by the Branchettes, The Long Branch Disciple Church in rural Johnston County, North Carolina.

[18] Nancy Ammerman, *Congregation and Community* (New Brunswick, N.J.: Rutgers University, 1997); Roozen et al., *Varieties of Religious Presence;* and Alan Mock, "Congregational Religious Styles and Orientations to Society: Exploring our Linear Assumptions," *Review of Religious Research* 34 (1992) 20–33, all found that downtown churches had the strongest sense of identity.

[19] I have in mind here the "Rational Actor" theories employed to explain religious behavior. For a discussion and some representative arguments, see Lawrence A. Young, ed., *Rational Choice Theory and Religion: Summary and Assessment* (New York: Routledge, 1997).

ready assure that membership in this congregation makes a difference (we are "people living church" or "the church at work in the
city" or the church where "Jesus saves—lives and communities").

A related aspect of these churches that both derives from the
members' choices and in a sense produces them is a common
legacy of strong leadership. In fact, the strength of congregational
identity in each directly parallels the relative strength of its leadership. Central's is strongest, set a century ago through the key
leadership of elder John J. Eagan and fostered by a string of out-
standing pastors committed to developing that same strong identity. Big Bethel's is also strong but has ebbed and flowed with the
quality and commitment of the ministers assigned to it by the
bishop. Its current strength is in large part due to successive dynamic and committed pastors who have had relatively long
tenures, given the rotational bias of the Methodist system of itinerant ministry.[20] The Shrine's identity is weakest, built up under the
strength of one pastor's tenure and strongly supported by a large
percentage of the parish that joined during his leadership.

It stands to reason, then, that especially for leader congregations,
strong leadership (lay and not just clergy—John J. Eagan was a lay-
man) is essential. A hierarchical polity can aid this by the relative
strength it places in the position of pastor but can undermine it,
too, by the influence of a bishop's power over pastoral appoint-
ments. This was a significant concern for the Shrine during the end
of Father Adamski's tenure. This led to the parish council's powerful letter to their new pastor even before learning who he was, attempting to state who they understood themselves to be as an
implicit request that he lead them forward rather than set them
back with changes they would not welcome. A Presbyterian polity
does not structurally afford the pastor the same high place of un-
questioned authority—that would undercut their commitment to a
democratic form of governance—yet Central has fostered very

[20] This system of moving ministers from church to church every few years
has its roots in the early days of Methodism in the U.S., when pastors rode a
"circuit" of churches by horseback and a "settled ministry" was looked down
upon. See James T. Campbell, *Songs of Zion: The African Methodist Episcopal
Church in the United States and South Africa* (Chapel Hill: University of North
Carolina Press, 1998) 33ff.

strong leadership through its ability to carefully choose its new leadership, and it has done this job well.

In the above examples, the communal identity worked in varied ways to structure the possible ways members offered themselves, their gifts, and abilities toward three different styles of having a "sense of public church." I mean by that phrase that each congregation, through its social context, membership demographics, polity, local culture/history, and especially its dominant ecclesiology, engages in public work—concern for others who share in common its present place and time—that makes "sense" to them because it seems the only, or better, the right thing to do. This sort of sensibility comes from the second-natured judgments rooted in "who we are" and does not require the conscious questioning of assumptions at every point.

These judgments about each congregation's "sense of public church" are met by various forces that influence the ways its ideals can be met. Such a view does not repeat the idea, implied in the "linear model" of relating worship and ethics, that such forces create competing counter-formations. What Don Saliers and others writing on character ethics and worship refer to as "social forces" are in fact often turned to "social resources" by the uses members make of their gifts, knowledge, and abilities gained through their upbringing and family, education, connections and skills on the job, and others. While it is possible, as Saliers worries, that business sensibilities learned in the economic sphere can turn the church toward market metaphors, thus flattening Christian practices in favor of increasing its market share, skills and language from business can *also* be turned toward the church's mission of buying drug-infested properties with an eye toward neighborhood redevelopment in Jesus's name.

Such an example of a "sense of public church" seems natural to Big Bethel. How could they not, they would argue with Saliers, use business members' abilities in living their mission that "Jesus saves"? As I explicate these themes in terms of an "interaction model" for relating worship and ethics, I can more carefully defend how social forces do indeed become social resources, contributing to each congregation's particular "sense of public."

COMMUNAL IDENTITY, WORSHIP, ETHICS:
AN INTERACTIVE MODEL

Here I come full circle to the question that began my research: How does participation in corporate worship form significant Christian communities that enact a public commitment, that become, to paraphrase Bonhoeffer, a "church for others"? The answer begins by saying that worship's power, or at least its effect on those gathered, depends in significant ways on the identity of the gathered community. I claimed this just above, offering extended examples of how this worked out in my case congregations. But still, what specifically does worship do? Does it form Christians, as character ethics claims?

Certainly worship does not always and equally enact such formative power. I found in my case congregations that for most people most of the time, worship is less formation as con-formation, a reinforcement and reminder of what is important in life as they envision it in that place. At times, especially for young children and for converts (e.g., those for whom the communal style of ritual enactment is new and attractive), worship can be strongly formative, giving shape to one's senses, affections, habits of feeling and thinking and believing and behaving.

Furthermore, if Ann Swidler is correct, in unsettled times during life liturgy may be more formative in the way it is for a new convert; old patterns have broken apart, and new ways can be found in the patterns of the worshiping community.[21] One could think, for example, of the effervescence in worship forms and experimental communities during the upheaval of the 1960s or the current growth of "contemporary worship" in the face of declining Protestant mainline churches. Even so, however, such formation happens in ways that "fit" the dominant ethos of a congregation, the acquired habitus of the members.

Thus, I would argue, liturgy does not dramatically form or change the Christian as moral agent most of the time. It certainly does not effect any dramatic "transformation," as some theological

---

[21] Ann Swidler, "Culture in Action: Symbols and Strategies," *American Sociological Review* 51 (April 1986) 278–279.

and liturgical writing indicates.[22] In thinking through what I understand worship's power to be on the basis of my fieldwork, I arrived at an "interaction model" of the relation between worship and ethics (Figure 6.3). I'll briefly spell out how this model can illumine the way worship works, and fails to work, drawing briefly on case material for illustration.

The model begins with "what's there" in the church, seen through the dominant communal identity in all its complexity. Generally those who join, no matter how they came to know of the church, join because they feel a fit between their vision of church and the vision embodied in the congregation's communal identity. Those joining may not be a perfect fit, as with those Catholics joining Central Presbyterian or the Lutheran woman who joined Big Bethel, but they find sufficient resonance that they accept the work of shedding the layers of "misfit" assumptions they bear and taking on new sensibilities that fit their current reality.

The next stage in the model comes as particular churches worship in a certain way, a way that embodies a vision of who they understand themselves to be, or at least who they feel they ought to be. When this happens, people are often drawn more deeply into what they have already committed to in their initial involvement with the church. This happens, when it happens, because the churches take the things they did not "make up," such as their denominational worship as a pattern of word and gesture; the Scripture texts; their architecture; their congregational history, etc., and through a process of interpretation, adapt these "givens" to their purpose by their own strategies of artful improvisation. They are doing this not so much in a calculated way as because this reflects "who we are" and thus "how it should be done."

At the Shrine, Central, and Big Bethel, worship services resonate powerfully not only because they are thoughtfully prepared and aesthetically powerful but also because they lift up and ritually embody the common ideals constituting each community as church. In this regard, for instance, Father Adamski's liturgical leadership had been of central importance for the development of the Shrine's life. His twelve-year effort to strengthen the Holy

<hr/>

[22] For a prominent example of such a tendency, see my discussion of Stanley Hauerwas in chapter 1, pp. 30–35, above.

Week liturgies in the parish's life marks a key example of this. Numerous people I interviewed said that they had experienced being drawn deeper into their faith, and in most cases directly tied this to liturgical experience, especially the Triduum. Fernando and others in a RENEW group suggested that the deepening of their faith has led to changes at work—efforts, in their words, to make work "a ministry, something meaningful." It was striking, however, to see the way in which the fellowship of worship worked most effectively when, as in the case of the RENEW group, layers of other meals shared together aided the work of building the interconnections within the community gathered for worship on Sunday morning.

Such claims that worship drew participants' own lives more deeply into the life and mission of their particular congregation were common across my three case congregations. In each, distinctive elements of their communal identity had to be present in worship for such an effect to have its power. Yet it is important to note that this pattern does not always hold. At times, especially at the Shrine and at Central, I spoke with members whose joining was

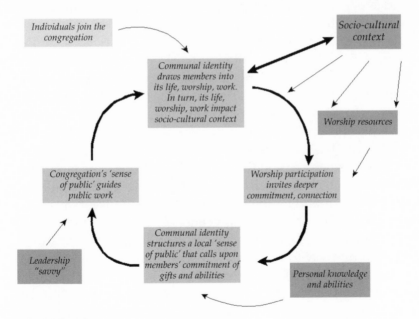

FIGURE 6.3—
AN INTERACTIVE MODEL OF THE RELATIONSHIP OF
WORSHIP AND ETHICS

tied to a moral commitment to the congregation's stand for justice in the world. They described their commitment in joining being deepened through becoming active in the public work of the congregation, and their appreciation for worship grew more slowly. This was often the case with young adults who had had bad experiences with church growing up, had come to see "the church" as hypocritical, and had come to see worship anew in the context of congregations that tried to live out their lofty ideals. In either case, it was the strong identity of the churches that overcame initial reluctance and drew initial commitment.

The third and fourth moments in the "interactive model" try to show how, as members experience a desire for deeper commitment, such a desire is structured by a local "sense of public" that calls on members' lives, knowledge, and abilities in particular ways that connect to the sorts of public commitments that make sense for the particular congregation. I'll offer an example drawn across my three cases to elaborate on these two interconnected moments in the model.

In each of my three case congregations, members told me in varying ways that their participation in worship filled them, moving them to find opportunities to offer their knowledge and abilities on behalf of the church's life and work. What response the members offer in the end depends both on the communal identity and on members' knowledge and abilities learned through family life, in school, through participation in civic groups, or on the job. A key to this process is the leadership (what I call "leadership savvy") needed to facilitate good use of the skills members offer.

Central Presbyterian and the Shrine share similar demographics and impulses when it comes to responding to needs of the urban community surrounding them. Yet how these impulses play out differs greatly. The Shrine's congregational identity, including its local culture and history of struggle for survival, its hierarchical polity tending away from shared leadership, and its small membership, including relatively lower numbers of highly educated professionals, tends toward heartfelt emotional appeals and volunteer actions of care, such as volunteering at Central's Night Shelter. Central's congregational identity, in contrast, including its strong ecclesial ideal as "the church at work in the city," its Presbyterian polity of democratic participation, and large membership, including very high numbers of highly educated professionals (eighty lawyers, for example), plays out in lofty rhetoric, fund-raising, and institution-building, as in their health center and new transitional shelter for women and children.

Big Bethel, however, has somewhat different impulses in responding to needs. They engage in charity, including programs for homeless people, but their congregational identity, especially rooted in their theology and polity and the emphasis on racial uplift and economic development, leads them to draw on the professional skills of members differently. They have engaged in a systematic campaign to buy dilapidated lots (thirteen so far) in the neighborhood and, by becoming the landlord, offer positive economic opportunities for the community.

Coming full circle, then, the model suggests that each congregation—its life in public worship and public work—makes an impact on its sociocultural context. Yet it does so in ways, as I argue above, that fit its understanding of itself. Such a conclusion echoes an old point, explicitly made twenty years ago by the title of David Roozen, William McKinney, and Jackson Carroll's book, *Varieties of Religious Presence: Mission in Public Life*. Yet, both in Roozen's arguments and in the arguments of theologians discussed in chapter 1 above (pp. 43–46), the habit of employing church-world distinctions has led to an assumption that the church is somehow pure, a resource for a counter-formation against the corrosive formation of the world. They hold out the hope that the church's influence can offer something more lofty and noble than the prospect that we will all become self-centered consumers or *homo economicus*, relentlessly maximizing our self-interest in order to make a million dollars. I share the hope that the church could provide an alternative to these visions of life. Yet the church cannot provide hope separate from the material shape given to it by people who make up its membership.

When one tries to move beyond church-world thinking, I argue, this hope for the church's distinctive witness becomes both more realistic and more compelling. For the "one, holy, catholic and apostolic church" exists as the incarnate Body of Christ, taking on kinds of faithful worship and work in its various locales throughout the world. Understanding the ways in which a congregation is worldly allows more careful attention to those places where it is possible to lose its distinctiveness—or where it has already lost it. Patrick Clayborn pointed to this when he outlined for me the various pitfalls of the music employed at Big Bethel. With the popular contemporary gospel music, which draws heavily on contemporary grooves in hip-hop music, you are in danger of "getting caught up in the entertainment and so the loud music, you're popping your fingers, swinging on your feet, thinking you're at the club on Saturday night and not trying to worship." Yet, exactly because of this musical echo of popular African American culture and music, the church can reach a young post–civil rights generation not interested in singing the staid hymns of their fathers' and mothers' church. The point is that a church's worldliness offers both potential for mission and the temptation to abandon mission by becoming just like the rest of the world.

CHURCHES IN PUBLIC: FURTHER RESEARCH

Let me conclude by suggesting further lines of research on the basis of my findings here. That such varied "senses of public church" exist in these three churches should not be a surprise. Further study would surely find that churches exhibit an even broader variety, including many, I suspect, with less explicit styles of public engagement. Yet, in the context of increasing church membership based on expressive commitment among churches today, it is heartening to see the ways in which these churches draw in new members and very often offer public worship that inspires them, claims them even, for deeper commitments (though not always) through the existing repertoire of public work in that place. At the very least, this study contributes a more realistic model for studying the relation of worship, character, and commitment in local congregational life.

In *Better Together: Restoring American Community*, the follow-up study to the influential study *Bowling Alone*, Robert Putnam and his coauthors offer a series of case studies that offer hope for a renewed commitment to community.[23] One chapter deals with two

---

[23] Robert Putnam, Lewis Feldstein, and Don Cohen, *Better Together: Restoring the American Community* (New York: Simon and Schuster, 2003).

contrasting churches in southern California, each in its own way examples of a vital "sense of public," as I have called it here.[24] This study offers three additional installments of hope for a vital "sense of public church" today. Their witness that the church is to be a "church for others" and that such public spiritedness can be expressed in a variety of ways, yes, must be expressed in a variety of ways, itself makes a sort of mini-case for vitality of the church as a public institution in and for the world God loves.

[24] The two are Saddleback Church in Lake Forest, California, an Evangelical megachurch led by Pastor Rick Warren, and All Saints Episcopal in Pasadena, California, also very large, though not quite in the megachurch category (two thousand worshiping per week). See Putnam, *Better Together*, 119f.

Appendix

Data and Methods

During the fall of 1998, I began reading histories of Atlanta and doing site visits at various churches in and around the old city center. Early on I decided to take as my bounded geographic area the so-called "Olympic Ring" comprising the central business district, since this was a preexisting definition of the downtown area and is widely disseminated through its adoption by the MARTA transit system as its map (see illustration in the introduction to part 2, p. 73, above). While at an early stage, I considered using two case congregations from downtown and two from suburban communities for comparison, in the end I chose a cross-comparison between three downtown churches. Why? First, because I love downtown churches—their history, their pluckiness in keeping on despite difficulty, and the fact that they very often have strong visions of their mission. This last point leads to the second reason for a focus on downtown churches. Because they are often churches with strong visions of their mission, I hypothesized that they would be just the sort of places to investigate how worship forms Christian witness. If it did not happen in these churches, I did not think it would happen elsewhere, either.

THE PROCESS OF RESEARCH
I have followed a mixed approach to method. On the one hand, I have largely shaped the "how" of my project after "extended case method," an ethnographic approach that requires testing a specific theory in a case study while understanding that forces outside the

case impact and are impacted by the case (thus "extension" beyond the confines of the case is assumed necessary).[1] Yet the defensiveness of this method that it is "truly scientific" does not strike me as worth defending with rigor. So, on the other hand, I borrow an interpretive approach learned from my teachers Paul Rabinow, Robert Bellah, and Steve Tipton.[2] This approach finds validity more in its descriptive power, the way in which it rings true to the reader, than in its openness to repetition and falsification.

My approach is complicated further by my explicit theological commitments and arguments. While I can't claim that this work would fulfill his intention, I've had in my mind the sort of venture hinted at thirty years ago in Robert Bellah's well-known text *Beyond Belief*. There, in his concluding essay, he argues for a rapprochement between the theologian and the scientist, an approach that would employ a sort of phenomenological double vision.[3] He laments the "radical split between knowledge and commitment that exists in our culture." In following this agenda, I have attempted to approach my subject with just this sort of double vision.[4]

Research on each case congregation is based on four to five months of participation in the parish's life. I first met with Father Adamski about working at the Shrine in January 1999. After his agreement and his presentation of my project to the parish council, I began research there just before Ash Wednesday. My object was to spend a "season" in each church, and for the Shrine, the Lent-Easter cycle is very important to their life. It also was to be Father Adamski's last five months in the parish after a tenure of twelve years. This, no doubt, contributed to his interest in my doing the study; I would be a part of his own stock-taking as he contem-

[1] Michael Burawoy et al., *Ethnography Unbound: Power and Resistance in the Modern Metropolis* (Berkeley: University of California Press, 1991), and "The Extended Case Method," *Sociological Theory* 16 (March 1998) 4–33.

[2] Paul Rabinow and William M. Sullivan, *Intepretive Social Science: A Second Look* (Berkeley: University of California Press, 1987).

[3] One model of this is the sort of sociology of morality pursued by Steve Tipton, combining descriptive ethics and interpretive sociology in an effort to understand how people think out their morality and how they live it out in everyday life.

[4] See Robert N. Bellah, *Beyond Belief: Essays on Religion in a Post-Traditional World* (New York: Harper and Row, 1970) 237–259.

plated his departure. I met with the pastors of Big Bethel and Central Presbyterian in August 1999, proposing my study and asking what might be the best season to spend with them. For Big Bethel, Rev. Davis recommended fall, leading into Christmas, when they undertake their main "outreach" focus for the year and hold numerous Christmas programs. I began there in September and finished in December. For Central, Rev. Wardlaw happily suggested spring, leading up to Easter. I began at Central in January and finished in April.

As in the other congregations, at the Shrine I focused my early research on attending worship and talking with people informally before and after worship, trying to learn the local language and style of worship and the range of activities involved. As I began to know my way around, a month or so into the field, I would branch out, attending educational events, committee meetings, social gatherings, and outreach activities. By the end of month two, I was drawing up a list of members for formal interviews. I gained these names partly from my intention to interview the minister, music director, and a few other staff members, as well as the local parish historian and then some of the members involved in social ministry projects. The rest were snowball interviews, usually people suggested by my first list. I was attentive to the goal of "representative diversity," especially in terms of generational cohorts and gender (and at the Shrine, race and sexual orientation). I taped interviews as a general rule and transcribed the tapes myself. When quotes are used in the text, they are someone's verbatim words. When I was not sure, I did not quote.

To supplement my observations and interviews, I collected historical materials, documents of all sorts (worship programs, devotional guides, meeting handouts, membership directories, educational materials, worship planning materials, and other ephemera of all sorts) and used this material both to fill in details and check my own observations.

While explicitly identifying myself as an Emory doctoral student conducting dissertation research, I nonetheless fully participated in the life of the parish, to the extent a non-member could. At the Shrine this meant that I could take communion but was warned by Father Adamski not to talk about it. At all the congregations, it meant begging my way into places and meetings that even members might not attend (ministerial planning meetings, for example). While I think my subject is something that many Christians, including some of my case study members, reflect on, my explicit self-identification did lead to stylized responses. People love their churches and wanted me to know that they are doing good things. Yet, remarkably, they were also fairly self-reflective about the challenges they face. As members at the congregations have read my chapters about them, they have on the whole said, "Yes, you've got it. This sounds like us." Such a response is a welcome compliment.

INTERVIEW SCHEDULE

Semi-structured interviews allowed me to follow the basic movement of my schedule, asking my core questions listed below, but following directions offered by my interviewees and their particular place in and knowledge of the church. For example, when I interviewed older members who formally or informally held the role of "church historian," I spent a lot of time on questions one to four compared with the rest of the questions, while with people involved in music ministry, questions went in deeper around issues of worship and music, and so on. This approach had good and bad sides in retrospect. At times I gained valuable information because the person went off on a tangent, and I followed it to my gain. Other times, however, people just went off on a tangent. Such is the nature of interviewing. My interview schedule is below.

Date:_____

Interview with_____

1. I'd like to start with your background—some autobiography if you will. What things combined to lead you to your present involvement at Central?

   Prompts: Family of origin
             Education
             Work
             Key relationships

2. If you had to choose a word to describe Central church, what would it be?

3. How were things when you first came to Central?

4. How have things changed?

5. What things are you (or have you been) involved in at Central?

6. How would you describe worship to a friend who had never been to Central Church?

7. What are the most meaningful things about worship for you?

FOR STAFF, ASK:

8. How do you prepare for worship on a given Sunday?

9. What is good worship? How do you know if it happened?

10. Is it important to you that Central is a socially committed church, serving the needy?

11. Does worship at Central have anything to do with those commitments to serve?

12. Has participation at Central impacted your own ethical ideals?

13. Does your participation at Central influence your work? Your family?

14. Do your involvements outside Central impact your participation at Central?

15. Are there things that prevent you from fulfilling your ethical ideals?

That's all—Thanks so much! Any final thoughts or reflections?

Bibliography

THEOLOGY AND SOCIAL SCIENCE

Alexander, Jeffery C., ed. *Durkheimian Sociology: Cultural Studies*. New York: Cambridge University Press, 1988.

Ammerman, Nancy T. *Congregation and Community*. New Brunswick, N.J.: Rutgers University, 1997.

Becker, Penny Edgell. *Congregations in Conflict: Cultural Models of Local Religious Life*. New York: Cambridge University Press, 1999.

Bellah, Robert N. *Beyond Belief: Essays on Religion in a Post-Traditional World*. New York: Harper and Row, 1970.

———. "Introduction." In Robert N. Bellah, ed., *Emile Durkheim on Morality and Society*, vii–lv. Chicago: University of Chicago Press, 1973.

———. "Is There a Common American Culture?" *Journal of the American Academy of Religion* 66 (Fall 1998) 613–626.

———. "Max Weber and Word-Denying Love: A Look at the Historical Sociology of Religion." *Journal of the American Academy of Religion* 67 (June 1999) 277–304.

Bellah, Robert N., Richard Madsen, William M. Sullivan, Ann Swidler, and Steven M. Tipton. *Habits of the Heart: Individualism and Commitment in American Life*. Berkeley: University of California Press, 1996 [1985].

———. *The Good Society*. New York: Alfred A. Knopf, 1991.

Burawoy, Michael. "The Extended Case Method." *Sociological Theory* 16 (March 1998) 4–33.

Bourdieu, Pierre. *Outline of a Theory of Practice*. Trans. Richard Nice. New York: Cambridge University Press, 1977.

———. *Distinction: A Social Critique of the Judgement of Taste*. Trans. Richard Nice. Cambridge, Mass.: Harvard University Press, 1984.

———. *The Logic of Practice*. Trans. Richard Nice. Stanford, Calif.: Stanford University Press, 1990.

———. *Pascalian Meditations*. Stanford, Calif.: Stanford University Press, 2000.

Bourdieu, Pierre, and Jean-Claude Passeron. *Reproduction in Education, Society, and Culture*. 2nd ed. Thousand Oaks, Calif.: Sage Publications, 1990 [1977].

Bourdieu, Pierre, and Loïc J. D. Wacquant. *An Invitation to Reflexive Sociology*. Chicago: University of Chicago Press, 1992.

Camic, Charles. "The Matter of Habit." *American Journal of Sociology* 91 (1986) 1039–1087.

Casanova, José. *Public Religions in the Modern World.* Chicago: University of Chicago Press, 1994.

Demerath, N. J., III, and Rhys H. Williams. *A Bridging of Faiths: Religion and Politics in a New England City.* Princeton: Princeton University Press, 1992.

Durkheim, Emile. *The Division of Labor in Society.* New York: The Free Press, 1984 [1893].

———. *The Evolution of Educational Thought.* London: Routledge and Kegan Paul, 1977 [1904–1905].

———. *The Elementary Forms of Religious Life.* New York: The Free Press, 1995 [1912].

———. *Moral Education: A Study in the Theory and Application of the Sociology of Education.* New York: The Free Press, 1961 [1925].

Durkheim, Emile, and Marcel Mauss. *Primitive Classification.* Chicago: University of Chicago Press, 1963 [1903].

Farley, Margaret A. "Beyond the Formal Principle: A Reply to Ramsey and Saliers." *Journal of Religious Ethics* 7:191–202.

Geertz, Clifford. *The Interpretation of Cultures.* New York: Basic Books, 1972.

Gustafson, James M. "Christian Faith and Moral Action." *The Christian Century* 82 (November 3, 1965) 1345–1347.

———. "Context Versus Principles: A Misplaced Debate in Christian Ethics." *Harvard Theological Review* 58 (April 1965b) 171–202.

———. *Christ and the Moral Life.* New York: Harper and Row, 1968.

———. "Spiritual Life and Moral Life." *Theology Today* 19 (Winter 1971) 296–307.

———. "The Sectarian Temptation: Reflections on Theology, the Church, and the University." *Catholic Theological Society of America Proceedings* 40 (1985) 83–94.

———. "Response to Critics." *Journal of Religious Ethics* 13 (1985) 185–209.

Hammond, Phillip E. *Religion and Personal Autonomy: The Third Disestablishment in America.* Columbia: University of South Carolina Press, 1992.

Hauerwas, Stanley. *A Community of Character: Toward a Constructive Christian Social Ethic.* Notre Dame, Ind.: University of Notre Dame Press, 1981.

———. *The Peaceable Kingdom: A Primer in Christian Ethics.* Notre Dame, Ind.: University of Notre Dame Press, 1983.

———. "Introduction: On the Alleged Popularity of an 'Ethics of Character.'" In *Character and the Christian Life: A Study in Theological Ethics,* 2nd ed., xiii–xxxiii. Notre Dame, Ind.: University of Notre Dame Press, 1985.

———. *Christian Existence Today: Essays on Church, World, and Living in Between.* Durham, N.C.: The Labyrinth Press, 1988.

———. *In Good Company: The Church as Polis.* Notre Dame, Ind.: University of Notre Dame Press, 1995.

—————. *Sanctify Them in Truth.* Nashville: Abingdon, 1998.

Hauerwas, Stanley, and Charles Pinches. *Christians Among the Virtues: Theological Conversations with Ancient and Modern Ethics.* Notre Dame, Ind.: University of Notre Dame Press, 1997.

Henriot, Peter J., S.J. "Liturgy and Social Concerns." In *The Awakening Church: 25 Years of Liturgical Renewal,* 115–120. Ed. Lawrence J. Madden, S.J. Collegeville, Minn.: The Liturgical Press, 1992.

Jones, Sue Stedman. "The Concept of Belief in the Elementary Forms." In N. J. Allen, W. S. F. Pickering, and W. Watts Miller, eds., *On Durkheim's Elementary Forms of Religious Life,* 53–65. New York: Routledge, 1998.

—————. "Representation in Durkheim's Masters: Kant and Renouvier." In W. S. F. Pickering, ed., *Durkheim and Representations,* 37–79. New York: Routledge, 2000.

Lichterman, Paul. *The Search for Political Community: American Activists Reinventing Commitment.* New York: Cambridge University Press, 1996.

Lukes, Steven. *Emile Durkheim: His Life and Work, A Historical and Critical Study.* Stanford, Calif.: Stanford University Press, 1985.

Luther, Martin. "The Large Catechism." *The Book of Concord.* Ed. and trans. Theodore G. Tappert et al. Philadelphia: Fortress Press, 1959 [1529].

Milbank, John. *Theology and Social Theory: Beyond Secular Reason.* Cambridge: Blackwell, 1990.

Potter, Ralph B., Jr. "The Logic of Moral Argument." In Paul Deats, Jr., ed., *Toward a Discipline of Social Ethics,* 93–114. Boston: Boston University Press, 1972.

Putnam, Robert. *Bowling Alone: The Collapse and Revival of American Community.* New York: Simon and Schuster, 2000.

Putnam, Robert, Lewis Feldstein, with Don Cohen. *Better Together: Restoring the American Community.* New York: Simon and Schuster, 2003.

Roozen, David, Jackson Carroll, and William McKinney. *Varieties of Religious Presence: Mission in Public Life.* New York: Pilgrim, 1982.

Saliers, Don E. "Liturgy and Ethics: Some New Beginnings." *Journal of Religious Ethics* 7 (1979) 173–189.

—————. "Symbol in Liturgy, Liturgy in Symbol: The Domestication of Liturgical Experience." In Lawrence J. Madden, S.J., ed., *The Awakening Church: 25 Years of Liturgical Renewal,* 69–82. Collegeville, Minn.: The Liturgical Press, 1992.

—————. "Afterword: Liturgy and Ethics Revisited." In E. Byron Anderson and Bruce T. Morrill., eds., *Liturgy and the Moral Life: Humanity at Full Stretch Before God,* 209–224. Collegeville, Minn.: The Liturgical Press, 1998.

Spohn, William C. *Go and Do Likewise: Jesus and Ethics.* New York: Continuum, 1999.

Stamps, Mary E., ed. *To Do Justice and Right Upon the Earth.* Collegeville, Minn.: The Liturgical Press, 1993.

Swidler, Ann. "To Revitalize Community Life, We Must First Strengthen Our National Institutions." *The Chronicle of Higher Education* (May 16, 1997) B4–5.

———. "Culture in Action: Symbols and Strategies." *American Sociological Review* 51 (1986) 273–286.

———. *Talk of Love: How Culture Matters.* Chicago: University of Chicago Press, 2001.

Tipton, Steven M. *Getting Saved from the Sixties.* Berkeley: University of California Press, 1982.

———. "Review of Robert Wuthnow, Meaning and Moral Order: Explorations in Culture Analysis." *Review of Religious Research* 30 (1989) 307–309.

———. "Public Theology." *The Encyclopedia of Politics and Religion.* New York: Congressional Quarterly Press, 1998.

———. "Social Differentiation and Moral Pluralism." In Richard Madsen, William Sullivan, Ann Swidler, and Steven Tipton, eds., *Meaning and Modernity: Religion, Polity, Self.* Berkeley: University of California Press, 2002.

Wacquant, Loïc J. D. " Solidarity, morality and sociology: Durkheim and the crisis of European society." *The Journal of the Society for Social Research* 1 (1993) 1–7.

———. "Durkheim and Bourdieu: The Common Foundation and its Fissures." *Critique* 51 (1995) 646–660.

Wallwork, Ernest. *Durkheim: Morality and Milieu.* Cambridge: Harvard University Press, 1972.

Weber, Max. "Science as a Vocation." In Gerth and Mills, eds., *From Max Weber: Essays in Sociology,* 129–156. New York: Oxford University Press, 1946.

———. "Religious Rejections of the World and Their Directions." In Gerth and Mills, eds., *From Max Weber: Essays in Sociology,* 323–359. New York: Oxford University Press, 1946.

Wenger, Etienne. *Communities of Practice: Learning, Meaning, and Identity.* New York: Cambridge University Press, 1998.

Wuthnow, Robert. *Restructuring of American Religion.* Princeton: Princeton University Press, 1988.

———. *Loose Connections: Joining Together in America's Fragmented Communities.* Cambridge, Mass.: Harvard University Press, 1998.

ATLANTA

Allen, Frederick. *Atlanta Rising.* Atlanta: Longstreet, 1996.

Bayor, Ronald H. "Planning the City for Racial Segregation: The Highway-Street Pattern in Atlanta." *Journal of Urban History* 15 (November 1988) 3–21.

Bradley, Donald. S. "Back to the City?" In Andrew Marshall Hamer, ed., *Urban Atlanta: Redefining the Role of the City,* 113–126. Atlanta: Georgia State University, 1980.

Bullard, Robert D., J. Eugene Grigsby III, and Charles Lee. *Residential Apartheid: The American Legacy.* Los Angeles: Center for Afro-American Studies, UCLA, 1994.

Carter, Jimmy. "Preface." In *The Atlanta Project, Because There Is Hope: Gearing Up the Renew Urban America.* Atlanta: Carter Collaboration Center, 1993.

Frey, William H. "Minority Suburbanization and Continued 'White Flight' in U. S. Metropolitan Areas." *Research in Community Sociology* 4 (1994) 15–42.

Hartshorn, Truman, and Keith Ihlanfeldt. *The Dynamics of Change.* Atlanta: Research Atlanta, Policy Research Center, Georgia State University, 1993.

Holmes, Bob. *The Status of Black Atlanta, 1996–1997.* Atlanta: The Southern Center for Studies in Public Policy, Clark Atlanta University, 1997.

Preston, Howard L. *Automobile Age Atlanta.* Athens, Ga.: University of Georgia, 1979.

Rutheiser, Charles. *Imagineering Atlanta.* New York: Verso, 1996.

Saporta, Maria. "The Middle Ground: Push for Intown Housing." *Atlanta Constitution-Journal* (September 28, 1998) E1, 7.

———. "Let's Keep Goizueta's Dream for Atlanta Alive." *Atlanta Constitution-Journal* (September 28, 1998) E7.

Smith, John Robert. *The Church That Stayed.* Atlanta: The Atlanta Historical Society, 1979.

Soto, Lucy, and Matt Kempner. "The New Suburbanites." *Atlanta Constitution-Journal* (January 3, 1999) A1, 10–11.

Walker, Mary Beth. *A Population Profile of the City of Atlanta: Trends, Causes, and Options.* Atlanta: Research Atlanta, Policy Research Center, Georgia State University, 1997.

White, Dana F. "The Black Side of Atlanta: A Geography of Expansion and Containment, 1870–1970." *The Atlanta Historical Journal* 26 (Summer-Fall 1982) 199–225.

———. "Landscaped Atlanta: The Romantic Tradition in Cemetery, Park, and Suburban Development." *The Atlanta Historical Journal* 26 (Summer-Fall 1982) 95–112.

White, Dana F., and Timothy J. Crimmins. "How Atlanta Grew: Cool Heads, Hot Air, and Hard Work." In Andrew Marshall Hamer, ed., *Urban Atlanta: Redefining the Role of the City,* 25–44. Atlanta: Georgia State University, 1980.

Index of Names and Topics